THE TURKISH DINING TABLE

H. GÜLER VURAL

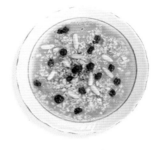

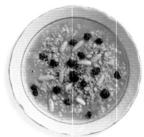

Author
H. Güler Vural

English translator
Carol Stevens Yürür

Editor and Photographer
İbrahim Ethem Vural

Designer
Ayhan Ogan

Production Manager
Bilal Temur

Printed in
China
ISBN: 978-1-58980-419-7
Gretna, Louisiana,
April 2006

Published in Turkey by SariPapatya Publications/ TÜRDAV A.Ş., 2002, 2004
Published by arrangement in the rest of the world by
Pelican Publishing Company, Inc., 2006
1000 Burmaster Street, Gretna, Louisiana 70053

THE TURKISH DINING TABLE

Recipes for Health and Happiness

H. GÜLER VURAL

PELICAN PUBLISHING COMPANY
GRETNA 2006

4

CONTENTS

FISH   159-166

bonito fillets – bonito with Russian salad – steamed fish – fish with tomatoes – fish with onions and tomatoes – fried mackerel – grilled whiting – Trabzon sardine casserole – Black Sea sardine omelette –bonito in olive oil – chopped sardine balls

RICE PILAFS   167-185

plain – with vermicelli – with chick peas – Uzbek – chestnut – Izmir – eggplant – tomato – Buhara – Sultan Reshat – liver – Iran – Cyprus – with kebab – latticed – Bursa pilaf stuffed in fat – sardine – peas – vegetable – curtain – Persian with carrots

MACARONI AND RAVIOLI   187-198

macaroni and ground meat – macaroni and vegetables – baked macaroni and cheese – macaroni and cheese – macaroni in dough – macaroni in sesame sauce – macaroni in bechamel sauce – macaroni and ground meat – homemade egg noodles – macaroni and liver – mock ravioli – ravioli – ravioli macaroni – Amasya cheese ravioli – chicken ravioli – Bosnian ravioli – Çanakkale ravioli

WHEAT DISHES   199-222

Gaziantep keshkek and chick peas – Çorum keshkek and chicken – Tokat keshkek and marrow bones – Denizli keskek – tutti pilaf – cracked wheat pilaf – cracked wheat tomato pilaf – cracked wheat pilaf and lentils – cracked wheat pilav and chickpeas – stuffed potato-wheat balls – Maraş stuffed meatballs – Bitlis stuffed meatballs – Gaziantep stuffed meatballs – Urfa stuffed meatballs – Mardin stuffed meatballs – Siirt liver patties – ground wheat balls – Harput cracked wheat balls – Elazığ grilled meat rings – lady's meatballs – Elazığ lentil patties – Urfa raw meatballs – potato wheat patties – Urfa wheat patties with egg – Tokat lentils and ground wheat (bat) – Malatya wheat balls – Malatya wheat balls in sauce – chick peas and ground wheat – Siirt chick peas and ground wheat stew – Malatya picnic balls – Adana falafel – Malatya stuffed meatballs – rolled loaf – Siirt fried meat patties – Gaziantep meatball shish kebab – garlic wheat patties with stewed lamb – wheat balls in garlic yoghurt – Urfa meatballs and chick pea stew – Muş meatballs – Gaziantep meatballs in yoghurt-chick-pea sauce – Adana mother-daughter meal – rice meatballs – ground wheat salad – Adana wheat balls in chick-pea stew

STUFFED VEGETABLES   223-238

Stuffing for vegetables in olive oil *– stuffed eggplants– stuffed cabbage– stuffed peppers – celery root in olive oil – stuffed grape leaves in olive oil.* **Meat stuffing for vegetables** *– zucchini –dried sweet peppers –dried eggplants – red and green tomatoes –potatoes –artichokes –grape leaves –celery roots –cabbage leaves with lentils –black cabbage with corn meal – Erzurum cheese-stuffed peppers – cheese-stuffed peppers – Siirt sour stuffed vegetables – Malatya stuffed leaves in yoghurt – Yozgat stuffed leaves with broad beans – stuffed lamb intestines (bumbar)*

LEGUMES   239-245

white beans with lamb – lentils with lamb – chick peas with lamb – pinto beans with lamb – black-eyed peas with lamb – dried okra with meat – mixed beans with lamb – pinto beans in olive oil – white beans in olive oil – broad beans in olive oil

DIET DISHES   247-262

Main dishes: *squash boats – grated squash with milk – eggplant with milk – steamed leeks – boiled meat with bouquet garni – cauliflower with cheese.* **Diet sweets:** *pumpkin in bourek – semolina banana pudding – semolina milk pudding – semolina cheese pudding – Uludağ frozen chocolate delight – mock chicken breast pudding – baked fruit – bread pudding – frozen fruit yoghurt – fruit salad – fruit pudding – kadayif dessert – rice pudding – fruit compote – plain cake – oatmeal cookies – quince preserves*

FRUIT DESSERTS   263-270

fruit salad – carrot-cookie dessert – carrot dessert with pudding – chestnut dessert – pumpkin dessert –baked quince – baked apple dessert – pears and cream – figs in syrup– dried apricots in syrup – orange dessert – candied chestnuts – bananas and honey – eggplant dessert

PUDDINGS AND CUSTARDS   271-281

strawberry pudding – orange pudding – crème caramel – rice pudding (sütlaç) – oven rice pudding – vanilla-almond pudding (keşkül) – cocoa crème – chocolate pudding (supangle) – chocolate sauce – apple balls in sauce –chicken breast pudding – mock profiteroles – bottom-of-the-pan pudding (kazandibi) – starch wafer dessert (güllaç) – milk fondant –cream & cookies dessert – quick oven custard (tez pişti)

DESSERTS   283-310

Noah's pudding (aşure) – saffron pudding (zerde) – Erzurum flour sweetmeats – iron dessert – flour sweetmeats with ginger – flour sweetmeats with syrup – Nuriye milk dessert – flour sweetmeats with powdered sugar – semolina sweetmeat with milk – semolina sweetmeat with cheese – kadayif dessert – çim dessert – Hatay cheese künefe – kadayif with pudding – fried vizier's fingers (lokma) – Erzurum stuffed kadayif – baklava – turban twists – cheese baklava – fried ears in syrup – Laz bourek – revani cake no. 1 – revani cake no. 2 – yoghurt cake with syrup – quick breadcrumb dessert – shambaba sweet – press to the sieve – pretty girl's lips – "date" dessert – hazelnut şekerpare – plain şekerpare – fried tulumba – baked bohça with walnuts – Samakol cake in syrup – Bosnian dessert (sulpita) – hazlenut dessert – bullseye rolls – Bosnian cookies – Siirt İmçerket – mutton neck dessert – Balıkesir hoşmerim dessert –sweet cheese dessert – sweet eggs – rose dessert – oven egg custard – molasses dessert

A THANK YOU

Dear readers ...

The decision to write this book was made with the support of my close friends and family. Only recipes that had been tried were included. However, it was by no means an easy task to experiement with this volume of recipes. The support and assistance of my friends sustained me throughout this effort. Since the photographs were taken during recipe testing sessions and the recipes selected for this book were prepared during those sessions, I present them here with a light heart.

I can not possibly present here an integral list of every one of the valued friends who contributed to this work, and so must limit myself here to mentioning the support of relatives Canan Aksoy and Handan and my adopted daughter Hülya Alp, as well as Süheyla Yılmaz who prepared attractive dishes for the photographer, and all those who contributed their own original recipes: Saime Sertbaş, Remziye Dingiloğlu, Ayşe Esenkal, Müşerref Kaya, Neş'e Erşenkal, Nermin Turcan, Gülsenem Demirci, Asiye Demirci, Ayşe Baysal, Aysel Kahraman, Güler Kıdeş, Sabite Şahin, Hatice Dikmen, Hatice Eren, Nahide Aksoy, Necibe Yeşildağ, Fatma Çalışkan, İnci Akyar, Münevver Doğan, Nurgül Ersönmez, Febiha Şedele and Saliha İmik. I wish to express my gratitude and heartfelt thanks to all of these ladies.

For their valuable contributions in the preparation of the Diet Foods chapter, I wish to single out two friends for special thanks: my medical doctor Prof. Fatma Sevil Ozan and dietician Ayşe Özkarabulut.

I look forward to receiving all my readers' criticisms and suggestions for the further improvement of this book in its future editions.

H. Güler VURAL

EDITOR'S PREFACE

Why and for what purpose and what type of a recipe book?

1. To eat and drink is not only for nourishment. Its social meaning is also very important today. It is closely tied to high-level political and economic life, as well as weddings and many other types of social activities that are crowned with a dinner.

2. One way of avoiding disease is good nutrition. The great variety of foods that nature provides serves as a pharmacy for human beings. On the other hand, nowadays artificial additives are taking over the food scene. For this reason, people's sensitivities and care with regard to food and drink are on the rise. (Excessively high-calorie foods and foods with hormones are harming us more than they help us.) In other words, nutritional issues have come to be regard-ed as overwhelmingly important for health.

3. In these times, increasingly wider varieties of tastes and more selectivity with regard to food have increased the general awareness of the saying, "the way to the heart is through the stomach." (A good cookbook has become an essential item in the dowries of young girls.)

4. Mankind's experiences in eating and drinking have come down to us through masterpieces of art. That is to say, one branch of our rich culture is cuisine. The Turkish culinary art has a heritage no less rich than those of marbling, calligraphy, ceramic, rug weaving etc. In order to revive the old dishes, original cookbooks have to be published and spread to every home. It was our wish to take a step in that direction with this book. In the creation of these recipes, the departure point has been the Turkish palate.

5. Cookbooks are necessary even for a thorough understanding of the concept of "provider and sustenance". We particularly sought to reflect this dimension in our book.

6. In the old times in our society, more varieties of fruits, vegeta-bles and grains were grown but the production was limited. Today, both purchasing capacity and volume have increased. For this rea-son the available selection in the market is much broader. Our educational institutions as well as families are becoming increasingly aware of this fact. In other words, the richness of our cuisine has brought a need for an overall assessment of our gastronomic wealth. (This book provides recipe and ingredient examples from all parts of Turkey from east to west.)

7. We can not do without recipe books in planning balanced menus. Of course, there is a difference between attractive food and eating right. The main thing to be considered is one's need for vitamins, protein, carbohydrates and calcium in the foods we eat. For this reason a carefully designed dinner table depends on one's knowledge about food.

8. The way the food is served to others, the arrangement of the dining table and the presentation of the food are as important as the cooking. A few simple details can make the food much tastier and more appealing. These factors make an illustrated cookbook important. (All of our photographs are originals taken especially for this book.)

9. The purpose of writing a cookbook should be to provide awareness and understanding of satisfactory and balanced nutrition.

a. For whom are the pleasures of life not enriched by foods that are pleasing first to the eye, then to the palate and then the stomach? People whose lives have lost their zest can gain a new lease on life through tasty foods. This is one more factor pointing to the importance of cookbooks.

b. Food also has to be assessed from the standpoint of afford-ability. (It is necessary to explain in cookbooks how to find and select the best ingredients for each recipe.)

We present for your evaluation and criticism this work that we believe is an important one. We sincerely hope you find it useful and express our best wishes for a good appetite.

İbrahim Ethem Vural (Editor)

TRANSLATOR'S PREFACE

To sit at the Turkish dining table is to treat onself to a plethora of tastes to surprise and delight the palate. When asked to translate Güler Vural's work, I was both pleased and challenged. Here is no simple collection such as those sold in tourist shops. Mrs. Vural has undertaken to cover the entire Turkish cuisine with its variety of regional recipes. Here you will discover the foods of East and West. You will recognize the French, Italian, Persian and Arab influences. You will find recipes of the Ottoman palace as well as more familiar Mediterranean dishes. Are you dieting for health, or are you seeking non-meat recipes? Here are special sections for you.

Any cook anywhere, novice or expert, will find this book a valuable source of information and ideas for food and drink preparation. Do you wonder about buying meat or cheese or how best to whip egg whites? Do you need advice about what to serve with the main dish or with tea or how to use stale bread? The answers to such questions are included in this book. Social scientists and scholars too will find in this work insight into Turkish society and culture through the folk wisdoms and parables about nourishment, food preparation and dining that are inherent in Turkish cuisine traditions.

The Turkish Dining Table: Recipes for Health and Happiness brings to mind my first years as a young American housewife when I regularly consulted that culinary classic, Joy of Cooking. When I moved to Turkey in 1986, how I would have appreciated Mrs. Güler's book. I came to admire the Turkish cuisine, was impressed by the abundance and variety of fresh food available here, and sought to learn the recipes from my new family and friends in order to show my culinary skills. Now, after nearly 20 years, it is as though I have rediscovered Turkish cooking in this book. If you are new to the Turkish cuisine, I welcome you to our fabulous dining table.

Carol Stevens Yürür

ABOUT BREAD

ABOUT BREAD

Bread is an essential part of any meal. It enhances the pleasure of eating any dish. The smell of bread wafting in the air signals in people feelings of motherly compassion and blessings. It's as if all the other gifts from nature are surrounding her on the dining table. Bread is the staple of every home, in all cultures, rich and poor. Some possess all the wealth but are dreaming of her. Some avoid bread for reasons of status. For most it is the basic nourishment. Because of the primary place of bread in the Turkish cuisine, it was selected as the first topic to be addressed in this book.

HELPFUL HINTS ABOUT BREAD
- If you pinch the bread and it soon returns to its original shape, it is well-baked.
- If you store fresh bread in a bread box, it will become stale less quickly.
- If you place 2-3 sugar cubes in the bread box, the bread will become stale less quickly.
- It is best not to buy more bread than is needed at the time. However, there are many useful ways to make use of excess or stale bread.

1. Bread cut in small cubes and baked lightly
a. The cubes may be kept in a glass jar in the refrigerator and when needed, reheated and used with soup.

b. The cubes may be crushed or passed through a food processor to make fine crumbs for meatballs or various sauces.

2. Bread "ravioli"
Saute in some oil: finely chopped onion and ground meat. Add some tomato paste and black pepper and stir a little. Add tiny bread cubes, then a dash of water, and stir the mixture once or twice. Place the lid tightly on the pan and turn off the fire. After 5-10 minutes the bread cubes have softened. Spread garlic yoghurt on top. When ready to serve, drizzle over the top some red pepper sauteed in oil.

3. Open-faced hot pittas
Mix well together: equal amounts of onion and ground meat, some chopped green pepper, salt, a little tomato paste or chopped tomato, black pepper and a little oil. Cut in half the hard heels of leftover bread or thick bread slices. Spread the mixture on the bread pieces and either place them under the broiler or in a lightly oiled pan in the oven. They are ready to serve when browned well on top.

4. Bread pizza
Put small slices of bread in a flat greased baking pan. Pour a mixture of beaten egg and milk all over the bread and press down the bread by hand. Spread over the top a mixture of chopped onion and ground meat, either sauteed or not. Salami or bacon can be added. Place the pan in the oven for 10-15 minutes. Remove and sprinkle on grated kashar cheese is added, then return pan to the oven. When the cheese is lightly browned, serve the pizza hot. (This is an excellent surprise for the Sunday breakfast table as well as a way to use up the stale bread.)

5. Bread dessert

Soak slices of stale bread briefly in milk and remove. Dip in beaten egg, fry in hot oil and lay the slices in a glass pan. Pour a sweet syrup over it and let it set until serving time.

6. Tiny pieces of stale bread are placed in a dish and milk or yoghurt are put over them (and sugar if desired) for a tasty snack.

7. Tiny pieces of bread can be added to soups.

8. Seasoned bread cubes (croutons). Ground red pepper is fried lightly in oil and the bread cubes fried a little in the oil. (If desired, before adding the bread, add some sliced garlic to the oil). The cubes are then added to each serving of hot soup.

9. Sandwich varieties. Thin slices of kashar cheese are placed on top of bread slices, followed by a slice of salami or bacon in the center of each, then placed in the oven. Or, beaten egg with cheese mixed in may be spread on the slices and placed in the oven.

10. Steamed bread (Benmari). Put a little water in a wide pan and heat, place a strong perforated skimmer over the pan and bread slices on top. Cover the pan and turn heat on simmer for the bread to soften in the steam. This method both softens the bread and brings out its nice smell.

11. Bread balls with cheese. Remove the crusts of 4-5 bread slices. Grate 250 grams (1/2 lb) white cheese. Add the cheese to the slices and mix well. Beat 2 eggs with finely chopped parsley, dill and black pepper. Mix the bread and egg mixtures together and form tiny balls. Fry in hot oil and serve.

12. Bread with poached eggs (Çılbır). In proportion to the amount of stale bread at home: onion, tomato paste, oil, egg, salt and pepper are needed. Fill a large bowl with bread cubes. Slice the onions in rings and saute a little in oil. Add the tomato paste and cook a little more. Add a little water and when it boils break a few eggs (or to taste) directly into the pan. Bring to a boil again and remove from heat. Place on top of the bread.

Notes:

1. The amount of water used is adjusted according to the amount of bread to be moistened.

2. In place of eggs cubed potatoes may be added. After simmering a little in the tomato sauce add enough water to moisten the bread. When the potatoes are cooked place on top of the bread and cover for about 10 minutes until the bread is soft.

13. When bread is called for in recipes in the Eggs Section, stale bread may be used.

To appreciate the fragrance and taste of fresh bread it is good to use stale bread from time to time.

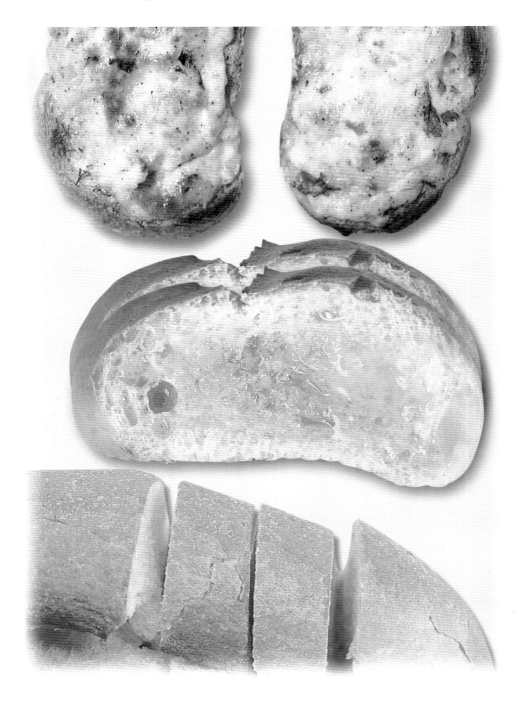

CANAPES

CONTENTS

SPICY WALNUT SPREAD (TARATOR) CANAPES

Ingredients:

1/3 cup walnut pieces
3/4 cup tahin
2-3 garlic cloves
1 teaspoon red pepper
juice of 1/2 lemon
salt
3-4 sprigs parsley
3-4 sprigs fresh dill
bread slices

1. Crush the garlic in salt and mix together well with walnut pieces, pepper, tahin and lemon juice.

2. Add finely chopped parsley and dill and mix a little more. Spread on bread slices.

TAHIN CANAPES

Ingredients:

1/3 cup tahin
1/3 cup lemon juice
1 teaspoon or more red pepper
1/3 teaspoon cumin
2-3 cloves garlic
2-3 pickling cucumbers
bread slices

1. Crush the garlic in salt and mix well with the tahin, red pepper and cumin. Gradually add the lemon juice while stirring. Spread the mix on bread slices.

2. Slice cucumbers very thin and spread on top of the canapes.

BREADCRUMB CANAPES

Ingredients:

1/2 package prepared (fine) bread-crumbs (about 2 cups homemade)
1/3 cup walnut pieces
2 tablespoons red pepper flakes
2 tablespoons cumin
3 tablespoons olive oil
juice of 1/2 lemon
water as needed
bread slices

1. Mix together well all ingredients, gradually adding enough water to bring to spreading consistency.

2. Spread on bread slices.

POTATO PUREE AND WALNUT CANAPES

Ingredients:

4-5 potatoes
1 handful walnut pieces
2-3 garlic cloves
2 tablespoons tomato paste
juice of a lemon
6 oz. olive oil
salt
bread slices

1. Wash, boil, and peel the potatoes. Mash with a fork. Add crushed garlic, walnut pieces, tomato paste, salt and lemon juice. Mix well.

2. Spread on toasted or fresh bread slices.

HUMMUS CANAPES

Ingredients:

2 cups chickpeas
4-6 tablespoons tahin
5-6 garlic cloves
lemon juice and cumin to taste
1 tablespoon olive oil
1 tablespoon butter
red pepper, 1/2 bunch parsley
bread slices

Wash and soak chickpeas for 8-10 hours. Boil chickpeas and drain. Press through a sieve all ingredients except the oil and butter. Mix in the oil and butter. Put in blender and spread on bread.

TOMATO-PEPPER SPREAD (ÇEMEN) CANAPES

Ingredients:

1/3 cup tomato paste
1/3 cup pepper sauce
1/3 cup walnut pieces
100 grams (about 3 oz.)
cheese
2 slices of bread, crusts
removed
3-4 garlic cloves
black pepper, oregano and
dried mint
1/2 cup olive oil
1/2 bunch parsley
1/2 bunch fresh dill
bread slices

1. Moisten the 2 bread slices and squeeze out the water (or use crushed, stale bread or hard biscuits and put in the food processor).

2. Crush the garlic in a dash of salt. Finely chop the parsley and dill. Grate the cheese.

3. Mix all ingredients in a deep bowl. Add a little more oil if desired, depending on the type of bread used.

4. Spread on bread slices.

Haydari canapes

EGG CANAPES

Ingredients:

5 eggs

2 tablespoons

mayonnaise

salt

pepper

bread slices

1. Boil the eggs. Remove the yolks and crush with a fork. Add mayonnaise and salt and mix well.

2. Spread on bread slices. Slice the whites of the eggs matchstick thin and arrange them on the canapes. Place on serving plate and sprinkle on black pepper.

Cheese canapes

CHEESE CANAPES

Ingredients:

100 grams (3 oz) white cheese
2-3 cloves garlic
1 lemon
1/4 cup olive oil
red pepper
bread slices

1. Grate the cheese or press with a fork. Crush the garlic. Mix all ingredients together well.

2. Spread on bread and arrange parsley sprigs on top.

SPICY YOGHURT (HAYDARİ) CANAPES

Ingredients:

1 heaping cup strained yoghurt or sour cream
5-6 cloves garlic
1/3 cup walnut pieces
1 teaspoon oregano
3 tablespoons olive oil
1 1/2 tablespoons red pepper flakes
1/3 teaspoon black pepper, salt
1/3 teaspoon ground red pepper
bread slices

1. Mix all ingredients together until the consistency of a very thick sauce.

2. Spread on bread slices and serve.

HOT PEPPER-POTATO PUREE CANAPES

Ingredients:

4-5 medium sized potatoes
1/2 bunch green onions
3 tablespoons pepper sauce
2-3 cloves garlic or to taste
1/4 cup olive oil
juice of 1 lemon
salt
bread slices

1. Wash the potatoes and pierce with a knife. Place in pan with just enough water to cover and boil.

2. Chop the onions very thin. When potatoes are cooked remove skins, crush and add pepper sauce, salt, lemon juice and crushed garlic. Mix well. Add onions and olive oil, stir and spread the mix on bread slices.

HOT PEPPER SPREAD CANAPES

Ingredients:

4 tablespoons red pepper flakes
4 tablespoons fine bread crumbs
1 teaspoon cumin
1/3 cup walnuts
olive oil
thin bread slices

1. Place red pepper flakes in a pan with a few drops of water and turn flame high. When water 2 evaporates remove pan from heat to cool.

2. Add to pan the bread crumbs, cumin and walnuts and mix. Gradually drizzle olive oil onto this mixture until spreading consistency.

3. Spread to desired thickness on bread slices. These canapes will add color and taste to an attractive table of boureks and savory pastries.

Eating and drinking – essentials for life

*- Provide **heat and energy** for your body (carbohydrates, oils and proteins)*

*- Help your body **grow and become** strong and repair your internal organs (proteins, vitamins and water)*

*- Keep your body functioning for a **long and healthy life** (vitamins, minerals and water)*

EGGS AND OMELETTES

CONTENTS

HINTS WHEN PURCHASING EGGS

When purchasing eggs examine them carefully:

1. If the egg shines when held up to the light it is fresh, if it appears cloudy and spotted it is not fresh.

2. If the inside shifts around or gurgles when shaken, the egg is not fresh.

3. When placed in salted water if the egg goes to the bottom it is fresh, if it remains half way it is a little old and if it floats to the top it is very old.

4. Fresh eggs weigh more than unfresh eggs.

HINTS FOR COOKING EGGS

1. The freshness of eggs is important for health as well as for the enjoyment of eating them.

2. Remove the eggs from the refrigerator about 5-10 minutes before adding to boiling water to prevent cracking in the pan.

3. For soft-boiled eggs, first rub them in the hands or brush them while washing, then slowly add to boiling water and cook for 1-2 minutes.

4. For half-cooked eggs place in boiling water for 5-6 minutes.

5. 10-12 minutes are required for fully cooked eggs. If left to boil longer the yolks will turn black and the eggs will be tough.

6. When preparing poached eggs add vinegar to the boiling water before breaking the eggs. For 5 eggs use 1 liter of water, 1/4 cup vinegar and a little salt.

7. Remove poached eggs with a slotted spoon and serve with a vegetable or meat.

PLAIN OMELETTE

Ingredients:

4-5 eggs
1 tablespoon butter
1/2 bunch parsley
salt
black pepper

1. Crack the eggs into a glass or porcelain dish. Beat slightly. Add chopped parsley, salt and pepper and mix a little more.

2. Melt butter in a skillet (teflon is recommended). When butter is sizzling pour in all or a portion of the egg mixture (if a separate omelette is desired for each person divide accordingly.) Do not allow the eggs to become hard. Turn off the fire and fold the omelette over once or twice. Turn the omelette onto a serving plate.

Note: If desired additions to the omelette may be made while cooking. Before folding add cheese, spinach puree, potato puree, cooked ground meat or sliced mushrooms.

BREAD AND EGGS

Ingredients:

5-6 eggs
5-6 thin bread slices
cooking oil
1 tablespoon tomato paste
1 tablespoon butter
1 large tomato
salt
pepper
5-6 slices of salami, pastrami or kashar cheese

1. Fry the bread slices in an oiled skillet. Arrange on a platter. Oil a skillet and fry the eggs lightly, then gently place them on top of the bread slices. Place the salami, pastrami or cheese slices on top of each egg.

2. Remove the skin from the tomato and chop the tomato well. Melt the butter in a pan, add the tomatoes and stir. Add the tomato paste and cook a little longer. Add salt and pepper. Spoon the sauce on top of the eggs.

Note: The thin strips of salami or pastrami can be added to the tomato sauce and then spooned over the eggs.

FRIED EGGS

Ingredients:
5 eggs
1 tablespoon butter
salt, pepper

1. Melt the butter in a pan.

2. Carefully break the eggs one by one into the pan. Add salt and pepper. Cook until the whites turn white.

3. If well-cooked eggs are desired, cover the pan and cook 1-2 minutes.

Fried Eggs

PALACE EGGS

Ingredients:
4 onions
4 eggs
3 tablespoons olive oil
salt

Slice the onions in half-moons and cook in the olive oil until translucent. Break the eggs on top. Add salt and stir briefly. Transfer immediately to a serving plate.

EGGS WITH TOMATOES AND PEPPERS (MELEMEN)

Ingredients:
3-4 eggs
5-6 tomatoes,
3-4 small green peppers
2 tablespoons oil
salt, black pepper

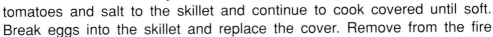

1. Wash and remove seeds from the peppers. Slice very thin. Place oil in a large skillet and saute the peppers. Peel the tomatoes and slice thinly. Add tomatoes and salt to the skillet and continue to cook covered until soft. Break eggs into the skillet and replace the cover. Remove from the fire before the eggs are hard. For a softer yolk, cook the eggs without covering the pan. Add black pepper and transfer to serving plate.

Note: *If desired, the eggs may be broken into a bowl and beaten slightly before adding them to the pan.*

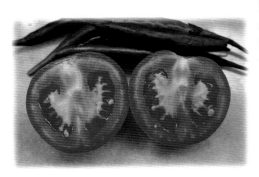

EGGS WITH SAUCE

Ingredients:

300 grams (9.6 oz) tomatoes

1 egg

1 celery stalk

1/2 bunch parsley

fresh basil leaves

2 tablespoons olive oil

salt

black pepper

1. Peel the onion and trim and wash the onion, celery, basil and parsley. Chop all very thin.

2. Saute in oil until just as the color is changing. Add the peeled and chopped tomatoes. Add salt and saute a little longer. Continue to cook covered until the water has evaporated (about 10-15 minutes). Spoon sauce onto serving plate.

3. Gently boil the eggs and plunge into cold water. Remove shells and slice in two the long way with a sharp knife being careful not to displace the yellows. Place the eggs on top of the sauce. Spoon some of the sauce over the eggs. Add black pepper and serve immediately.

HOLIDAY MORNING SURPRISE

Ingredients:

4 eggs

1-2 fresh green onions

1-2 small green peppers

1 sausage

1/2 bunch parsley

1 tablespoon oil

1. Remove stems and seeds from peppers and wash them. Slice the sausage into tiny pieces and slice the onions very thin and set aside. Slice the peppers very thin and saute in the oil. Add the sausage pieces, stir and continue to cook.

2. Crack the eggs into bowl and pour over the peppers. Add the sliced onions and cover the pan, continuing to cook until the eggs are ready. Add the finely chopped parsley on top and serve hot.

CHEESE OMELETTE NO. 1

Ingredients:
1/3 cup grated kashar cheese
2-3 eggs
salt, black pepper
1 1/2 tablespoons oil

1. Heat the oil in a skillet and add the grated cheese.
2. When the cheese starts to melt break the eggs into the pan and stir twice. Remove from the fire as soon as the cheese starts to become transparent.

Note: *A teflon skillet is preferred to prevent the cheese from sticking.*

OMELETTE WITH FLOUR (MURTOGE)

Ingredients
1/2 packet of margarine or butter
4 tablespoons flour
3-4 eggs
salt, red pepper flakes

1. Cook the flour in oil until it has become smooth. Add salt and break the eggs on top. Stir lightly.
2. When the eggs are cooked, transfer to a serving plate and sprinkle the red pepper flakes on top.

MOCK BACON OMELETTE

Ingredients:
100 grams (3.2 oz.) ground meat
2-3 garlic cloves
1 1/2 tablespoons oil
2-3 eggs
salt, black pepper

1. Heat the oil in a pan and add crushed garlic and meat. Cook on high heat until the meat is done. Add salt and cook a little longer.
2. Break each egg carefully into the pan and cook to desired doneness. Transfer to serving plate and add pepper.

*How **egg white** is handled is critical. Some dishes call for fluffy egg white. The volume increases considerably when food with egg white is beaten. However, excessive beating could cause the ingredients to separate. If cream or sugar are combined with egg white, the whipping takes longer to complete.*
Measurements *and measuring containers can vary considerably in the Turkish kitchen. For example, the amount in "one handful" depends on whose hand is used. One pinch = 10-30 grams; one handful = 100-600 grams; one coffee spoon = 4-5 grams; one dessert spoon = 10-12 grams; one soup spoon = 12-15 grams; one coffee demitasse = 25-75 grams; one tea glass = 100-125 grams; one water glass = 200-250 grams. In this book we have translated these to approximate American and European measurements.*

GROUND MEAT OMELETTE

Ingredients:

1 1/2 tablespoons sauteed ground meat and 2 eggs (per serving)
4-5 sprigs of parsley
oil

1. Oil a teflon skillet.

2. Wash the parsley and chop finely. Add to the sauteed meat and blend well.

3. Break two slightly beaten eggs into the heated pan along with a pinch of salt. Tip the pan so the eggs spread across the pan surface. Break any bubbles in the eggs. When cooked, add cooked ground meat, fold over the omelette and transfer to a serving plate.

Note: 1. *To prepare a family sized omelette the amount of meat and eggs may be increased proportionately. Cook half of the eggs, place without folding onto the serving platter and spread all of the cooked meat and parsley on top. Cook the other half of the eggs and lay it on top. Slice and serve.*

2. *For additional flavor, add tomatoes and peppers.*

3. *Cheese may also be used by mixing it in with the parsley.*

Cheese Omelette

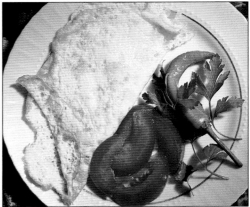

SWEET EGGS (SEFİRE)

Ingredients:
5 eggs
1 tablespoon flour
1 cup sugar
1/2 cup water
1 tablespoon oil

1. Mix the flour and egg well. Heat the oil in a pan. Break the eggs in the pan and tip the pan to spread over the entire surface.

2. Melt the sugar in the water and mix. Add the mixture to the pan when the egg is cooked. Serve immediately.

Note: *Molasses can be used in place of sugar.*

Plain Omelette

CHEESE OMELETTE NO. 2

Ingredients:

2 eggs and 1 1/2 tablespoon white cheese (per serving)

4-5 sprigs parsley

oil

1. Oil a teflon skillet
2. Grate the cheese. Wash the parsley and chop finely. Mix the cheese and parsley well.
3. Break the slightly beaten eggs with a pinch of salt into the hot skillet and tip the pan to spread the eggs evenly. Punch out any bubbles. . When cooked, add cheese-parsley mixture, fold over the omelette and transfer to a serving plate.

Note: To prepare a family sized omelette the amount of cheese mixture and eggs may be increased proportionately. Cook half of the eggs, place without folding onto the serving platter and spread all of the cheese and parsley on top. Cook the other half of the eggs and lay it on top. Slice and serve.

POTATOES AND EGGS

Ingredients:

3-4 potatoes

1 onion

4 eggs

2 tablespoons oil

salt, black pepper

1. Peel and wash the onion and chop finely. Wash and peel the potatoes and cut in small cubes. If possible use a no-burn pan. Place the onions and potatoes in the pan with oil and salt. Cook on a very low fire stirring often until transparent or slightly browned.

2. Break the potatoes into a bowl and add to the pan while stirring a little. When the eggs are cooked add black pepper and transfer to a hot serving plate.

EGGS WITH DATES

Ingredients:

250 grams (8 oz.) dates

3-4 eggs

2 tablespoons butter

1. Remove pits from dates and slice very thin. Saute a little in the butter.
2. Break the eggs over the dates. Stir as the eggs cook and transfer to a hot serving platter.

TOMATO EGGS (ÇILBIR)

Ingredients:

2-3 tomatoes
1 onion
4 eggs
2 tablespoons oil
salt, black pepper
3-4 sprigs parsley, if desired

1. Chop the onions into cubes. Saute a little in the oil. Peel the tomatoes and chop small. Add to the onions and cook a little longer. Add 1/3 cup water and salt. Bring to a boil.

2. Break the eggs one by one so that they remain separate and cook without stirring.

3. Transfer each egg with a portion of the sauce onto the serving platter. Add black pepper and parsley if desired. This dish can be served at breakfast or become a lunch or evening meal.

Note: *Add eggs one by one into a pan of 1-2 cups boiling water and cook until soft. Transfer to serving plate and spread over the eggs plain yoghurt or garlic yoghurt. Red pepper that has been fried in oil can be drizzled over the eggs. Prepared this way the dish is called "yoghurt çılbır".*

Sayings about honey

"*Sweet honey dissimulates so many powerful poisons.*" Ovidius

"*Don't be fooled by the enemy's sweet words; there may well be poison in the honey.*" Sheikh Sadi

"*The honey of one with a sour face will taste bitter.*" Sheikh Sadi

"*Where there's honey the flies are plentiful.*" Cervantes

"*The one who handles honey has sticky fingers.*" Balzac

"*Too much of even the sweetest honey is too much.*" Shakespeare

"*Honey tastes sweet to any mouth.*" Mevlana

"*Poison comes with honey as hatred comes with love.*" Firdevsi

"*Yunus how nicely you said it / you ate the honey and the sugar / I already found the honey of honeys / let my beehive go to plunder.*" Yunus Emre

SALADS

CONTENTS

HELPFUL HINTS ABOUT SALAD PREPARATION

Salads may consist of only green leafy vegetables (leaf lettuce, romaine, rocket, parsley, garden cress etc.) as well as a whole variety of raw roots and flowers. Many types of fruits as well add zest to salads.

The type of dressing selected for a salad depends on which vegetables or fruits it contains.

1. It is very important that all implements used in preparing a salad are very clean. The folds of many vegetables can be nests for bacteria. Therefore they should first be separated, sorted and trimmed, then placed in water for 5 minutes. This procedure eliminates any mud that might be remaining on the leaves and give the vegetables a lively appearance.

2. If very muddy, it is not sufficient to place the vegetables in water. In this case each leaf must be passed under running water.

3. Washed vegetables should be placed in a colander to drain well. (Undrained water between the leaves will dilute the dressing put on the salad. Therefore it is advised to place the vegetables on a clean cloth or paper towel to absorb the remaining water.)

4. To prevent loss of vitamins and food value, wash the vegetables before cutting.

5. The smaller the vegetables are cut the more vitamins are lost. Cut in large pieces whenever possible.

6. Greens and certain flowers suitable for salads (pansies, roses, honey-suckle, etc.) should be processed when fresh and shortly before the meal.

7. Add the dressing just before serving and toss the greens gently.

8. The usual proportions of 1 part vinegar to 2 parts oil for salad dressings may be altered according to taste. Various herbs and spices and mayonnaise-yoghurt mixtures add zest and color to salad dressings.

9. Mix the ingredients of the dressing without the oil first, then slowly add the oil. If the dressing is then beaten a little it will thicken.

10. Salad dressings containing such ingredients as oil, vinegar, salt and pepper may be prepared and stored in a jar or glass bottle and kept at room temperature for a week. If artificial sweetener is to be added, add just before serving to avoid a chemical taste.

11. Just as various spices add flavor, so do finely chopped onion or crushed garlic.

12. A little bit of flavored oil or vinegar added to a salad dressing or to a marinade enhances the flavor.

13. It is better when adding onion to a salad to cut the peeled onion in two, placed the cut sides down on the board and slice thinly.

14. The stems as well as the leaves of the parsley are very good. Parsley may be brewed like a tea that helps the body ride itself of poisons. It is also good against body aches and high blood pressure.

15. To keep the parsley fresher longer, trim the stems a little and dip in a bowl of water, then lay in damp paper before placing in a plastic bag.

16. The outer leaves of romaine are rich in vitamins. Do not discard them when cleaning. If a bit wilted dip in a dish of water and squeeze on a little lemon to liven them.

17. Unripe grapes may be squeezed and the juice used to add a sour taste to salads and other foods.

LEAF LETTUCE SALAD

Ingredients:

1 medium-sized curly leaf lettuce or romaine
1 bunch fresh green onions
1/2 bunch parsley or other fresh herbs such as
mint, dill, garden cress, rocket, salt
1/4 cup lemon juice or vinegar
1/2 cup olive oil

1. Wash greens three times and drain thoroughly.

2. Chop only when ready to prepare the salad. Mix lemon juice or vinegar with salt and oil and pour over greens. Toss and serve.

CUCUMBER-POTATO SALAD

Ingredients:

3-4 potatoes
1-2 large cucumbers
2-3 cloves garlic
1 cup yoghurt
1/2 cup mayonnaise
fresh dill, salt

1. Boil the potatoes, strain and cube. Scrub cucumbers and place unpeeled through a food processor. Strain well and add to the potatoes.

2. Mix together the crushed garlic, yoghurt, mayonnaise and salt and add to the potatoes. Add the finely chopped dill and stir again. Let the salad settle in the refrigerator. (Goes well with meat and fried dishes.)

CORN SALAD

Ingredients:

250 grams (8 oz.) each of canned
corn and canned peas
2 carrots
2 green peppers
1 cup mayonnaise
4 tablespoons olive oil
2 tablespoons vinegar
1 teaspoon sugar
1/3 teaspoon mustard, salt

1. Scrape and wash carrots. Parboil, drain and chop in small cubes.

2. Add peppers sliced about same size as carrot pieces. Drain corn and peas and add.

3. Mix together mayonnaise, sugar, salt, mustard and vinegar in a bowl. Slowly add olive oil while stirring. Add dressing to the vegetables and toss together.

Note: Salami slices may be placed around the border of the serving plate.

MAYONNAISE

Ingredients:
2 egg yolks
1 cup olive oil
juice of one lemon
dash of salt
a little mustard if desired

1.Remove eggs from the refrigerator at least 2-3 hours before using to be sure the yolks are at room temperature.

2. Beat egg yolks in a glass or porcelain bowl until they foam. Add olive oil drop by drop while continuing to mix. The last part of the oil may be added a little more quickly. Repeat with the addition of the lemon juice. Add a dash of salt and mustard if desired.

Notes:

1. If non-acidic olive oil is not available, corn oil may be used.

2. The oil and egg should be at the same temperature and the eggs should be as fresh as possible.

3. If the mixture begins to separate, a spoonful of boiling water may be added gradually.

4. Try to mix evenly and maintain a steady pace.

5. A spoonful of flour or cornstarch can be mixed with a little water, brought to a boil for a minute or two and cooled. Later, if added to the egg yolks, it then becomes easier to make the mayonnaise according to the above recipe.

SALAD DRESSINGS

No. 1 Ingredients:
1/4 cup mayonnaise
1 1/2 tablespoons oil
1/4 cup vinegar
1 teaspoon sugar
1/3 teaspoon celerly seed, oregano or dill weed, salt

Mix all ingredients together and pour on salad. (This dressing will not last long.)

No. 2 Ingredients:
1 part mayonnaise to 2 parts yoghurt
1/4 cup oil
4 tablespoons vinegar, salt

Mix all ingredients together and pour on salad. (This dressing will not last long.)

No. 3 Ingredients:
1 part vinegar to two parts oil
Salt and red pepper flakes

Mix all ingredients together and pour on salad. (A large amount may be prepared and refrigerated for 1-2 weeks.)

No. 4 Ingredients:
1 bunch parsley
1/4 cup olive oil
juice of 1/2 lemon

Mix all ingredients in a blender and pour in a glass jar. (A large amount may be prepared and refrigerated for 1-2 weeks.)

FLAVORED OILS

HERB OIL Ingredients:
3-4 cups oil
1 bunch fresh tarragon or basil
A few sprigs of oregano or another fresh herb (If dried is used, 1/4 cup) Do not be tempted to mix in more types of herbs. Select one.

Crush the fresh herbs slightly to bring out the flavor. If dried, pound the herbs. Place them in a jar and pour the oil over them. Cap tightly, shake a little and store in the cupboard (Keeps 1-2 weeks).

PEPPER OIL Ingredients:
3-4 cups oil
2-3 fresh or dried hot peppers

Crush the fresh peppers slightly to bring out the flavor. If dried, pound them. Place them in a jar and pour the oil over them. Cap tightly, shake a little and store in the cupboard (Keeps 1-2 weeks. Shake from time to time.)

GARLIC OIL Ingredients:
3-4 cups oil
4-5 garlic cloves

Peel and wash the garlic. Crush a little, place in a jar and pour the oil over them. Cap tightly, shake a little. (Keeps a long time if stored in a cool place.)

FLAVORED VINEGARS

SPICY VINEGAR Ingredients:
3-4 cups vinegar
1 bunch tarragon
basil
a bit of oregano or another herb

Crush the fresh herbs slightly to bring out the flavor. If dried, pound the herbs. Place in a jar. Bring the vinegar to the boiling point and pour over the herbs. After it cools, cap the jar and shake from time to time. Store for 1-2 days. Strain and pour into another jar or bottle for use as needed.

GARLIC VINEGAR Ingredients:
3-4 cups vinegar
4-5 garlic cloves

Peel, wash and crush the garlic, place in a jar. Bring the vinegar to the boiling point and pour over the herbs. After it cools, cap the jar and shake from time to time. Store for 1-2 days. Strain and pour into another jar or bottle for use as needed.

FRUITY VINEGAR Ingredients:
3-4 cups vinegar
250 grams (1/2 lb) raspberries, apple or pear

Wash and crush the fruit and place in a jar. Bring the vinegar to the boiling point and pour over the herbs. After it cools, cap the jar and shake from time to time. Store for 1-2 days. Strain and pour into another jar or bottle for use as needed.

MUSHROOM SALAD

Ingredients:

1/2 kilogram (1 lb) mushrooms
3-4 small cucumbers
2 medium size carrots
1/2 bunch parsley
1/3 cup canned peas
1/3 cup olive oil
6 tablespoons vinegar or lemon juice
1 teaspoon sugar
salt

1. Wash mushrooms, drain off excess water, place in an iron skillet and cook on low heat until their own juice is released. Set aside to cool.

2. Slice large mushrooms in four and small ones in two.

3. Scrape, wash and grate the carrots. Saute in a tablespoon of oil, stirring occasionally. Spoon on top of the mushrooms.

4. Drain the peas and add to the mixture.

5. Add finely chopped parsley and thinly sliced cucumbers. Mix together the lemon juice or vinegar, salt and sugar, then slowly stir in the olive oil. Pour on the salad and serve.

BEAN SALAD (PİYAZ)

Ingredients:

250 grams (1/2 lb) white beans
2-3 tomatoes
3-4 small peppers
2 dry onions
1/2 bunch parsley
1/3 cup olive oil
6 tablespoons vinegar or lemon juice, salt

1. Soak beans 8-10 hours. Drain and add fresh water. Boil until done, drain and set aside to cool.

2. Chop or slice the onions. Press into them 1 1/2 tablespoon salt, rinse 2-3 times and drain.

3. Chop tomatoes, slice peppers in thin rings, chop parsley. The salad may be prepared in two ways:

a) Place the boiled beans on the salad plate and lay the onions over them. Arange the tomatoes and peppers. Mix together the lemon juice, olive oil and salt and pour on top.

b) Mix all ingredients except the dressing and parsley in a deep bowl and turn onto the salad platter. Spread the parsley over it and then pour the dressing on top.

Notes:

1. If desired cooked egg slices may be added, as well as black olives. Thin radish slices may be placed around the salad. Then the sauce is added.

2. A dressing of mayonnaise mixed with vinegar, sugar, salt and a little olive oil can be used.

CARROT SALAD

Ingredients:
3-4 carrots
1/2 bunch parsley
5-6 black olives
3-4 tablespoons mayonnaise
1 teaspoon olive oil
1 teaspoon sugar
salt
4 tablespoons vinegar

1. Scrape, wash and grate the carrots. Add salt.
2. Mix together the mayonnaise, vinegar, olive oil and sugar. Pour the dressing over the carrots and mix together. Spoon the carrots into a serving dish.
3. Spread finely chopped parsley over the carrots and arrange the olives on top.

SHEPHERD SALAD

Ingredients:
3-4 medium sized tomatoes
2 small green peppers
2 cucumbers
1 onion or 1/2 bunch fresh green onions
1/2 bunch parsley
salt
1/2 cup olive oil
1/4 cup vinegar or lemon juice.
(fresh mint, if desired)

Trim and wash the vegetables. Chop to the desired size. Mix the lemon or vinegar with olive oil and salt. Pour the mixture over the cut vegetables and mix together well. Serve.

Note: *This salad should be prepared just before serving.*

BRUSSEL SPROUT SALAD

Ingredients:
1 package brussel sprouts
2-3 carrots
5-6 black olives
1/3 cup olive oil
6 tablespoons vinegar or lemon juice
1/3 teaspoon sugar
1/2 bunch parsley
1/2 bunch fresh dill, salt

1. Trim the brussel sprouts and place in pan with twice the water needed to cover it. Cook 3-4 minutes, drain and set aside to cool.
2. Place brussel sprouts on a serving plate and spread finely chopped dill over them. Mix the vinegar or lemon juice, olive oil, salt and sugar together and pour over the brussel sprouts.
3. Peel, wash and grate the carrots.

Saute in a spoonful of oil in a skillet (preferably teflon) until they soften. Add to the platter and arrange the olives amid the carrots. Place sprigs of parsley on the carrots and serve.

Note: *Instead of the oil and vinegar mixture, mayonnaise and yoghurt dressing may be used.*

ICEBERG SALAD WITH MAYONNAISE

Ingredients:

1 head iceberg lettuce
1/2 bunch fresh green onions
1 head leaf lettuce
1 tomato
50 grams (1 _ oz) cheese
50 grams (1 _ oz) corn (canned may be used)
10 green olives
2 teaspoons olive oil, salt
4-5 spoonsful yoghurt
mayonnaise

1. Wash and chop the iceberg lettuce into a deep bowl.
2. Chop small the onions, slice the cucumbers and tomatoes and add to the bowl. Add grated cheese. Cut olives into 2 or 3 pieces and add. Add the corn and finely chopped parsley.
3. Mix in a small bowl the olive oil, vinegar, lemon juice and salt and pour over the salad. A mixture of mayonnaise and yoghurt may be spread over the top. Serve the salad without tossing it.

CELERY ROOT SALAD

Ingredients:

2 medium sized celery roots
4-6 tablespoons mayonnaise
4-6 tablespoons yoghurt
juice of half a lemon
2-3 garlic cloves, salt

1. Wash, trim and grate the celery roots. If they smell strong they may be placed in lemon water and brought just to the boiling point. Drain and place in a dish.
2. Add crushed chopped garlic, yoghurt, mayonnaise, lemon juice and salt. Mix well and turn onto serving platter. (Goes well with meat or fish dishes.)

CABBAGE SALAD

Ingredients:

a small head of cabbage
4-5 tablespoons mayonnaise
6 tablespoons vinegar
1/3 cup olive oil
1 teaspoon each of sugar and salt
celery seed or fresh celery leaves
or mint

1. Trim the outer cabbage leaves, wash the cabbage and grate it.
2. Wash the celery leaves (if used) and add to the cabbage (or add the celery seed or mint).
3. Mix together in a bowl the mayonnaise, oil, vinegar, sugar and salt. Be sure the mayonnaise is blended in well. Pour over the cabbage and blend in well. (Goes well with meat dishes, especially meatballs.)

MACARONI SALAD

Ingredients:

*1 package (500 grams or 1 lb)
elbow macaroni
250 grams (1/2 lb) canned corn
3-4 tablespoons mayonnaise
3-4 tablespoons yoghurt
1 tablespoon vinegar
1 teaspoon sugar
1 bunch dill, salt
5-6 small pickling cucumbers*

1. Boil the macaroni, drain and cool. Add drained corn, sliced cucumbers and finely chopped dill.

2. Mix in a bowl the mayonnaise, yoghurt, vinegar, salt and sugar and toss with the macaroni. Place salad in a serving bowl. Serve with meat dishes.

RICE SALAD

Ingredients:

2 cups rice
2-3 cups water
1/4 cup peas, canned or fresh
2 medium sized carrots
1/2 bunch dill
7-8 green onion stalks
3 tablespoons olive oil
juice of 1/2 lemon, salt
5-6 small pickling cucumbers
1/3 teaspoon sugar

1. Soak the rice in hot water for 20 minutes. Rince 3-4 times until the water is no longer white. Depending on the type of rice, put 2 or 3 cups of water in a pan and bring to a boil. Add the washed rice and salt. When the rice comes to a boil add the lemon juice and sugar and cook on high heat until the water is gone. Cover and let it sit. (Addition of the lemon and sugar makes the rice shine.)

2. Peel, wash and boil the carrots. Drain. When cooled cut into small cubes. Drain the peas. If fresh peas are available, boil, drain and chill. Add the vegetables to the cooled rice. Mix together the finely sliced onions, cubed cucumbers and finely chopped dill and add. Mix well and serve well chilled.

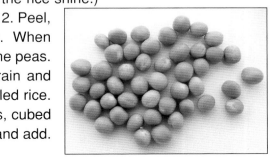

PURSLANE SALAD

Ingredients:

1 bunch tender purslane
2 cups yoghurt
1 cup walnut pieces
1 cup mayonnaise
1/2 bunch dill, salt
3-4 garlic cloves, if desired

1. Wash the purslane and cut the thicker stems. Wash 3-4 times and drain.
2. If using garlic, crush in salt. Mix with yoghurt and mayonnaise and add walnuts.
3. Place the finely chopped purslane in a large bowl and mix in the dressing. Add the finely chopped dill and transfer to a serving dish.

POTATO SALAD

Ingredients:

5-6 potatoes
1 1/2 cups thick yoghurt
3-4 pickling cucumbers
2 medium sized carrots
3-4 cloves garlic
4 tablespoons oil, salt
red pepper

1. Wash and cook the potatoes. Cool and peel. Mash, adding a little salt. Work in 3 tablespoons oil and spread the potatoes into a glass dish.
2. Wash, peel and grate the carrots and put over the potatoes.
3. Crush the garlic in salt and add to the yoghurt. Put this mixture over the vegetables.
4. Chop the cucumbers in cubes and arrange on top of the yoghurt.
5. Fry the red pepper a little in the remaining tablespoon of oil and drizzle over the top. Place the salad in the refrigerator for about a half-hour before serving.

Note: *The cucumbers may be sliced very thin and mixed with the potatoes.*

EGGPLANT SALAD

Ingredients:

1 kilogram (2 lb) large eggplants
2 cups yoghurt
3-4 garlic cloves
salt, red pepper flakes

Grill the eggplants over an open flame to remove the peel. Mash and allow to cool. Mix the crushed garlic and yoghurt and add salt. Mix well with the mashed eggplant. Spoon onto a serving dish and sprinkle on the red pepper.

BEAN-POTATO SALAD

Ingredients:

500 grams (1 lb) white beans
1 bunch curly leaf lettuce
4-5 potatoes
1/2 bunch parsley
lemon
olive oil, salt

1. Boil the potatoes, then peel and slice. Set aside to cool.
2. Boil and drain the beans and set aside to cool.
3. Wash the lettuce and parsley and chop finely.
4. Mix all vegetables and place in the salad bowl. Mix lemon, olive oil and salt and pour over the salad.

VEGETABLE MACARONI SALAD

Ingredients:

500 grams (1 lb) macaroni
5-6 green onion stalks
2-3 small green peppers
3 crisp and fresh tomatoes
1/2 bunch parsley
2 cups yoghurt
1 cup mayonnaise
1/4 cup vinegar
1/3 cup olive oil, salt

1. Boil, drain and chill the macaroni. Wash and drain the vegetables.
2. Cut the onions and the parsley very thin. Chop the tomatoes in cubes and the peppers in thin slices. Mix all the vegetables together and add to the macaroni.
3. Mix together well the mayonnaise and yoghurt and add the vinegar, oil and salt. Add to the macaroni mixture and mix well before transferring to a serving plate. (Goes well with meat, meatball and fish dishes.)

SAUSAGE MACARONI SALAD

Ingredients:

500 grams (1 lb) macaroni
3-4 sausages
1 cup yoghurt
3-4 tablespoons mayonnaise
2 tablespoons olive oil, salt

1. Boil. Drain and chill the macaroni. Add the finely sliced sausages.
2. Mix well the mayonnaise, yoghurt, salt and olive oil and pour over the macaroni. Mix well and transfer to a serving plate. (Goes well with meat dishes. May also be offered at tea time along with bourek.)

LEEK SALAD WITH EGG

Ingredients:

6 medium sized leeks
2 small white onions
1/3 cup mustard
3/4 cup olive oil
4-5 tablespoons vinegar
ground red pepper, salt
1 egg
5-6 parsley sprigs

1. Trim the leeks, cut into 7-8 cm lengths and wash well. Tie them together in threes.

2. Put salted water in a pan and bring to a boil. Add the leeks and cook 15-20 minutes. Drain and set aside to cool.

3. Slice the onion and mix with the mustard, olive oil, vinegar, red pepper and salt. Marinate the leeks in this mixture at least one hour in the refrigerator. Drain the leeks and place on a salad plate.

4. Boil the egg and separate the yolk and white. Pass the yolk through a sieve and place in a line on top of the leeks. Arrange a parallel line of finely chopped parsley. Chop the egg white and place it in a line next to the parsley. This presentation may be altered as desired. The salad is ready to serve.

COLD DISHES

CONTENTS

GAZİANTEP PEPPER SAUCE

Ingredients:

1 cup tomato paste

1 onion

2-3 small green peppers

1 1/2 tablespoons ground red pepper

1 1/2 tablespoons red pepper flakes

1/3 teaspoon black pepper, salt

1. Peel, wash and grate the onion.

2. Trim and remove seeds from peppers and slice thin.

3. Add spices, onions and peppers to the tomato paste and blend well.

SESAME SAUCE

Ingredients:
6 tablespoons sesame seeds
3 tablespoons soy sauce or
  mayonnaise
2 tablespoons vinegar
2 garlic cloves
scant teaspoon sugar

1. Toast the sesame in a dry pan until golden. Set aside to cool.

2. Add to the cooled seeds the soy sauce or mayonnaise, vinegar, crushed garlic and sugar. Stir until the mixture is creamy or mix in food processor.

Note: If processing by hand, it is recommended to chop the toasted seeds in a coffee grinder or use a pestle to crush them.

Goes well with macaroni, meat and chicken dishes.

BROAD BEAN PUREE (FAVA)

Ingredients:
2 cups dried broad beans
1 cup (scant) olive oil
2 onions
1/3 cup sugar
1 lemon, salt
1 handful parsley sprigs
8-10 black olives

1. Sort and wash the beans and soak for 8-10 hours. Saute lightly the thin-sliced onions in 1 tablespoon of olive oil, and add to the drained beans. Add the sugar, salt and 3-4 cups of water and cook the beans until soft.

2. When the beans have cooled, press them through a sieve or put in the food processor. Place on a serving plate and drizzle the olive oil over it. Arrange lemon slices and olives on the plate and spread parsley sprigs on top.

Note: Goes well with macaroni, meat and chicken dishes.

MUHAMMARA SPREAD

Ingredients:
1/2 package fine bread crumbs
1/3 cup walnut pieces
3 tablespoons red pepper flakes
3 tablespoons cumin
3 tablespoons olive oil
juice of 1/2 lemon
water

1. Combine all ingredients and add water as needed for desired consistency.

2. Spread on bread slices or place on the table in a bowl.

HOT PEPPER SAUCE (Adana)

Ingredients:
5 tablespoons red pepper flakes
4 tablespoons fine bread crumbs
1 teaspoon cumin
1/3 cup walnut pieces
olive oil

1. Put the red pepper in a pan of water finger deep and boil on high flame until the water is gone but the pepper is not too dry.

2. When the pepper has cooled slightly add the bread-crumbs, cumin and walnuts and mix. Slowly add sufficient oil to bring to desired consistency. Leave a layer of oil on top until ready to spread the sauce on bread.

3. Spread on bread and serve. This tasty sauce can be served next to boureks and savory pastries to make an attractive cold appetizer table before the main course.

VINEGAR AND WALNUT SAUCE (HAYDARİ)

Ingredients:
1 heaping cup goat's milk curd
or strained yoghurt
5-6 garlic cloves
1/3 cup walnut pieces
1 teaspoon oregano
3 tablespoons olive oil
1 1/2 tablespoons red pepper
flakes
1/3 teaspoon ground red pepper
1/3 teaspoon black pepper, salt

Mix together all ingredients, spread on bread slices and serve.

SPICY TOMATO SALAD

Ingredients:
3-4 tomatoes
1 large onion
2 small green peppers
1 teaspoon red pepper flakes
1/3 teaspoon black pepper
1/3 teaspoon oregano
1/4 cup fermented pomegranate juice
or vinegar (if vinegar is used add a
scant teaspoon sugar)
1/3 teaspoon cumin
salt, sumach to taste

1. Chop tomatoes and onions very fine. Remove seeds from peppers and cut into thin (2 mm) pieces.

2. Combine vinegar, salt, pepper flakes, black pepper, cumin, oregano and sumach. Mix well with vegetables. This goes well with raw meatballs. Also, lentil balls, egg meatballs and some meat dishes.

CURD SALAD

Ingredients:
500 grams (1 lb) goat's milk curd (lor) or strained yoghurt
6-7 green onions, salt, red pepper flakes
1/2 bunch parsley

1. Trim, wash and slice the onions very thin. Mix in a bowl with the curd or yoghurt with salt and transfer to a serving plate.

2. Spread finely chopped parsley and red pepper on top.

Note: *Cucumbers may be used in place of onions.*

SLICED ONION SALAD

Ingredients:
3-4 onions
1/2 bunch parsley
1 tablespoon ground sumach
2 tablespoons red pepper flakes
2 tablespoons olive oil
1 tablespoon salt

1. Peel, wash and cut the onions in two. Thinly slice the onions in half-moons. Place in a bowl and add the salt. Set aside until the bitterness is gone and stir well. Wash three times and drain.

2. Mix the oil, pepper and sumach and pour onto the onions. Mix well and transfer to a serving plate. Spread finely chopped parsley over the onions.

Note: *This goes well with meat dishes such as shish kebab, meatballs or doner and rice pilaf.*

FALAFEL

Ingredients:
1 cup chickpeas
2 onions
1 bunch parsley
2-3 garlic cloves
1/3 teaspoon black pepper
1/3 teaspoon cumin
1/3 teaspoon salt
ground red pepper
2 tablespoons flour
1/2 teaspoon soda

1. Wash chickpeas and soak 8-10 hours. When softened, push through a sieve or mash in a food processor.

2. Slice the onions very thin and mix together in the food processor with the garlic, parsley, cumin, salt, black pepper and red pepper flakes. Add this mixture to the chickpeas and mix well. Add the flour and soda and mix a little more.

3. Form into patties and fry in hot oil. Excellent as a hot appetizer.

POTATO BALLS

Ingredients:
1 kilogram (2 lb) potatoes
25 grams (1/4 lb) margarine
4 tablespoons flour
1/3 cup water
1/3 cup kashar cheese
5 eggs
1 1/2 tablespoons coconut, salt

1. Boil and mash the potatoes. Combine the water, margarine and salt in a pan to boil.

2. When the water boils add the flour and stir. Cook 10 minutes.

3. Remove from the fire and cool slightly. Add the eggs and stir. Return to the fire and stir a little more. Remove from fire and add to the potatoes. Mix in the salt, pepper and coconut.

4. Divide into small parts and serve cold.

Note: *The potato balls can also be fried or a ground-meat filling added and fried.*

CELERY ROOT WITH WALNUTS

Ingredients:
1/2 kilogram (1 lb) celery roots
1/3 cup walnut pieces
1 cup yoghurt
2-3 garlic cloves
2-3 tablespoons mayonnaise
2 tablespoons olive oil
1 tablespoon vinegar
1 teaspoon sugar, salt

1. Peal, wash and grate the celery roots. Add the walnut pieces.

2. Mix the crushed garlic with the yoghurt. Add the mayonnaise, vinegar salt and sugar. Gradually mix in the olive oil. Mix well and transfer to a serving plate.

3. Chopped dill may be spread on top.

AMERICAN POTATO SALAD

Ingredients:
4-5 potatoes
10 cm. (4 in.) long piece salami
1 cup mayonnaise
1/3 cup strained yoghurt
1 tablespoon olive oil
1/3 teaspoon sugar, salt

1. Wash and boil the potatoes and set aside to cool. Chop in cubes and place in refrigerator for about 15 minutes.

2. Cut salami into matchstick size pieces and add to potatoes. Mix together well the mayonnaise, yoghurt, salt and sugar and add. Mix well and transfer to salad dish.

SPICY TAHINI (TARATOR)

Ingredients:
*1 cup walnut
pieces
1/4 cup tahin
3 garlic cloves
juice of
1 lemon
1/2 bunch
parsley
salt,
ground red pepper*

1. Crush the garlic in salt. Mix the walnuts, tahin and red pepper in a bowl, add the garlic and squeeze the lemon juice over it. Transfer to serving plate.
2. Spread parsley leaves over the top. Pickles, olives and lemon slices may be arranged on the plate.

FRIED ONIONS

Ingredients:
*4-5 onions
2 eggs
6 tablespoons flour, salt,
black pepper, frying oil
ketchup*

1. Cut the onions in half rings and mix with salt, wash and drain.

2. Add flour, salt, pepper and eggs and mix.

3. Spoon into hot oil until golden brown and remove to a serving plate. Add bottled or homemade ketchup.

POTATO PUREE WITH WALNUTS

Ingredients:
4-5 potatoes
1 handful walnut pieces
2-3 garlic cloves, salt
2 spoonfuls tomato paste
juice of a lemon
1/4 cup olive oil

1. Wash and boil the potatoes and remove the skins. Mash with a fork.

2. Add crushed garlic, tomato paste, salt and lemon juice. Serve spread on toast or fresh bread slices or in a dish.

HUMMUS

Ingredients:

2 cups chickpeas
4-6 tablespoons tahin
5-6 garlic cloves
lemon juice to taste
cumin to taste
2 tablespoons olive oil or butter
ground red pepper, salt
1/2 bunch parsley

1. Wash chickpeas and soak 8-10 hours. When softened, push through a sieve. Add all remaining ingredients except the oil and mix in a food processor. Transfer to serving dish.

2. Place parsley springs around the dish. Fry the red pepper in the oil and pour in the middle. Cut thin lines into the hummus to let the oil penetrate.

Note: *If olive oil is used, pour cold, if butter, pour hot.*

CARROT-BEET SALAD

Ingredients:
3 beets
3 carrots
2-3 tablespoons oil
1 tablespoon walnut pieces
1 tablespoon mayonnaise
1 tablespoon strained yoghurt
1/2 bunch parsley
2-3 garlic cloves, salt

1. Trim, peel, wash and grate the beets and carrots into a pan. Add the oil and cook 15-20 minutes, stirring frequently. Remove from heat.

2. Mix together well the crushed garlic, yoghurt, mayonnaise and salt. Add to the vegetables.

3. Add the walnuts and mix together. Transfer to serving plate and spread the finely chopped parsley over the top.

CIRCASSIAN CHICKEN

Ingredients:
1 medium sized chicken
1/2 kilogram (1 lb) white walnut pieces
Stale bread (about 1/2 lb loaf)
1/3 teaspoon ground red pepper
1 tablespoon oil
salt, black pepper

1. Clean and wash the chicken, cover it with water and boil. Add some salt when almost done. Remove from water and allow to cool.

2. Remove skin and bones and cut into very small pieces.

3. Crush the walnuts in food processor.

4. Moisten the stale bread with chicken broth. When softened place in food processor with a pinch each of red and black pepper. Add the crushed walnuts and some salt and mix in the processor until creamy, adding chicken broth as needed.

5. Mix in the chicken pieces and transfer to serving plate.

6. Place the oil and red pepper in a bowl and mix frequently for 5-10 minutes. When the oil takes on the color of the pepper, strain it and drizzle it over the chicken. Place parsley sprigs around the dish if desired.

RUSSIAN SALAD

Ingredients:

2-3 potatoes
1-2 carrots
1/2 cup cooked peas (fresh or canned)
10-12 small cucumber pickles
3-4 slices salami
1 teaspoon mustard
1-2 tablespoons vinegar
1-2 tablespoons olive oil
1/2 cup mayonnaise, salt
1 teaspoon sugar

1. Scrape and wash carrots. Peel and wash potatoes. Boil the vegetables separately just until softened. Allow to cool and cut into tiny cubes. Combine and add strained peas. Cut salami and pickles into tiny pieces and add.

2. Mix together mayonnaise, sugar, mustard, vinegar and a little salt, keeping in mind the saltiness of the pickles. Add to vegetables, mix together and transfer to a serving bowl. Finely chopped dill may be spread on top.

ÇEMEN SPREAD

Ingredients:

1/3 cup tomato paste
1/3 cup pepper sauce
1/3 cup walnut pieces
A small chunk of cheese
2 slices bread, crusts removed
3-4 garlic cloves

Black pepper (red pepper flakes if pepper sauce is not hot), oregano, dried mint
6 tablespoons olive oil
1/2 bunch parsley
1/2 bunch dill

1. Moisten bread and squeeze out water (or use prepared fine bread crumbs or put stale bread in the food processor).

2. Crush the garlic with a dash of salt. Finely chop the dill and parsley. Grate the cheese.

3. Mix all the ingredients in a deep bowl. Add a little more oil if needed, depending on which type of bread is used. Spread the mixture on bread slices. If desired, omit putting bread in the mixture.

PINTO BEANS IN SAUCE (BARBUNYA PİLAKİ)

Ingredients:
1/2 kilogram (1 lb) pinto beans
1 large red pepper
2 tomatoes, 1/2 bunch parsley
2 tablespoons olive oil
juice of 1 lemon, salt, cumin

1. Boil and drain the beans and transfer to a serving dish. Mix in a food processor: tomatoes, pepper, cumin, parsley, olive oil and lemon juice.

2. Pour the sauce over the beans.

Note: *Serve with macaroni and meat dishes.*

SOUPS

CONTENTS

HELPFUL HINTS

1. Some of the soup recipes call for one of the many ways to add flavor, or "educate", the soup. When doing this, it is necessary to mix the ingredients very well. The following are some of the mixtures for "educating" soup:

a. Egg and milk: Separate the yellow from the white carefully. After being well beaten with the milk it should be added to the boiling soup very gradually.

b. Egg and lemon: Separate the yellow from the white carefully. After beating the yolk well stir in the salt and lemon. Add a cup of cold water and stir again before slowly adding to the boiling soup.

c. Yoghurt, flour, lemon and egg
d. Yoghurt flour, and egg
e. Yoghurt and flour
f. Milk and flour
g. Garlic and vinegar
h. Flour browned in oil

2. **With yoghurt and flour mixtures,** first either beat in a mixer or pass through a sieve as you add to the soup in order to avoid yoghurt particles or flour lumps in the soup.

3. **When adding egg to hot liquid,** it starts to cook and tiny yellow particles can form. To avoid this, add to the soup a little at a time while stirring the soup. Or take a spoonful of soup from the pot and mix with the egg and then stir into the soup.

4. **With oil and flour mixtures,** it is important to brown the flour lightly. If browned too much it will change the color of the soup and give a burnt taste. If not browned enough it will give a floury flavor to the soup.

5. **If the soup is too thick,** add a little boiling water. If it is too watery let it boil longer, but if it has already cooked long enough and to cook much longer would ruin

it because of such ingredients as meatballs, peas or chickpeas, a little thin vermicelli can be added, or some lightly browned flour.

6. With flour and yoghurt soups, the addition of boiled chickpeas or peas can make the soup tastier and look more appetizing.

7. Add salt to the soup when the cooking is almost finished, as is the case with all dishes you cook.

8. With milky soups, finely chopped parsley goes well in place of mint.,

9. If the water is reduced when cooking lentils, as with cooking meats, boiling water should be added. If cold water is added the color of the lentils changes.

10. If the soup is too salty, a little sugar can be added. Or, before serving, one or two cooked and cubed potatoes can be added.

11. Meat and chicken broth are fattening and should be avoided by those on diets. The soup can be cooked rather thick and a portion for the dieting person taken out and water added. Then meat or chicken broth can be added to the remaining soup for the non-dieters.

12. Because chicken and meat broth give flavor to a soup, it is not necessary to use butter with them and it is healthier as well.

13. When ingredients are not exact in the recipes, such as 1-2 or 2-3 pieces, cups or spoonfuls, using the smaller amount for whatever reason will not have a negative effect on the taste.

14. Stale bread – as explained in the Breads chapter – can be used to make an excellent and tasty accompaniment to soup.

15. Chicken skin and a few slices of garlic can be put in the food processor and sauteed a little, then added to the soup, offering a way to both use the chicken skin and add flavor to the soup.

HOW TO MAKE YOGHURT

Ingredients:
2 kilograms (2 quarts) milk
1 tablespoon yoghurt
2 tablespoons water (3 if yoghurt is very thick)

1. Put the milk to boil. After it reaches the boiling point continue to boil for at least 15 minutes while stirring.

2. Set aside until the milk is lukewarm, about 45° C (110° F). (Skim cream off top if desired, but be sure to use a sterilized spoon to avoid bacteria.)

3. Mix yoghurt with water and beat until all the lumps are gone. Add to milk. Stir only once or twice.

4. Cover with a clean cloth or paper towel. (This is important to avoid condensation from dripping back into the mixture.) Place the cover on the pan and over that wrap a towel or table cloth. Let it sit at least 2 1/2 or 3 hours.

5. After removing cover, carefully lift the pan without shaking it and put in a cool place or refrigerator until ready to serve.

6. As yoghurt is dished out from its container, whey accumulates in the empty space. Thus the remaining yoghurt thickens. The whey may be drained off if thick yoghurt if desired. Whey, however, is an important source of nourishment that can be added to soups or used to make a yoghurt drink (ayran), etc.

PLATEAU (YAYLA) SOUP

Ingredients:
1 cup rice or whole wheat
2 cups yoghurt
1 tablespoon flour
6 cups meat broth or water
1 egg yolk
juice of 1/2 lemon, salt, fresh mint

1. Sort and wash the rice or wheat and cook in the broth or water. If wheat is used, put to soak the night before.

2. To educate the soup, beat together in a bowl the yoghurt with the flour, lemon juice and egg yolk. Add gradually to the boiling broth, stirring constantly. Boil and stir 1-2 minutes longer.

3. Spread mint on top and serve.

Note: *If meat broth is not used, pepper sauteed in oil can be added to the top.*

TOMATO SOUP

Ingredients:
3 tablespoons flour
2 tablespoons oil
3 tomatoes or 1 tablespoon tomato paste
5 cups meat broth or water
salt, mint

1. Brown the flour lightly in oil. Add the finely chopped tomatoes or tomato paste and cook a little longer. Add the water while stirring and stir until the mixture comes to a boil.

2. Add salt and turn the flame on low to simmer for 5-6 minutes. Add mint and serve.

PLATEAU POTATO SOUP

Ingredients:

3 potatoes suitable for frying
3 1/2 cups yoghurt
3 1/2 tablespoons flour
1 egg
2 tablespoons oil
mint, red pepper flakes, salt

1. Peel potatoes and place in cold water for a little while. Then cut into tiny cubes.

2. Add oil to a frying pan and heat. Add the potato cubes to the hot oil and when almost browned add the flour and fry together a little longer. Stir in 4-5 cups of water. When the mixture comes to a boil add salt. After coming to a full boil again remove from heat.

3. Mix together well the yoghurt, mint, pepper and egg. Add to the soup and stir once. The soup is ready to serve.

Note: a) Instead of using flour, thin vermicelli may be added after the water comes to a boil. b) This soup may also be made by frying the flour in the oil first and not frying the potatoes.

RICE SOUP

Ingredients:

1 cup rice

2 tomatoes or 1 tablespoon tomato paste

6 cups meat broth or water

2 tablespoons oil

1 egg yolk

juice of 1 lemon, salt

1/2 bunch parsley or mint

1. Grate the tomatoes and fry in a little oil. Add the broth or water and set aside without boiling.

2. Sort and wash the rice and add to the broth. Bbring to a boil.

3. Beat the egg yolk into the lemon juice. Slowly add this mixture to the boiling soup while stiring. Add the salt.

4. Remove the soup from the stove and add finely chopped mint or parsley.

Note: *If a white soup is desired, omit the tomatoes.*

FLOUR SOUP

Ingredients:

3 tablespoons flour

2 tabvlespoons oil

5 cups meat broth or water

2-3 egg yolks

1 cup milk, salt, parsley

1. Fry the flour in oil until light brown and slowly add the broth or water. Stir until it boils. Add salt. Simmer 6-7 minutes longer.

2. Beat the egg yolks into the milk and add to the boiling soup, stirring constantly. Boil 1-2 minutes longer. When ready to serve, sprinkle chopped parsley on top.

Note: *If a sour taste to the soup is desired, omit the milk and mix some lemon juice with the egg yolks.*

FLOUR-YOGHURT (TARHANA) SOUP

Ingredients:

3 tablespoons flour

2 tablespoons oil

2 cups yoghurt

1 tablespoon tomato paste

5 cups meat broth or water

salt, mint

1. Fry the flour in the oil until light brown. Blend in the yoghurt and tomato paste. Add the broth and stir until the mixture comes to a boil.

2. Add salt and boil 8-10 minutes longer. Just before removing from the heat sprinkle mint on top of the soup.

FLOUR SOUP WITH ONIONS

Ingredients:

3 tablespoons flour
5 cups meat broth or water
2 tablespoons oil
2 small green peppers
3 tomatoes
1/2 bunch green onions
3 garlic cloves
1/4 cup vinegar, salt

1. Remove tomato skins and finely chop tomatoes and peppers. Saute them a little, add the broth and bring to a boil.

2. Place the flour in a dish and moisten. Veryu slowly add the flour to the boiling broth stirring constantly. Add salt. To eliminate the floury taste continue to boil for 7-8 minutes.

3. Add to the boiling soup finely chopped onions and boil 3-4 more minutes.

4. Mix the crushed garlic with the vinegar and stir into the soup when ready to serve.

WEDDING SOUP

Ingredients:

1/2 kilogram (1 lb) boneless lamb
or chicken
3 tablespoons flour
2 cups yoghurt
2 tablespoons oil
5 cups broth or water
1 onion
1 egg yolk
juice of 1 lemon, salt

1. Grate the onion and fry lightly in oil. Add the broth and bring to a boil.

2. Combine the flour, yoghurt, egg yolk and lemon juice, mix well and slowly add to the boiling soup, stirring constantly.

3. Add to the soup the cooked and chopped meat or chicken and salt. Boil for 10 minutes and serve.

DAYBREAK SOUP

Ingredients:

3 tablespoons flour
1 cup milk
2 tablespoons oil
4 tomatoes
1 egg yolk
5 cups meat broth or water, salt

1. Brown the flour lightly in oil and add the broth. Add the chopped tomatoes and cook for 5 minutes.

2. Pass this mixture through a sieve and bring to a boil again. Add slowly a mixture of well-beaten egg and milk, stirring constantly. Add salt and boil 2-3 minutes.

3. When ready to serve add toasted bread cubes, if desired.

LENTIL AND MINT (EZO GELİN) SOUP

Ingredients:

1/3 cup green lentils
1/3 cup rice
1 onion
2 tablespoons tomato paste
2 tablespoons oil
6 cups meat broth, salt
mint, ground red pepper

1. Grate the onion and fry lightly in oil. Add the broth and bring to a boil. Add the lentils, rice and tomato paste. Cook well.

2. Add salt and mint. When ready to serve fry the pepper in a little oil and drizzle over the soup.

Plateau Potato Soup

LENTIL SOUP

Ingredients:
1 cup green lentils
1/3 cup linguini egg noodles or oval-shaped vermicelli
2 tomatoes or 1 tablespoon tomato paste, 1 onion
2 tablespoons oil
6 cups water or broth, salt

1. Saute a little the finely sliced onion and grated tomatoes. Add the broth and bring to a boil. Sort and wash the lentils and add to the boiling broth.

2. When the lentils are cooked add the noodles or vermicelli and salt. When cooked, the soup is ready to serve.

ZUCCHINI SOUP

Ingredients:
2 medium sized zuchinni squash
1 large potato
1/3 cup rice
1 cup milk
2 tablespoons oil or butter
5 cups broth or water
2 tablespoons grated kashar cheese, salt

1. Wash the squash and potato and cut in chunks. Boil in salted water and drain.

2. Mix the oil or melted butter with the milk and add to the vegetables. Add water and bring to a boil. Add the rice and continue cooking.

3. When soup is ready serve with grated cheese on top.

VERMICELLI NOODLE SOUP

Ingredients:

1 cup thin vermicelli (star or oval-type may also be used)
3 tomatoes or 1 tablespoon tomato paste
6 cups broth or water
2 tablespoons margarine or butter, salt, mint

1. Peel the tomatoes and chop or grate finely. Saute a little in the oil and add the broth. Bring to a boil and addthe vermicelli, cooking 10 minutes longer. Add salt.

2. Finely chopped mint or parsley may be sprinkled on top before serving.

Note: *If desired, educate the soup with an egg yolk beaten into lemon juice.*

CARROT-LENTIL SOUP

Ingredients:

1/3 cup green lentils
1/3 cup rice
3 tablespoons oil
1 onion
2 medium sized carrots
salt, ground red pepper

1. Wash the carrots well and scrape lightly. Cut the carrots and the onion into small pieces and place in a pan. Sort and wash the lentils and rice and add. Cook all together in a small amount of water until soft.

2. Push cooked soup through a sieve or place in a food processor. Add water and bring to a boil, cooking for 1-2 minutes. Fry some red pepper in a little oil and drizzle over the soup just before serving.

ADANA SOUP

Ingredients:

1 cup chickpeas
3 tomatoes or 1 tablespoon tomato paste
150 grams (about 1/4 lb) ground meat
6 cups meat broth
1/4 cup vinegar
black pepper, salt, oregano

1. Soak the chickpeas 8-10 hours. Boil until soft. Chop the tomatoes. Mix chickpeas and tomatoes and drain well through a sieve. Add salt and broth and bring to a boil.

2. Add a little salt to the ground meat and form small meatballs and place them in a bowl with a little flour in it. Drop them into the boiling broth and boil until done.

3. Remove the soup from the heat and stir in the vinegar and oregano. Sprinkle pepper over the soup and serve.

SOUR MALHITA SOUP

Ingredients:
1 1/2 cups lentils
6 cups water
1 head of garlic
2 tablespoons olive oil, salt, ground red pepper, 1 lemon
sumach or sour grape molasses

1. Placed the lentils and half the garlic in a pan with the water. Cook until soft and add salt and some pepper.

2. Saute the rest of the garlic in the olive oil and add to the lentils. Boil 1-2 minutes more. Add ground red pepper, lemon juice, and sumach or sour molasses.

TRIPE SOUP

Ingredients:
1/2 kilogram (1 lb) beef or mutton tripe
2 tablespoons oil
2 tablespoons flour
1/3 cup vinegar
5-6 garlic cloves
2 egg yolks
1 lemon, a little salt

1. Soak the tripe 1-2 hours in salt water, strain, scrape with a knife and wash thoroughly. Place in a pot with 10 cups water. Boil until well cooked.

2. Strain and reserve the hot liquid. Cut the tripe into tiny pieces.

3. Brown the flour lightly in the oil and slowly add to the broth, stirring constantly until it returns to a boil. Add salt and the chopped tripe.

4. To educate the soup, beat the egg yolk in lemon juice and add gradually to the soup while stirring. Boil 1-2 minutes. If desired, mix the crushed garlic in vinegar and add when ready to serve.

TARHANA SOUP

Ingredients:
1/2 cup tarhana (a dried yoghurt and flour mixture available in stores or see recipe, page 450)
2 tablespoons oil
1 tablespoon tomato paste
3 garlic cloves
5 cups broth or water

1. Brown lightly in oil the finely chopped or crushed garlic and tomato paste. Add the cold broth or water to the pot. Add the tarhana before heating. Stir until the mixture comes to a boil.

2. Add salt, turn down the fire, simmer for 10 minutes and serve.

Note: *Fry some ground red pepper in oil and add it to the cooked mixture of tarhana, tomato paste and water, if desired. (Also this can be done before adding the garlic.)*

WHEAT AND BEANS SOUP

Ingredients:

1/3 cup whole wheat
1/4 cup red lentils
1/4 cup green lentils
1/3 cup chickpeas
1/3 cup white beans
6 cups water or broth
1 onion
5 tablespoons butter
1 tablespoon pepper sauce, salt
ground red pepper, red pepper
flakes, mint

1. Wash the chickpeas, wheat, and beans and put to soak separately the evening before. Drain and place in a large pot or pressure cooker. Wash green and red lentils and add. Add the pepper sauce. Cook about 2 hours (or until done in pressure cooker).

2. When the beans are almost done, chop the onion finely and brown lightly in butter, add salt, mint and ground red pepper and sauté a little more. Add to the boiling soup and boil two more minutes before removing from the stove.

OVMAÇ SOUP

Ingredients:
3 tablespoons flour
1/3 cup yoghurt
3 tablespoons vinegar or
juice of 1 lemon
5-6 garlic cloves
100 grams (3 oz.) ground
meat
1 small onion, black
pepper
6 cups water, salt
3 tablespoons oil

1. Mix well in a pan the flour, crushed garlic, vinegar or lemon, and yoghurt. Place on the fire adding the water. Bring to a boil stirring constantly.

2. Grate the onion and mix with the ground meat, a little salt and pepper and form tiny meat balls. Add the meat balls to the boiling liquid. Add salt and cook until meatballs are done.

3. Saute the mint in the oil and drizzle over the soup before serving.

Note: *This can be made without meatballs.*

LEBENİYE SOUP

Ingredients:
1 cup whole wheat
1/3 cup chickpeas
1 kilogram (2 lb) whole milk
yoghurt
1 egg

1. Soak the wheat and chickpeas the night before. Wash once or twice in water and place in a pot full of water. Cook until soft on a high flame.

2. Beat the egg and beat well into the yoghurt. Place this mixture into a large pot and slowly bring to a boil while stirring. Add the cooked wheat and chickpeas and salt. Bring to a boil twice more. Serve warm or cold.

SOUR SOUP

Ingredients:

1/3 cup red lentils
1/3 cup whole wheat
(add 3 tablespoons chickpeas if
desired)
1/2 kilogram (1 lb) kale or spinach
(or eggplant)
4-5 cups meat broth or water
3 tablespoons oil
3-4 garlic cloves, ground red pep-
per, mint, salt
1/3 cup sumach juice or lemon juice

1. Put the wheat (and chickpeas if used) to soak the night before.
2. Mix the wheat, (chickpeas), and lentils in a pan and cover with water 4 fingers above the level. Cook until soft.
3. Wash and chop the kale or spinach finely (or cube the egg plant). Place in a pan in salted water and soak 10-15 minutes. Rinse in several waters until salt is gone.
4. When the wheat and lentils are almost done add the vegetable and the sumach or lemon juice. When everything is finished cooking add the crushed garlic.
5. Saute the red pepper and mint in the oil and drizzle over the top.

Note: *If desired 10-15 pearl onions can be used instead of the vegetable.*

MUSHROOM-YOGHURT SOUP

Ingredients:

250 grams (1/2 lb) fresh mushrooms
2 tablespoons flour
2 tablespoons oil
1 cup yoghurt
6 cups meat broth or water
salt, mint

1. Brown the flour lightly in the oil. Add the yoghurt and mix well. To avoid the flour from separating use a wire whip if necessary. Add the water and allow to boil.
2. Immerse the mushrooms in salted water for 5-10 minutes, rinse well and drain. Chop the mushrooms into very small pieces and add to the boiling broth. Add salt and boil until the mushrooms are cooked.
3. Sprinkle mint on the soup before serving.

CIRCASSLAN SOUP

Ingredients:

1/3 cup cracked wheat
6 tablespoons cracked corn
4 cups chicken broth
1 chicken breast
2 tablespoons oil
1 egg yolk
1 cup yoghurt, salt, mint

1. Soak the wheat and corn over night. Drain.
2. Cook the chicken breast. Boil the chicken broth and add the wheat and corn and cook until done.
3. Slice the chicken and add to broth. Put the yoghurt in a dish and beat in the

egg yolk. Slowly add this mixture to the soup. Add the oil or butter and boil 3-4 more minutes. When almost finished add salt.

4. Sprinkle dried mint over the soup when ready to serve.

ARAB SOUP

Ingredients:

1 whole chicken
1 cup flour
6 cups water, 2 cups chicken broth
1 onion
1 carrot
3 dried red peppers
2 tablespoons oil and 2 tablespoons butter
salt, ground red pepper

1. Clean, wash and dress the chicken and place in a pan. Broil the peppers, remove the skins. Add them with the onion, carrot and water to the pan and bring all to a boil. Cook until the chicken is done, adding more boiling water as necessary. Strain off the broth in a pan and place the chicken and vegetables in a bowl. When cooled, remove the chicken breast and slice very small. (The remaining ingredients may be used in another dish.)

2. Brown 2 tablespoons flour in 2 tablespoons oil. Gradually add 2 cups of the chicken broth, stirring constantly. When bubbling, simmer to taste. Add salt and the chicken breast slices.

3. Put the remaining chicken broth in another pan to boil. Mix remaining flour with a little water until it forms a very thick sauce. Slowly add this to the boiling broth, stirring until it thickens.

4. Empty this mixture into a bowl to cool. When ready to serve, sauté some red pepper in the butter, place two spoonfuls of the pudding-like mixture in the soup bowl, add a ladle of the hot soup on top and drizzle over the top some of the red pepper-butter mixture.

HOMEMADE NOODLE (KIKIRDAK) SOUP

Ingredients:

500 grams (1 lb) flour
1 egg, salt, water
1 kilogram (2 lb) yoghurt
3 tablespoons butter or margarine or 1 1/2 of each, mint

1. Make a soft dough with the flour, egg, salt and water. Divide the dough in two and cover the bowl with a damp cloth for 1/2 hour.

2. Roll out one part of the dough 1/2 cm thick and cut into parallel strips 2 cm wide. Lay the strips one on top of the other and cut 1/2 cm crossways (like noodles).

3. Roll the other part of the dough 1 cm thick and cut it into 1 cm wide strips. Cut the strips crossways in 1 cm lengths to make cubes.

4. Fill a large pot just over halfway with water, add salt and bring to a boil. Add the dough strips (noodles) to the boiling water. When the water returns to a high boil turn the heat down and cook until the smell of flour is gone. Remove from the heat for about 10 minutes.

5. Beat the yoghurt well and stir into the soup. Cover the pot.

6. Heat the butter or margarine and fry the dough cubes. Remove them from the butter. Five minutes before serving the soup, stir in the fried cubes.

7. Put mint in the remaining butter and heat a little. After pouring the soup into the bowls, drizzle a little of the minted oil over each serving.

SPINACH SOUP

Ingredients:

1/2 kilogram (1 lb) spinach
1 cup chickpeas
1/3 cup rice or oval vermicelli (or ground wheat)
1 small onion
6 cups water or meat broth
1 teaspoon red pepper flakes
1/3 cup sour sumach or 1 lemon
1 tablespoon tomato paste or
2 tomatoes
oil, salt, sweet basil

1. Cover the sumach with warm water for 15 minutes.

2. Sort the spinach and wash 3-4 times. Chop finely and place in a pan. Add finely chopped onion and tomatoes (or tomato paste), rice, salt, pepper flakes, and a little oil. Pour the water or broth over it and add the strained sumach. Bring to a boil.

3. When the rice is cooked, turn down the flame and add the basil. Cook 1-2 minutes more and remove from heat.

VEGETABLE
DISHES

CONTENTS

Vegetables with meat

HELPFUL HINTS

1. In order to take full advantage of the food value of the root vegetables such as potatoes, radishes, carrots and Jerusalem artichokes, it is recommended to peel them as thinly or as little as possible.

2. In order to take full advantage of the food value of vegetables which we use in their entirety, such as lettuces, cabbages, spinach, celery, and kale, use as much of the greener parts as possible, and it is best to use them cut into large rather than small pieces.

3. When using lettuces and cabbages it is necessary to wash each leaf separately. For other vegetables, immerse them in water for 1-2 minutes, drain and wash again in more water. Particularly for such vegetables as spinach and kale and any vegetable that has mud or sand on it, wash 3-4 times.

4. The food value is reduced if the vegetables remain in water a long time.

5. After trimming the vegetables, wash only once, if possible.

6. When trimming vegetables for a salad, adding lemon and olive oil resists vitamin C loss and protects them from vitamin A loss.

7. When preparing to boil potatoes, add them to hot water and the water will remain clear.

8. Before adding the potatoes to the water, pierce them in one or two places so they will cook evenly throughout.

9. Peel onions over a full bowl of water to keep your eyes from watering.

10. When sauteing onion, add a little salt to increase the flavor of the dish.

11. Saute the tomato paste a little before adding to keep the dish from having a sour taste.

12. To make peeling a tomato much easier, first penetrate it with the point of the knife, then either dip the tomato in boiling water for 10 seconds or rotate it briefly over an open flame.

ABOUT GARNITURES AND SAUCES
FOR VEGETABLE DISHES

1. SAUCES: These are used to add body to or increase the flavor of soups, sautes or vegetable and meat dishes cooked in water.

a. MEYANE: Flour or fine bread crumbs are sauteed in oil to make a roux (See BREADS chapter, p. 12).

b. VELOUTE: Meat broth or a beaten egg is added to the meyane.

c. BECHAMEL (WHITE SAUCE) – 1: Flour is lightly browned in oil and salt and milk added and then stirred until thickened.

BECHAMEL – 2: Flour is lightly browned in oil, salt and water are added and then stirred until thickened. When cool an egg is beaten in and some coconut sprinkled on top.

2. SAUTE: Cut vegetables, fish or meat pieces all the same size and cook uncovered in oil without adding water. If the pieces are large turn them over.

3. FOR STEWS: Peel onions and cut in half. Turn the cut sides onto the board and slice thinly top to bottom to make half-moons.

4. REMOVING TOMATO SEEDS AND SKINS: Place tomatoes in boiling water until the skins are loose. Transfer to a bowl of cold water and remove the skins. If the seeds are not wanted squeeze them out and cut the tomatoes into 1cm cubes to use for meat dishes or some vegetable sautes.

5. SALAMANDER: For lightly browning the food or carmelizing it (as in baking briefly with a cheese or sugary topping)

COOKING METHODS

A. BOILED DISHES

Before boiling:

1. Use as little water as possible in order for it to be used up by the end of the cooking. Adding salt and lemon juice to the boiling water improves the color and nutritional value of the food.

2. It is best to keep the lid on the pan as much as possible during cooking.

3. Boiling in copper or iron pans eliminates the vitamin C from foods.

4. If additional water is needed during cooking, add hot water.

5. Spinach and watercress may be cooked with only the water remaining from washing if put on a very low flame and covered tightly.

6. When cooking vegetables such as celery root, cauliflower and cabbage, allow the lid to remain off for 1-2 minutes to reduce excess gas and odor.

7. Do not throw out the water after cooking. Use it in soups or sauces.

8. Cook vegetables only until just soft, not until they fall apart. If cooked too long they lose much of their food value.

9. With vitamin C-rich vegetables, cook only enough for one meal because each time they are reheated they lose much of the vitamins.

10. Crushing garlic in salt is easier than without and this process adds to the flavor of the dish.

11. If you want the peppers to be bright green, first put them in hot water for 10 minutes.

B. FRIED DISHES

Before frying:

1. Foods fry more quickly in a deep pan with a lot of oil than in a skillet.

2. Instead of margarine, butter or olive oil, which smoke at lower temperatures, use corn, soy, or sunflower oil for frying. The result is a better color and much more healthful food.

3. After frying with corn, soy or sunflower oil, you may strain the oil and use once or twice more.

4. Adding a dash of salt or flour to the hot oil helps prevent spattering.

5. Placing the fried food briefly on paper towels eliminates excess oil from the food. Then transfer to the serving plate.

6. Fresh yellow potatoes are best for frying. Slice and wash until the starch begins to come up, drain and fry. This keeps them from sticking together in the pan.

7. For dry and harder fried potatoes do not use a lid; for softer fries, use the lid.

8. Because fried foods are generally rather heavy, serving them with tomato sauce or yoghurt with or without garlic lightens the taste.

FRIED DISHES

Frying is done in three ways.

a. Vegetables cut and fried in hot oil

A large amount of cooking oil is needed.

FRIED ZUCCHINI

Ingredients:
1 kilogram (2 lb) zucchini
oil, salt

1. Scrape, wash and dry the squashes. Cut in rounds or long strips and fry in hot oil.

2. When cooked on both sides drain and place on paper towels to drain. Remove to serving plate. If desired put garlic yoghurt over it. Can be served along with meat dishes.

FRIED POTATOES

Ingredients:
1 kilogram (2 lb) potatoes
oil, salt

1. Peel potatoes and immediately put in a bowl of water. When ready to begin frying, remove and cut each potato and fry in hot oil.

2. By slicing the potatoes and putting in water before frying, the excess starch will come out and prevent the potatoes from sticking. It is important in doing this to dry the potatoes well before adding to the hot oil. Fried potatoes go well with meatballs and meat dishes.

Note: Potato chips can also be done in this way.

FRIED PEPPERS

Ingredients:
1 kilogram (2 lb) small green
peppers
oil, salt

Wash the peppers, dry and fry in hot oil without removing the stem and seeds. Drain on paper and remove to a serving platter. Goes well with garlic yoghurt. Goes with some meat dishes.

Note: If the stems and seeds are removed, wash the peppers before doing this in order to avoid water getting inside the peppers and causing them to crack apart when frying.

FRIED EGGPLANT

Ingredients:
*1 kilogram (2 lb)
eggplants
oil, salt*

1. Wash and dry the eggplants. Peel strips lengthwise about a finger width apart. Cut in rounds. Add salt when about ready to fry.

2. Deep fry in oil. When fried on both sides drain on paper towels. When drained sufficiently transfer to a serving plate. Serve with tomato sauce or garlic or plain yoghurt. Also goes well with meat dishes.

FRIED CAULIFLOWER

Ingredients:
*1 cauliflower
oil, salt*

Boiled Cauliflower

1. Wash and parboil the cauliflower in a little water. When cooled separate the flowerets and drain well. Fry in hot oil.

2. When fried well on both sides place on paper towels and drain. Transfer to a serving plate. Serve with garlic yoghurt or plain. Goes well with boiled meats or pilafs.

ZUCCHINI-EGG PATTIES (MÜCVER)

Ingredients:

3-4 zucchini squash
1 onion
2-3 small green peppers
3 eggs
3-4 tablespoons flour
1/2 bunch each of parsley
and dill
oil, salt, black pepper

1. Scrape and grate the squash. Grate the onion and chop finely the peppers, parsley and dill. Mix all together with the egg and flour.

2. Heat the oil and drop spoonfuls of the mixture into the oil. Turn once. Remove with a slotted spatula and to eliminate extra oil place on a paper towel.

Note: *Grated potatoes or leeks may be substituted for the zucchini.*

b. Breaded and fried dishes:

BREADED EGGPLANT

Ingredients:

1 kilogram (2 lb) eggplant
2 cups frying oil
3-4 eggs
2-3 tablespoons flour, salt

1. Wash and dry the eggplants. Peel strips lengthwise about a finger width apart. Cut in rounds or wide strips.

2. Mix the eggs, flour and salt in a glass bowl. Beat to pudding consistency. Dip the eggplant pieces in the batter and fry in hot oil. Transfer to paper towels and drain. Transfer to serving plate. Goes well with meat dishes.

BREADED ZUCCHINI

Prepare like breaded eggplant.

BREADED CARROTS

Boil the carrots and drain. Prepare like breaded eggplant.

BREADED CAULIFLOWER

Boil the cauliflower first and separate the flowerets. Drain and prepare like breaded eggplant.

BREADED FRIED ONIONS

Ingredients:
1 kilogram (2 lb) onions, oil
3-4 eggs
2-3 tablespoons flour, salt

1. Peel, wash, and dry the onions and slice into rings.
2. Mix the eggs, flour and salt in a glass bowl. Beat to a pudding consistency. Dip the onion rings in the batter and fry in hot oil. Drain on paper towels and transfer to a serving platter. Goes well with meat dishes.

c. Aux gratins dishes

Boil the vegetables and place on a baking pan. Add bechamel sauce. Grate some kashar cheese. 15-20 minutes before the meal add the cheese and place in the oven to brown.

d. Moussaka

Trim, wash and cut the vegetables and saute lightly in oil. Prepare a filling in another pan, such as the filling for Split eggplants with ground meat (karnıyarık). Layer portions of the vegetable and the filling alternately in the pan and add a little water or thin tomato sauce and cook. The best vegetables for making this dish are eggplant, zucchini, celery root or potatoes.

e. Moussaka aux gratins

Prepare as for moussaka above but use a pan suitable for the oven. Pour bechamel sauce over it, then add grated kashar cheese and heat until bubbling in the oven.

OLIVE OIL VEGETABLE DISHES

BROCCOLI IN OLIVE OIL

Ingredients:
350-400 grams (about 3/4 lb) broccoli
1 onion
1/3 cup rice or cracked wheat
1/3 cup water
2 tablespoons olive oil
red pepper flakes, salt

1. Cut away the thicker stems of the broccoli, separate the flowerets, wash it and place in a pan.
2. Add finely sliced onions and stir once. Add washed rice or wheat, pep-

per, salt and olive oil. Add the water, cover the pan and cook on high heat. Do not stir while cooking because broccoli cooks quickly and if stirred will fall apart. Remove from heat when the rice or wheat is soft. Shake the pan before transfering the broccoli to a serving plate. When cooled goes well with a meat dish or by itself.

Note: *Watercress may be prepared in the same way.*

SOUR LEEKS

Ingredients:
500 grams (1 lb) leeks
1/2 cup olive oil
3 onions
2-3 garlic cloves
2 tablespoons tomato paste
1/2 bunch parsley
1/2 bunch dill
1 lemon
1/3 cup sugar
salt

1. Trim and wash the leeks and cut into 3-4 inch pieces. Then cut each piece into thin slices. Place in a pan and boil in one-half cup of water on high heat until the water is gone.

2. Cut the onions into half rings and chop the garlic into small pieces. Saute in the olive oil until yellow. Stir in the tomato sauce, sugar and salt and the finely chopped dill and parsley. Stir.

3. Spread the boiled leeks on a small tray and the above mixture over it. Add a cup of water and place on the stove. Cook without stirring. May be served warm or cold. Before removing from the heat sprinkle the lemon juice over it.

BROAD BEANS IN OLIVE OIL

Ingredients:
1 kilogram (2 lb) broad beans
1 onion
3 tablespoons olive oil
1 lemon
2 tablespoons flour
1 teaspoon sugar
1 bunch dill

1. Wash and drain the beans. Heat oil in a pan. Saute the beans until their color begins to change. Add the thinly chopped onion and saute a little more.

2. Mix the lemon juice, flour and sugar well and add to the beans. Cover with hot water and add salt. To prevent the beans from turning black put a layer of parchment over them before covering. After cooking remove to a serving plate and spread finely chopped dill over it.

Note: *1. Half of the dill can be added during the cooking.*
2. May be served with garlic yoghurt.

ARTICHOKES WITH BROAD BEANS

Ingredients:

500 grams (1 lb) fresh broad beans
5-6 whole artichokes
1 onion
1/3 teaspoon sugar
1/2 bunch parsley or dill, salt
1 lemon
1/2 cup olive oil

1. Peel the artichokes. Remove the stems and chop the stems very small.

2. Remove insides with a spoon. Place artichokes whole in water with the salt and lemon juice added.

3. Saute lightly the thinly slice onion and add the chopped stems and the whole artichokes. Add 2-3 cups of water and boil until half-cooked.

4. Remove the ends of the fresh broad beans. Add salt and sugar to the beans and cook covered on high heat.

5. After the beans are cooled, stuff them into the artichokes. Sprinkle chopped dill or parsley on top.

Note: *Peas and carrots may be substituted for the broad beans.*

BRUSSEL SPROUTS IN OLIVE OIL

Ingredients:
500 grams (1 lb) brussel
sprouts
1 onion
1/3 cup rice or cracked
wheat
1/3 cup water
2 tablespoons olive oil
red pepper flakes, salt

1. Remove any bad outer leaves of the sprouts. Wash well and place in a pan.

2. Add finely sliced onion and stir once. Add the washed rice or wheat, red pepper and salt. Add the oil and water and cook covered over a high flame. Do not stir while cooking because the sprouts cook quickly and if stirred will fall apart. Remove from the fire as soon as the rice is soft. Shake the pan up and down and transfer to a serving plate. Serve cold with a meat dish or by itself.

Note: *Leeks may be substituted for the brussel sprouts. Slice them very thin and cook in the same way.*

Vegetable stew with meat

JERUSALEM ARTICHOKES IN OLIVE OIL

Ingredients:

1 kilogram (2 lb) artichokes
1 onion
3 tablespoons olive oil
1/2 bunch dill, salt

1. Peal the artichokes, wash and drain. Cut in cubes.

2. Saute the finely sliced onion in oil and add the artichoke cubes. Saute a little more and cover with hot water. Add salt and cook over a low flame. Transfer to a serving platter and sprinkle finely chopped dill over it. Goes well with meat dishes.

Note: If a red dish is desired add a spoonful of tomato paste to the onions after browning, then add the cubed artichokes.

EGGPLANT (İMAM BAYILDI)

Ingredients:

1 kilogram (2 lb) eggplant
2-3 onions
1 garlic clove
1 bunch parsley
1-2 tomatoes
1 teaspoon tomato paste
as many small green peppers as eggplants
oil, salt
black pepper

1. Cut off the stems of the eggplants. Peel strips lengthwise about a finger width apart. Fry the whole eggplants lightly in oil and transfer to a flat pan. Cut in halves lengthwise.

2. Wash, drain and dry the peppers and fry in the same oil.

3. Saute together the finely chopped onion, garlic, tomatoes and parsley and mix together a little.

4. Fill the eggplants halves with this mixture and place a pepper on top of each one.

5. Stir the tomato paste into 1/3 cup warm water. Add salt and black pepper and stir a little. Sprinkle over the eggplants, and either place them in the oven or cover and cook over a low flame.

POTATO-EGG SAUTE

Ingredients:

4-5 potatoes
2 medium sized onions
3 eggs, salt, black pepper
3 tablespoons olive oil

1. Wash, peel and cube the potatoes. Place the olive oil in a large pan and saute the thinly-sliced onions until light brown. Mix in the potatoes and cook a little more.

2. Break the eggs on top and add salt. Cook while stirring, transfer to a serving platter and add black pepper. Goes well with any vegetable saute or as a breakfast dish.

PEAS IN OLIVE OIL

Ingredients:
1 kilogram (2 lb) peas
1 onion
2-3 medium sized potatoes
3 tablespoons olive oil
1 bunch dill, salt

1. Shell the peas, wash and drain. Saute the thin-sliced onions lightly in the oil. Add the peas and cook a little longer. Cover with hot water and add salt. Bring to a boil.

2. Peel and wash the potatoes cut into tiny cubes. When the peas are almost cooked add the potatoes. Add half of the thinly chopped dill and cook until the water is about gone. Transfer to a serving dish and spread the remaining dill over the top. Goes well with fried chicken. Can be served with a pilaf.

GREEN BEANS IN OLIVE OIL

Ingredients:
1 kilogram (2 lb) tender green beans
2 onions
3-4 garlic cloves
4 tablespoons olive oil
1 tablespoon tomato paste or 3 tomatoes
1 tablespoon pepper sauce if available
salt

1. Trim and wash the beans and cut in desired lengths. Saute with finely chopped onions for 8-10 minutes.

2. Add the tomato paste or grated tomatoes. Slice 2 or 3 of the garlic cloves, add to the pan and cook a little longer. If using tomatoes do not add water. If using paste, add 1 cup water.

Put on the fire and cook over a low flame. When almost done add salt.

Note: *If using a pressure cooker use less water.*

Peas in olive oil

Green beans in olive oil

MEATLESS VEGETABLE DISHES

POTATOES BORANİ

Ingredients:

500 grams (1 lb) potatoes
1 cup yoghurt
3-4 garlic cloves, salt
1/3 teaspoon ground red pepper
2 tablespoons butter

1. Boil the potatoes and peel. Cut into small cubes and place on a serving platter.

2. Crush the garlic and mix it with yoghurt in a bowl. Add salt. Pour over the potatoes.

3. Fry the red pepper in oil and drizzle over the yoghurt. Serve hot.

Mushroom saute

Green bean saute

BLACK CABBAGE

Ingredients:
2 heads black cabbage
1 onion
1/3 cup cracked wheat or rice
6 tablespoons oil or olive oil
salt, black pepper

1. Trim the cabbage and wash well. Slice thinly and cover with water in a pan. Boil until cooked and drain.
2. Saute the finely sliced onion in a large pan and add the cabbage. Add the wheat and cook slowly.

Note: If desired, meat fat may be used in place of oil. Pinto beans may be used in place of the black cabbage and cracked corn used in place of the wheat.

BABAGANNUCH

Ingredients:
1 kilogram (2 lb) eggplant
3-4 small green peppers
3-4 garlic cloves
2 tablespoons oil (butter preferred)

1. Broil the eggplants and peppers. When cooled remove the skins. If desired broil the peppers less and not remove the skins. Mash the vegetables on a board or in a bowl and mix.
2. Heat oil in a pan and saute crushed garlic and alt. Add the eggplant and peppers and saute 4-5 minutes. Goes well with fresh bread or flat bread and also good eaten cold.

Note: If desired, break 2-3 eggs when sauteing the garlic, then add the eggplant.

BAKED CAULIFLOWER

Ingredients:
1 head of cauliflower
1 tablespoon oil
2 tablespoons butter or margarine
1 container of yoghurt
3-4 garlic cloves
1 tablespoon flour, salt
1/3 teaspoon ground red pepper

1. Wash and separate the flowerets and place in an iron pot. Add a dash of salt, cover and cook in its own water on very low flame.
2. When cooked transfer to an oiled oven pan and sprinkle the flour over it. Cook until light brown. When cooked slightly add a sauce made of garlic crushed with salt and mixed with the yoghurt. Saute the pepper in oil and drizzle on top.

CAULIFLOWER IN BECHAMEL SAUCE

Ingredients:

1 medium sized head cauliflower

3 cups milk

3 tablespoons margarine

3-5 tablespoons flour, salt

1/3 cup grated kashar cheese

1. Wash and separate the flowerets. Boil in water.

2. Melt the margarine in a pan and add the flour. Brown slightly and slowly add cold milk while stirring. Add salt and cook 3-4 minutes longer.

3. Place the cauliflower in a flat oven pan and pour the sauce over it. Spread the grated cheese on top and bake until the cheese is melted.

GREEN BEAN SAUTE

Ingredients:

1 kilogram (2 lb) green beans

1 cup water

2 eggs

2 tablespoons butter

salt, black pepper

1. Wash, trim and cut the beans. Place in a double boiler steel or copper pan. Add the water and cook on high flame until softened.

2. Melt the butter and break the eggs in the pan. Carefully remove the eggs with a spatula and lay them on top of the beans.

3. Add salt and continue to cook on high flame for 10 minutes. Serve hot and place in folded flat bread.

Note: Also goes well with pitta bread or a pilaf.

MUSHROOM SAUTE

Ingredients:

250-300 grams (8-10 oz)
mushrooms

1 onion

2-3 small green peppers

2 tomatoes

2 tablespoons fat or margarine

salt

black pepper, mint

3-4 slices kashar cheese

1. Cook mushrooms covered in own water and chop small.

2. Peel and chop the tomatoes. Cook thinly sliced onions in the fat and stir a little. Add sliced peppers and tomatoes and saute a little more. Add mushrooms, salt, pepper and mint and cook 10 minutes longer. Place in a flat oven pan, cover with the cheese slices and brown in the oven.

BAKED SPINACH

Ingredients:
1 kilogram (1 lb)
spinach
1 onion
3-4 eggs
2 tablespoons oil
black pepper, salt

1. Trim spinach and wash in 3-4 waters. Chop as desired.
2. Saute the thinly sliced onion in oil and add the spinach. Add a little salt and pepper and saute. Transfer to a flat oven pan.
3. Beat the eggs with a dash of salt and pour over the spinach. Place in oven. Remove when the eggs are cooked. Cut in squares and serve.

WINTER SQUASH (IR'İYYE)

Ingredients:
1 kilogram (2 lb) hubbard squash
or pumpkin
1 head onion
1/2 packet margarine
6 tablespoons rice
1 teaspoon sugar
juice of 1 lemon or a handful of
sumach juice
1 spoonful each tomato paste and
pepper sauce

1. Saute the very finely sliced onion in the margarine. Add the sauces and cook a little more. Cube the squash pieces and add. Cover with water and add lemon juice.
2. Bring to a boil and add rice. Add salt and sugar and stir a little. Cook on a high flame until done.

VEGETABLES WITH MEAT
ALİ NAZİK

Ingredients:
1 kilogram (2 lb) eggplant
500 grams (1 lb) yoghurt
250 grams (1/2 lb) ground meat
1 onion
3-4 small green peppers
3 tomatoes
4-5 garlic cloves
1 tablespoon each, butter and oil
1/3 teaspoon ground red pepper or pepper flakes
salt

1. Broil the eggplants and remove the skins. Chop finely on a board and place on a serving dish (a glass dish with a cover is recommended).

2. Saute the onion and ground meat in the oil. And add the chopped peppers and the tomatoes that have been skinned and chopped finely. Add salt and continue the saute. When well blended spread over the eggplant.

3. Crush the garlic in a little salt, mix with the yoghurt and over the sauce.

4. Fry the pepper in the butter and drizzle over the yoghurt. Serve hot.

FRESH OKRA WITH MEAT

Ingredients:
1 kilogram (2 lb) boneless lamb cubes
500 grams (1 lb) fresh okra
3 tomatoes or 1 tablespoon tomato paste
2 onions
2 tablespoons oil
juice of 1 lemon or 1 tablespoon vinegar
salt, black pepper

Note: *chickpeas may be added.*

1. Sort and wash the okra and pour over it the juice of a half lemon or vinegar. Set aside.

2. Cook the meat and finely chopped onion in some oil. When the juices begin to come out add the tomato paste or the skinned, chopped tomatoes. Add hot water and bring to a boil.

3. Drain the okra and put in a bowl of fresh water. Remove gently in handfuls from the bowl to a strainer and then add to the meat pan. Add remaining lemon juice, salt and pepper. Cook until the okra is done but not mushy.

OVEN EGGPLANT KEBAB

Ingredients:
1 kilogram (2 lb) eggplant
250 grams (1/2 lb finely ground
meat
1 onion
1/2 head garlic
3-4 small green peppers
2 tomatoes
2 tablespoons oil
salt, black pepper, oregano

1. Slice the eggplant in rounds but do not cut all the way through. Cover with salted water for 15 minutes. Remove to a board.

2. Cut the peppers lengthwise, then crosswise in 1 cm pieces. Remove tomato skins and cube. Cut the garlic in thin slices.

3. Mix together well finely sliced onion and ground meat. Place nut-sized pieces of the mix between the slices of eggplant. Then press together so the meat mixture spreads out between the slices.

4. Remove the eggplants to a wide flat oven pan. Put the pepper pieces between the slices. Mix together the tomato cubes and garlic slices and put on top of the eggplants. Add salt, pepper and a teaspoon of oregano. Drizzle two spoonfuls of oil over the top. Cover with aluminium foil and place in the oven. If desired, the dish may be cooked partially covered on top of the stove.

Note: *Goes very well with pitta, flat bread or a pilaf.*

EGGPLANT AND LAMB

Ingredients:
1/2 kilogram (1 lb) boneless lamb cubes
1 kilogram (2 lb) eggplants
2 onions
4-5 medium sized tomatoes
1 tablespoon tomato paste
4-5 small green peppers
5-6 garlic cloves
salt, black pepper, ground red pepper

1. Mix together sliced meat, finely chopped onion, tomato paste, salt, black pepper and red pepper and place in a wide pan.

2. Slice the eggplants in cubes and allow to remain 15 minutes in a bowl of salt water. Rinse and drain well and place on top of the meat.

3. Skin and finely slice the tomatoes, peppers and garlic and put on top of the eggplants. Drizzle 2 spoonfuls of oil over the top and add 1/2 cup of hot water. Cover and cook over a low flame until done.

EGGPLANT AUX GRATINS

(Award-winning recipe of Ms. İnci Akyar of Istanbul)

Ingredients:
1 kilogram (2 lb) eggplants
500 grams (1 lb) ground meat
2 tomatoes
1 onion
oil, salt, pepper
100 grams (3-4 oz) kashar cheese
Bechamel sauce:
3 tablespoons flour
2-3 cups milk
1 egg
2 tablespoons butter or margarine

1. Slice off the skins of the eggplant lengthwise in strips leaving equal amounts unsliced. Place in salted water for 15-20 minutes to remove the bitterness. Wash and drain. Squeeze out the water with paper towels or a clean kitchen towel.

2. Slice lengthwise and fry in hot oil. Lay half of the fried eggplant in a glass dish.

3. Saute the onion and ground meat lightly in a tablespoon of oil. Add salt and black pepper. Put on top of the eggplant in the dish. Put the rest of the fried eggplant over the top. Add the skinned and thin-sliced tomatoes. Finally pour the bechamel sauce over the top and sprinkle grated cheese over it. Bake in the oven until the cheese is light brown.

To make the sauce: Fry the flour lightly in the butter. Slowly add the milk and the egg. Cook until it thickens.

Note: *Goes well with a pilaf or cacık (chilled yoghurt soup).*

EGGPLANT WITH LAMB CUBES (Hünkarbeğendi)

Ingredients:

1 kilogram (2 lb) eggplant
1 tablespoon flour
3 tablespoons oil
2 tablespoons grated kashar cheese
1 cup milk
1 bunch parsley
750 grams (1 1/2 lb) lamb cubes
2-3 tomatoes, salt, black pepper

1. Saute the lamb cubes and coarsely chopped onion in oil. Skin the tomatoes and chop in cubes. Add to the meat and mix. Add 2-3 cups hot water and cook until the meat is tender. When almost done add salt.

2. While the meat is cooking broil the eggplants, peel and slice thin.

3. In another pan lightly brown the flour in oil and slowly stir in the milk. Add the cheese and eggplant slices. Add salt and pepper and remove to serving plate. Put the cooked meat on top and sprinkle on the chopped parsley. Serve hot. Goes well with a pilaf or a macaroni dish.

Note: *If desired place the eggplant to one side of the serving plate and the meat on the other without mixing together.*

Eggplant aux gratin

SPLIT EGGPLANTS WITH GROUND MEAT (Karnıyarık)

Ingredients:

1 kilogram (2 lb) eggplants
500 grams (1 lb) ground meat
1 onion
as many small green peppers as
eggplants
3-4 tomatoes
3-4 cloves garlic, salt, black pepper
oil, tomato paste

1. Saute ground meat and finely sliced onion in two tablespoons of oil. Add a little salt and pepper and the finely sliced garlic and stir.

2. Wash eggplants and cut skins off lengthwise in strips leaving equal amounts unsliced. Cut off stems. Cut only half-way through lengthwise. Fry a little in hot oil.

3. Lay eggplants in a flat pan and open them like boats. Add the meat filling. Cut tomatoes in half-moon slices and place over filling. Fry peppers whole and put one on each eggplant.

4. Mix some tomato paste in 1/3 cup water and pour over the eggplants. Place in oven.

SPLIT EGGPLANTS WITH CHICKEN

Ingredients:
1 kilogram (2 lb) eggplants
500 grams (1 lb) boneless chicken
1 onion
2-3 garlic cloves
1 cup cream
1 cup chicken broth
2 tomatoes
2 tablespoons flour
as many small green peppers as eggplants
50 grams (1 1/2 oz) mushrooms
frying oil
1 tablespoon butter or margarine

1. Boil the chicken until soft, remove bones and slice. Saute with thin-sliced onions and garlic in a tablespoon of oil. Chop the mushrooms small and add. Skin one of the tomatoes and squeeze out the seeds and juice. Cut the meat of the tomato in cubes and add to the saute.

2. Mix the chicken broth with the flour and cream and cook on a low flame for 10 minutes.

3. Meanwhile, while the above are being prepared, the skins of the eggplants have been sliced off lengthwise in strips leaving equal amounts unsliced, placed in salted water for 15-20 minutes, washed and drained and the water squeezed out in paper towels or a clean kitchen towel. Fry them in hot oil and cut only half-way through. Place the eggplants in a baking dish. Slice the remaining tomato in half moons and fry the peppers whole. Put the tomatoes and then the peppers on top. Pour the cream sauce over the eggplants and bake in the oven.

BAKED EGGPLANT

Ingredients:
1 kilogram (2 lb) eggplants
500 grams (1 lb) boneless mutton
4 tomatoes
1/2 tablespoon each of tomato paste and pepper sauce
1 onion
3-4 garlic cloves
salt, black pepper

1. Slice the skins of the eggplants off lengthwise in strips leaving equal amounts unsliced. Cut them in 3's or 4's lengthwise. Fry a little in hot oil and lay in an oven pan.

2. Boil the meat in very little water or cook in a pressure cooker. Spoon off the foam. Remove from heat and strain, reserving the broth.

3. Add thin-sliced onions and garlic, skinned and cubed tomatoes, salt and pepper to the meat and mix together. Put this mixture over the eggplants.

4. Mix the tomato paste and pepper sauce with 1/3 cup of the meat broth. Pour over the eggplants and bake in the oven for a half-hour.

Note: *Goes well with a plain macaroni or pilaf dish.*

CELERY ROOT WITH LAMB

Ingredients:
1 kilogram (2 lb) celery root
500 grams (1 lb.) lamb on the bone
2 onions, 1 carrot
2 tablespoons tomato paste
1 cup chickpeas
1/3 cup rice
2 tablespoons oil
3 cups hot water
salt, black pepper
1 lemon

1. Put the chickpeas to soak the night before. Boil them and drain. Fry lightly in oil the meat and one of the onions finely sliced. Add the tomato paste and cook a little longer. Add 3 cups hot water. When almost done, add the chickpeas. Cook together over a high flame.

2. Peel the celery roots and scoop out the insides. Mix this with the juice of the lemon.

3. Slice the other onion very thin and cut the carrot in small cubes. Fry these lightly in 2 spoons of oil. Drain off the lemon juice and discard. Add the celery pulp to the onions and carrots. Wash the rice and add, stirring a little. Add 1 cup hot water and a little salt and pepper. Cook until the water has evaporated.

4. Use the above mixture to fill the celery roots. Place them in a pan. If there is extra filling add it.

5. Pour the meat-chickpea stew over the celery roots and cook on a high flame until the celery roots are done.

CELERY ROOT WITH GROUND MEAT

Ingredients:
1 kilogram (1/2 lb) ground meat
1 onion
2 tablespoons tomato paste
2 cups hot water
2 tablespoons oil
salt, black pepper

1. Cook the very finely sliced onions with the ground meat in oil and add the tomato paste. Cook a little longer and add the hot water and put to a boil.

2. Peel and cube the celery root and add to the boiling stew. After coming to a boil once or twice, add salt and pepper and cook on a high flame until done.

Note: *The fresh green leaves of the celery root may be chopped and added to the pot.*

CABBAGE BOUREK

Ingredients:

*1 medium sized cabbage suitable
for making dolma
500 grams (1 lb) ground meat
2 onions
3-4 tomatoes
2 tablespoons cooking oil
4-5 garlic cloves, salt, black pepper
1 bunch parsley*

1. Add the finely sliced onions and garlic to the ground meat and cook a little in the oil. Skin and slice the tomatoes thinly, add to the meat and cook a little longer.

2. Add salt, pepper and 1/3 cup water to the mixture and cook 6-7 minutes longer. Add chopped parsley and mix, then remove from the stove.

3. Cut the core of the cabbage and remove 1 layer of the outer leaves. Cut in half and remove the heart.

4. Fill a pan of water, add salt and bring to the boil. Add the cabbage leaves to the boiling water and return to the boil. Remove from the heat and cover until the cabbage leaves are softened. Place in a colander, pour on cold water and drain.

5. Place the drained leaves in a large oven pan. Add a layer of the filling and continue to alternate the leaves and the filling. Drizzle a little oil on top and bake in the oven for 15-20 minutes.

Note: *If desired, when the bourek is almost done, sprinkle grated kashar cheese on top.*

ARTICHOKES WITH LAMB

Ingredients:
4 artichokes
300 grams (3/4 lb) boneless
lamb
2 onions
1 clove garlic
2 bunches parsley
1 cup peas
1 teaspoon sugar
2 tablespoons margarine
salt
black pepper
1 1/2 cups water

1. Saute the sliced onion and garlic and the chopped parsley in oil. Add the meat cubes and cook on high heat.

2. Cut the artichokes in 4's. Add to the meat the artichokes, peas, salt, pepper, sugar and water. Cook over a low flame until done.

Kapuska with meat

ERZURUM CASSEROLE

Ingredients:

1 kilogram (2 lb) lamb on the bone
500 grams (1 lb) onions
250 grams (1/2 lb) green beans
5-6 small green peppers
2 eggplants
1 zucchini squash
2 potatoes
1 kilogram (2 lb) tomatoes, salt
125 grams (1/4 lb) margarine

1. Select the most tender cut of lamb. Lay out the meat and place over it the onions that have been cut in half moons. Remove the ends and cut the beans to desired lengths and add. Remove the seeds from the peppers, cut crossways about 2 cm wide and add. Skin and cube the eggplants and squash and add. Place the entire mixture as is into a casserole.

2. Sprinkle salt and bits of margarine on top of the tomatoes. Cover the dish with aluminium foil and bake in the oven.

Note: *When done if there is too much juice add 1/4 cup rice, replace cover and leave in oven a little longer. The rice will soak up the excess juice.*

WINTER CASSEROLE

Ingredients:

500 grams (1 lb) tender mutton or lamb cubes
1 onion
3 carrots
1/3 cup peas
2 potatoes
3 tomatoes, salt, black pepper red pepper flakes or ground red pepper
2 tablespoons margarine
1/3 cup water or meat broth

1. Slice the onions very thin. Scrape and wash the carrots and cut into 1 cm rounds. Rinse the canned peas and strain. Peal and wash the potatoes and cut into large cubes. Skin the tomatoes and slice thin.

2. Mix all the vegetables with the meat and place in the casserole dish. Add salt and black pepper. Dot the top with the margarine and add the water or broth. Cover and bake in a low oven.

SUMMER CASSEROLE

Ingredients:
500 gram (1 lb) meat on the bone
1 onion
1 head garlic
2 small green peppers
1 red pepper
3 medium sized eggplants
6 tomatoes
2 tablespoons cooking oil
1 tablespoon margarine, salt
black pepper, red pepper flakes

1. Fry the meat a little in 2-3 spoons of oil. Add the chopped onion and 1-2 garlic cloves and continue frying.

2. Remove the stems and seeds from the peppers, add to the pan and cook a little more. Peel the eggplants, cut in 4's and and slice each piece into 2 cm long pieces (or cut in any way desired). Add the eggplant to the casserole and fry. Add salt, black pepper and red pepper flakes and mix well.

3. Transfer to a casserole dish. Skin and cut up the tomatoes small and add to the casserole. Dot the top with margarine and place uncovered in the oven. Remove from the oven before the tomatoes get too dark. Serve with bread, flatbread, pitta or a pilaf. Ayran (yoghurt drink) is an excellent accompaniment.

ÇANAKKALE MEATBALLS

Ingredients:
1 kilogram (2 lb) twice-ground beef
1 handful pearl onions
3 tomatoes
2 carrots
2 celery roots
2 zucchini squash
3 potatoes
1 bunch parsley
black pepper, salt, cumin, oregano
2 tablespoons oil
3 tablespoons flour

1. Add the finely chopped parsley, salt, black pepper, oregano and cumin to the ground beef and mix well. Prepare tiny nut-sized meatballs and roll in flour. Fry in hot oil for 5 minutes and drain.

2. Heat the oil in a pan and add the pearl onions, sliced rounds of carrots, potatoes, celery roots and squash and fry a little.

3. Remove the tomato skins and cut in cubes. Add to the vegetables and cook while stirring 2-3 minutes more. Add 2 cups water and bring to a boil. When boiling add the salt and meatballs.

4. Cover and cook on high heat for 20 minutes or until the vegetables are done. Transfer to a serving dish. Add the remaining parsley. Serve with a pilaf.

OVEN MUSHROOMS

Ingredients:

500 grams (1 lb) large mushrooms
100 grams (3 oz) ground beef
A small onion
2 medium size tomatoes
2-3 small green peppers
100 grams (3 oz) kashar cheese
a few sprigs parsley
salt, black pepper

1. Soak the mushrooms in water for 5-10 minutes, rince and drain. Gently pull out stems and gills to make room for filling.

2. Place the mushrooms insides facing up in an oiled pan.

3. Mix the ground beef and chopped onion. Add the washed and chopped parsley, salt and black pepper and mix.

4. Stuff this mixture into the mushrooms and in between them place sliced tomatoes and peppers. Spread grated cheese on top and cover with aluminum foil. Bake in the oven for 25-30 minutes.

Eggplant

RİZE BLACK CABBAGE

Ingredients:
1 head (about 1 kilogram or 2 lb)
black cabbage
1/3 cup cracked corn
250 grams (1/2 lb) fresh or dried
pinto beans
3-4 Albanian (hot) peppers (in Rize
known as red cabbage peppers)
1 matchbox size piece of meat fat
(or 2 tablespoons butter or oil)
1/3 cup corn flour

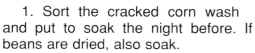

1. Sort the cracked corn wash and put to soak the night before. If beans are dried, also soak.

2. Trim the cabbage. If fresh use the stems. Wash each leaf and chop. (If desired, break apart by hand: hold the head in the hand and rotate removing the pieces.) Strain the soaked corn and beans and place together with the black cabbage in a large pot. Wash the Albanian peppers and add. Cover the contents of the pan in water and set to boil. After coming to a high boil once or twice, drain off the water. Add hot water to the pot and boil until cooked.

3. Remove the peppers from the cooked stew. With a knife called a "gudal" (in the Black Sea region) in one hand, and a long stemmed plant in the other, beat the cooked food. The loose stems can be wrapped around the gudal. Alternatively the mixture can be mixed in a food processor. Return to the fire and add the fat, butter or oil. Add salt and corn flour and cook over high heat, stirring constantly. Serve hot. Goes well with corn bread.

Notes: *1. If the gudal or food processor is not used, it becomes a soup and no corn flour is added.*

2. If you want the pinto beans to be very soft, cook separately, put through a food processor and add.

Dried fruit and lamb

TRABZON BLACK CABBAGE AND VEGETABLES

Ingredients:
1 black cabbage, about 1 kilogram
(2 lb)
1 cup cracked corn (preferably
roasted in the oven and dried)
250 grams (1/2 lb) dry pinto beans
or summer green beans
3-4 Albanian (hot) peppers
2-3 onions
5-6 small green peppers
2-3 carrots
1 matchbox size chunk of fat or
butter
2-3 tablespoons oil

1. Put the corn and dry beans (if used) to soak the night before.

2. Trim cabbage. Wash each leaf, drain and chop. Combine with pinto beans (if used), corn, hot peppers, cover with water and boil. While boiling add a little salt. (More salt may be added to taste later.) After coming to a full boil once or twice, drain off water.

3. Cut the onion in thin slices. Wash, trim and cut the green beans if used and cut the the carrots and green peppers in rounds. Mix the oil and the fat or butter in a pan and saute the cut vegetables. Add the cabbage and enough water to cook and some salt. If additional water is needed add it hot. Boil until cooked. Serve with cornbread.

Note: Cut the vegetables according to the recipe. If desired, put them in a pot with the cabbage mixture without the sauteing and, at that point, add the fat, oil and salt to the pot. Add sufficient water and cook without stirring.

DRIED FRUITS AND LAMB (HALAŞKA)

(Ms. Münevver Doğan of Yozgat won first prize with this recipe in a cooking contest in Ankara.)

Ingredients:
250 grams (1/2 lb) tender lamb
1 onion
2 tablespoons tomato paste
2 liters water
2 apricots, 8 plums
Dough:
2 eggs
4 spoons flour
salt, water

1. Cut the onion and the lamb in thin slices and fry in a little oil. Add tomato paste and cook a minute or two more. Add hot water. Cook until the meat is soft.

2. A soft dough is made with the egg, salt, flour and water. Knead by hand or with a spoon. Allow the dough to set 10 minutes. When the meat appears done spoon the dough 1/2 teaspoonful at a time onto the hot stew. (If each spoonful is slightly moistened with broth before adding, the stew will easily take in the dough.)

3. After adding all of the dough in this way, allow to boil. The dough balls will increase three times their size.

4. Wash the apricots and plums well and soak in hot water for 15-20 minutes. Add to the boiling stew. When the fruits are cooked, add a beaten egg

to the stew and immediately remove from the stove. Allow to set a little before serving.

KAZAKSTAN DISH

Ingredients:
250 grams (1/2 lb) flour
1 egg, a little water
250 grams finely chopped lamb or ground beef
1 onion, 2-3 small green peppers
2 tomatoes, 1 spoon tomato paste

1. Heat slightly together the meat, onion, peppers, tomatoes and tomato paste. Add hot water and cook until done. When almost done add salt. Continue to simmer.

2. Make a soft dough with flour, salt and water. Make small cuts a half cm apart and oil all sides. Roll thinly into a roll. Starting from the center of the boiling stew begin to wind the roll around and around until reaching the sides of the pot. Set over a low flame and cook until done.

3. When all is cooked and the broth is absorbed carefully transfer to a deep serving dish and sprinkle chopped green pepper and red pepper flakes over it.

POTATOES WITH GROUND MEAT

Ingredients:
1 kilogram (2 lb) potatoes
200 grams ground meat, 1 onion
2 tablespoons margarine
1 tablespoon tomato paste
2 cups water, salt, black pepper

1. Slice the onion thinly and cook in oil with the ground meat. Add the tomato paste and cook a little longer. Add hot water and allow to boil.

2. Cube the potatoes and add. Add salt and black pepper. Cook over a medium flame until done.

EGGPLANT SAUTE

Ingredients:
250 grams (1/2 lb) ground meat
500 grams (1 lb) eggplant
3-4 small green peppers
1 onion
2 tablespoons oil
3-4 garlic cloves
salt- black pepper
1/3 teaspoon oregano

1. Cook the onion and ground meat in oil. Chop the peppers in 1 cm pieces, skin and slice the tomatoes. Add these to the meat and stir a little. Cut the egg plants in cubes and crush the garlic. Add these to the mixture. Add salt and pepper and stir occasionaly, being careful not to crush or bruise the eggplant pieces.

2. Add the oregano, cover the pan and cook 1-2 minutes longer. Serve hot.

Note: *Goes well with a pilaf or macaroni dish.*

Mushroom saute

Fried onions

Green beans in olive oil

Eggplant puree

MEAT DISHES

CONTENTS

HELPFUL HINTS

1. When selecting meat pay attention to the following:

a. Mature beef cuts should appear firm and bright red.

b. Veal cuts should appear firm and pink.

c. Mutton meat should appear red and the fat white.

d. The best time for lamb is between February and May. The meat should appear pink and not too fibrous.

e. Goat meat has its own special strong odor.

In general if the meat appears yellowish and drab it is not fresh. If it starts to turn dark brown it is unsafe to use.

2. Ground meat and boiling meat can come from any part of the animal. The ground meat is better if part of it is taken from the breast portion.

3. Roasts are cut from the butt, leg or arm.

4. Lamb chops are cut from the arm.

5. Shish kebab is taken from the leg and the fillet.

6. Boneless meat cubes are taken from the butt, leg and arm.

7. Chops, shish kebab, steak and doner cook best on a charcoal fire but the oven or electric grill can also be used. If cooked too long they become dry.

8. To prevent meat and chicken that is cooked in the oven from getting too dry, place a pan of water in a corner of the oven.

9. When cooking meat in the oven baste the meat with its own juice to help prevent drying and to add to its flavor.

10. When preparing meatballs add a teaspoon of olive oil. This will make them soft.

11. Before grilling or broiling meat, oil the grill spit, or skewers. If using an oven moisten the meat first. Preheat the broiler or oven to a high temperature. In this way the juices that coagulate will layer on the meat and prevent loss of its nourishment value.

12. Grilling meat should not be overly fatty.

13. Normally when grilling, the meat is first pounded with salt and pepper and, if desired, oregano.

14. For breaded meats, sprinkle salt and pepper on the meat. Dip in beaten egg (if desired put some grated kashar cheese in the egg), then roll in fine bread crumbs and fry in hot oil.

15. For breaded lamb chops, sprinkle salt and pepper on the meat and braise a little on both sides in light oil. Mix grated cheese, flour and a little salt and pepper (remembering it was already used), and if desired some cold mashed potatoes. Add an egg and mix until consistency of yoghurt. Dip the chops in this mixture and fry in hot oil.

16. Marinades mixed with fresh herbs or spices add flavor as well as soften meats, fish and chicken. (such as onion juice, pepper, salt, oregano, flavored oils etc.).

Note: Recipes for flavored oils and vinegars are in the Salads chapter.

17. Remove the sinews from meat to be used for shish kebabs. Then put it in a marinade mixture of milk, olive oil, juice of a grated onion, salt and pepper. The marinade tenderizes the meat. For the most tasty and tender results, let the meat remain in the marinade at least 12 hours.

18. To prepare marinade for steak and lamb chops:

There are many excellent marinades, as for example the following commonly used in Turkey:

a. Oil, oregano, salt, black pepper and red pepper flakes.

b. Oil, oregano, salt, black pepper, crushed garlic, grated onion and tomato paste

If the meat is to be cooked right away, example (b) will bring a more flavorful result. However, for those who wish to avoid onion or garlic, example (a) can be used.

After the beefsteak, lamb chops or chicken steak are removed from the marinade they can be wrapped in wax paper or aluminium foil or a tightly covered glass dish and placed in the meat section of the refrigerator or in the freezer. About an hour or two before the meal remove from the freezer add vegetables such as mushrooms or potatoes, etc. and place in the oven.

19. Use only hot water when adding to meat cooking in water. If cold water is added, the broth and the meat will both lose flavor.

20. When the meat comes to a boil, spoon off the foam from the top in order to maintain an appetizing color to the meat and broth and to avoid a bitter flavor.

21. When frying meat brown it first on both sides and then continue to cook. In this way it maintains more juice and is softer.

22. A roast or kebab meat can also be browned a little, then some hot

water added and cooked. Or, the meat can be boiled first and then fried. When using this method, the meat broth is also very tasty and is good to use in making a pilaf or a soup.

23. If the lamb chops, beefsteak, fillet mignon etc. are to be fried use plenty of oil. Prepared this way makes it a little difficult to digest.

24. Oven fried meat is healthier and more flavorful.

25. The neck is the best part for boiling.

26. Veal bones make the best meat broth.

27. To make the meat dishes more delicious and make them cook faster, add a little vinegar to the pan or put the meat in vinegar before cooking.

28. Pour a little olive oil over the grilling meat to make it softer.

29. Meat cooked with vegetables in water has the highest food value and is easiest to digest.

30. For more flavorful meat, stick a few cloves in a whole onion and add to the water when cooking.

31. Adding a bouquet garni to the pot also adds flavor. Mix together bay leaves, parsley stems and wild oregano. Add celery root leaves and leeks if desired.

32. When preparing broth, to add more flavor there are some standard mixtures of vegetables and herbs that can be used.

Example:

Grate into a big bowl about 250 grams (1/2 lb) of carrots, onions and celery. Add a bay leaf and a little oregano. This mixture adds flavor to the meat broth. If desired strain off after cooking.

33. Placing liver or brain in ice water for 10 minutes before cooking eliminates any bitter taste.

34. When preparing oven-fried chicken a little tomato paste or just salt water may be added on top.

35. If the smell of chicken broth is undesirable, melt a little saffron in hot water and add to the chicken while cooking.

36. When chicken is left sitting hot or uncovered, the bacteria spread rapidly.

37. How to skin tomatoes (See the Vegetables chapter).

SIDE DISHES

Sauteed Side Dishes

Cut all the vegetables in cubes the same size and saute in oil. Salt and pepper may be added (beans, peas, cauliflower, carrots, etc.)

Bean Saute

Ingredients:

500 grams (1 lb) fresh tender beans
2 tablespoons butter
salt

1. Trim and wash the beans and chop to desired size. If using an iron pan cook on low flame in its own juice. With other pans a little water should be added.

2. When almost done add salt.

3. After cooking pour on some cold water to maintain lively appearance.

4. Melt the butter in a pan, add beans and stir awhile. Serve with a meat dish.

Peas saute

Ingredients:

1 kilogram (2 lb) fresh peas (or 2 cups canned peas, drained)
salt
1 1/2 tablespoons butter

1. Shell the peas and wash. Cook on low flame in very little water.

2. When almost cooked add salt.

3. Drain and pour on some cold water to maintain lively appearance. Saute in butter and serve with a meat dish.

Note: *Boiled cubed carrots may also be added to this saute.*

Zucchini squash saute

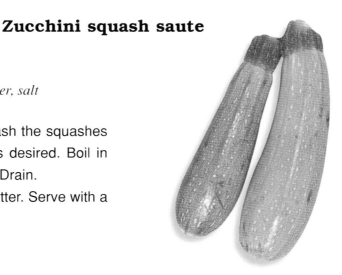

Ingredients:

2-3 squash
1 1/2 tablespoons butter, salt

1. Scrape and wash the squashes and cut in pieces as desired. Boil in very little salt water. Drain.

2. Saute in the butter. Serve with a meat dish.

Cauliflower saute

Cut the stem and separate all the flowerets. Prepare the same as for other vegetable sautes.

Carrot saute

Carrots look very nice if cut diagonally. After boiling prepare the saute as with the other vegetables.

Spinach saute

Wash 3-4 times in water. Cook over a slow flame in its own juice. Chop and saute in butter.

Pureed Side Dishes

Mash the cooked vegetables. Mix over a low flame with butter, milk or meat broth. (for example, potatoes, eggplants, spinach or carrots).

Mashed potatoes

Ingredients:
500 grams (1 lb) potatoes, 1 cup milk
2 tablespoons butter
salt, black pepper

1. Wash and boil the potatoes. Peel before they are cold. Pass through food processor or use a masher or fork.

2. Mix over a low flame with salt and butter. Slowly add the milk while stirring. Serve with a meat dish.

Oven hash browns

Ingredients:
5-6 potatoes, 3 eggs
1/3 cup grated cheese
salt, black pepper, 1 tablespoon butter

1. Boil the potatoes. Set aside to cool. Peel and grate.

2. Separate the yolk from one egg. Mix the rest with the salt, pepper and cheese and add to the potatoes. Mix well into a thick roux. Cut out rounds with the rim of a glass or separate by hand into pieces as desired.

3. Arrange in an oiled oven pan. Drizzle the beaten egg yolk over the top and place in oven.

Note: *If the mixture is too soft add a little fine bread crumbs.*

Eggplant puree

Ingredients:

1 kilogram (2 lb) seedless eggplants
1 1/2 tablespoons flour
2 tablespoons butter
1 cup milk
salt, black pepper

1. Broil the eggplants, peel off the skins and put them in cold water.

2. Wash and drain and slice thin.

3. Cook the flour in the butter until lightly browned and add the eggplant slices. Add the milk very slowly while stirring. Cook 15-20 minutes. Add salt and pepper and stir a little. If desired add grated cheese. Serve with a meat dish.

Fried side dishes

Slice the vegetables as desired and fry in oil (such as potatoes, eggplants, green peppers etc.)

Fried potatoes

The potatoes may be cut in cubes, matchstick pieces or slices as desired. Wash, drain and dry. Fry in hot oil.

Serve with a meat dish.

Fried eggplants

Peel the eggplants in strips, alternately leaving a strip. Cut in rounds or diagonals, soak a little in salted water, drain and dry well. Fry in hot oil. Serve with a meat dish.

Fried peppers

Wash, drain and dry the small green peppers. Fry without removing the stems or seeds. Serve with a meat dish.

Hash brown potatoes

Fried potatoes

Broiled or grilled side dishes

Trim the vegetables, wash and dry. Broil or hold over an open flame (eggplants, peppers, potatoes, tomatoes, etc.)

Grilled tomatoes and peppers

Broil or hold over an open flame. If the skins are not burned too much they may be served without peeling.

Note: *These may be served along with a cold garniture of tomatoes, peppers or cucumbers or with a meat dish.*

Grilled eggplants

Wash and dry the eggplants and broil or hold over an open flame. (This does not work with very fat type of eggplants. Use the long thin type.) Peel when cooled, add salt and pepper and serve as a side dish.

SAUCES

CREAMY SAUCE

Ingredients:

Extra chicken parts, skin, liver, etc.
1 onion
2-3 garlic cloves
1 celery root
1 carrot
2 tomatoes or 1 tablespoon tomato paste
2-3 bay leaves
2 tablespoons oil
4 cups water

1. Peel and wash all the vegetables.
2. Except for the tomatoes, saute until light brown the other vegetables and the chicken pieces in the oil. Then add the tomatoes or tomato paste and cook a little longer.
3. Add the water and cook on a medium high heat for 1 1/2 to 2 hours. Strain in a colander or, if there are no bones in the chicken, use a food processor.

Note: *Any type of poultry or meat can be used for this sauce.*

BÉARNAISE SAUCE

Ingredients:

3 tablespoons margarine
1/3 cup vinegar
1 onion
3 egg yolks
1 bay leaf
1 tablespoon potato starch or cornstarch
salt, black pepper

1. Chop onion coarsely and cook with vinegar, bay leaf, black pepper and onion in a little water until soft.
2. Mix the egg yolks with the starch. Gradually add a cup of water and mix well.
3. Add the egg mixture very slowly into the bubbling onion mixture. Add salt and whip very fast with a wire whip or mixer until it becomes the consistency of mayonnaise.
4. Add the margarine and stir occasionally.

Note: *This sauce goes well with meat or fish.*

LEMON SAUCE FOR FISH

Ingredients:

1/3 cup olive oil
1 1/2 lemons
1/2 bunch parsley
salt
pepper

Squeeze and strain the lemon and mix with the olive oil. Add the finely chopped parsley, salt and pepper and stir. Put on top of the grilled fish.

Note: *If a creamy sauce is desired put through the food processor.*

BLACK SAUCE

Ingredients:

500 grams (1 lb) mutton bones
2 onions
2 carrots
2-3 garlic cloves
1 celery root
5-6 tomatoes or 2 tablespoons
tomato paste
2/3 teaspoon peppercorns
3-4 bay leaves
2 tablespoons tomato paste
3 tablespoons oil
2 tablespoons flour

1. Ask the butcher to break the bones into very thin pieces. Saute with coarsely chopped onions, garlic, celery root, carrots and the bay leaves until lightly browned. Add chopped tomatoes or tomato paste and cook a little more.

2. Add 1 1/2 liters of water and cook on a slow flame about 1 1/2 to 2 hours. Drain through a colander.

3. If a finer mixture is desired put in food processor but be sure to remove the bones first. This will keep a long time in a tightly covered glass container. When ready to use heat while stirring in 2 tablespoons flour and cook until the flour taste is gone. Stir in the tomato paste and bring it to a very thick consistency.

Notes: *1. If desired, fry the flour in a little oil first, add the tomato paste and then mix into the sauce.*

2. This sauce can be used with poultry, macaroni and some bread dishes.

MEAT SAUCE

Ingredients:

2-3 onions
1 clove garlic
1/4 cup vinegar, salt, black pepper
2 tablespoons potato starch

1. Peel and slice the onion and garlic and boil in vinegar.

2. Add the starch gradually and add salt and pepper. Stir and bring to a boil. Mix in a food processor until smooth.

BECHAMEL SAUCE

See the recipe under the Vegetables - Sauces section.

MEYANE (ROUX)

After cooking the flour in the oil or butter if meat broth is added, it is a veloute sauce.

If the roux is too watery it thickens when added to meat. If it is a veloute, it can be used as sauce.

MAIN DISHES
ULUBORLU MEAT SAUTE

Ingredients:

500 grams (1 lb) boneless meat
1 head onion, salt, black pepper
2 tablespoons oil

1. The butcher can either prepare the selected meat as ground meat or cut it in very small pieces. Place in a pan and cover on a slow flame.

2. When the meat's own juices come out, add the oil and finely chopped onion and salt. Saute until light brown. Add black pepper and serve hot.

Note: *On the morning of the sacrifice this saute is cooked at home.*

SACRIFICE MEAT SAUTE

1. Place some thin slices off the sheep's tail into the pan and brown slightly, then add the sliced or cubed meat and cover.

2. Cook on slow flame until the meat's juices come out. When the juice is evaporated and only oil remains stir with a wooden spoon until the meat is lightly browned. Cut the kidney or liver into small pieces and add to the pan when the meat is almost done.

3. Add salt and pepper when done, mix well and remove from the heat.

Note: *If onion flavor is desired, peel an onion and brown it whole in 2 tablespoons of oil. Later add to the meat. When it softens remove from the pot.*

MEAT CUBE SAUTE

1. Heat the saç (a round, slightly convex pan made of sheet metal).

2. Put the meat cut in very small pieces in the saç and cook on slow flame stirring constantly with a wooden spoon until the juices come out.

3. Add ground red pepper and stir. Add half-moon slices of onion, chopped tomatoes if in season, rounds of chopped peppers, salt and pepper. Stir and cover. Cook for 20 minutes more.

Boiled meat

ROLLED MEAT LOAF

Ingredients:
500 grams (1 lb) twice-ground beef
1 onion
1 slice bread, crusts removed
1 bunch parsley
3 eggs
2 carrots
2 tablespoons cooked peas
1/3 cup water
1 tablespoon tomato paste
salt, pepper, meatball spice mix
3 cloves garlic

1. Put the ground beef in a large bowl. Grate the onion and crush the garlic. Chop the parsley finely. Moisten the bread and squeeze out excess water. Add all these ingredients to the meat along with salt, spices, and the white of one of the eggs slightly beaten. Mix well by hand, adding some water from time to time. Continue to mix a few more times until the fat of the meat sticks to the hands.

2. Form in a loaf and place in an oven pan press down with two fingers to make a valley in the middle.

3. Boil the carrots and cut thin like pencils. Boil 1 egg and peel. Cook the peas or strain if canned.

4. Lay the cut carrots in the valley, then the sliced egg and spread the peas between.

5. Close the opening in the loaf and roll it until it's round. Spread tomato paste over the top if desired. Spread the beaten egg yolk over the top and bake in a medium oven for 40-45 minutes. Serve hot.

Not: Goes well with mashed potatoes or carrot mayonnaise salad. A pilaf may also be served with the meat loaf.

BOILED MEAT

Ingredients:
500 grams (1 lb) meat
salt, black pepper
1-2 onions, 2-3 potatoes

1. Cut the meat in large pieces and put in a pan of water. Bring to a boil and remove the foam with a strainer. Cover and cook on a slow flame.

2. When almost done, peel the onions and cut in fours and add to stew. Add the potatoes whole. Season with salt and pepper.

3. To avoid breaking apart the onions and potatoes do not stir and cook on slow flame until the meat is done.

4. When ready to serve lay the meat on one side and the potatoes and onions on the other side. This goes well with shepherd's salad.

The remaining meat broth can be used to make a soup or a pilaf. Bread chunks can be added and eaten with the broth.

ULUBORLU BREAD CUBES AND MEAT IN BROTH
(A special dish for guests in Isparta and environs)

Ingredients:
For this dish no measurements are needed because the portions depend on the number of people invited. It may be served along with a platter of meat or when serving a sacrifice.

1. Use meat on the bone cut in large chunks. Cook until done. Cut large bite-size pieces

2. Pour the broth over the bread to moisten it but not too much. Put the meat on top. Sprinkle black pepper over it and serve hot.

Sliced onions, tomatoes and peppers go nicely with this dish.

WOMAN'S THIGH MEATBALLS

Ingredients:
500 grams (1 lb) lean ground veal
1 large onion
3 tablespoons rice
2 eggs
1/2 bunch parsley
4 1/2 tablespoons fine bread crumbs
salt, pepper, frying oil

1. Boil the rice in a little less than a cup of water and drain.

2. Grate the onion and saute with half of the ground meat without oil. Add to the rest of the ground meat. Add the boiled rice, salt, black pepper and

chopped parsley. Break the egg into the mixture and mix well. Let it set for awhile.

3. Form flat or oval patties the size of about two walnuts. Roll in the breadcrumbs and dip in the beaten eggs. Fry in hot oil.

CRISPY MEATBALLS

Ingredients:

500 grams (1 lb) ground meat
2 onions, 3 potatoes
1 egg
1/2 bunch parsley
3-4 garlic cloves
ground red pepper
cumin, black pepper, salt

1. Mix together well the ground meat, grated onion, crushed garlic, salt, black and red pepper, cumin, chopped parsley and egg. In place of using bread in the meatballs mashed potatoes are used. Mix together well.

2. If the meatballs are to be broiled or grilled, mix in a little grated kashar cheese. If the meatballs are to be fried, the cheese is not needed.

3. After mixing form balls the desired size and cook.

Note: *If desired, bread may be substituted for the potatoes and the meatballs put on skewers and grilled. This is called Shish Kebab Meatballs.*

HASAN PASHA MEATBALLS

Ingredients:

1 kilogram (2 lb) ground meat
3 slices bread
1 onion, 3 garlic cloves
black pepper, salt, cumin
3 potatoes, boiled and peeled
1 tablespoon margarine or butter
1 cup milk, ketchup

1. Cut away the crusts from the bread and soak in water for five minutes. Squeeze and add to the ground meat. Grate the onion and crush the garlic. Add these to the meat and add cumin, a little salt and pepper and knead well for five minutes.

2. Divide the meat mixture into egg-shaped pieces. Open each piece in the middle and place them on an oven pan.

Cook for 15-20 minutes. Remove from the oven.

3. While the meatballs are cooking, mash the potatoes with a fork or put through a sieve. Put the butter and milk in a pan and put the potatoes on top. Add salt and pepper. Mash them in the pan over a slow flame until blended well.

4. Spoon a little of the potato into the middle of each meatball. Dot the top of each one with ketchup - store-bought or homemade. Return the pan to the oven until the potatoes are lightly browned.

Note: *When the meatballs cook in the oven the first time, a little juice fills the openings at the centers. By placing the mashed potatoes on top the meat flavor penetrates the potatoes and makes the dish very tasty.*

OVEN MEATBALLS

Ingredients:

1 kilogram (2 lb) ground meat
1 onion
250 grams (1/2 lb) meat cubes
2 carrots
1/3 cup peas
100 grams (1/4 lb) mushrooms
3-4 tomatoes
3-4 small green peppers
2 tablespoons oil
2 tablespoons tomato paste
1/3 cup fine bread crumbs (or 3-4 slices stale bread)
black pepper, salt, meatball spice mix, oregano

1. Boil meat cubes and slice very thin or cut in very tiny cubes.

2. Chop carrots, mushroom and 2 tomatoes. Saute these with the peas and cooked meat.

3. Meanwhile, if stale bread is used remove crusts, wet the bread and squeeze out the water. Grate the onion. Then mix together well the ground meat, onion, salt, black pepper, meatball spice, and either the bread crumbs or squeezed bread. Divide this mixture into large meatballs each with an impression in the center. Arrange on a flat pan and bake 15-20 minutes. Remove from oven and fill each one with a spoonful of the meatcube-vegetable saute.

4. Cover each meatball with a slice of tomato. Slit peppers lengthwise, remove seeds and lay a half pepper on top of each meatball.

5. Mix tomato paste and 1 or 2 spoonfuls of the broth from boiled meat. Add a dash of salt, black pepper and oregano.

6. Spoon this sauce over the top of the meatballs and stick a toothpick from the top down through each one. Heat in oven until they sizzle. Serve with mashed potatoes or pilaf.

Hasan Pasha meatballs

DRY MEATBALLS

Ingredients:
500 grams (1 lb) ground veal
2 slices stale bread
1 large onion
1 egg
2 garlic cloves
1/3 teaspoon cumin
1/3 teaspoon black pepper, salt
1/2 bunch parsley
frying oil

1. Trim off the crusts and moisten and squeeze excess water from the bread. Mix well with the ground veal, grated onion, crushed gar-

Uluborlu meat and bread cubes

lic, salt, pepper, cumin, chopped parsley and egg.

2. Divide in walnut-size pieces and form into patties or shape as desired. Fry in plenty of hot oil.

Note: *For quicker frying use less bread. For a softer meatball add 2 spoonfuls of oil to the mixture.*

GROUND MEAT WITH EGGS

Ingredients:

250 grams ground meat
1 onion
1 tablespoon tomato paste
2-3 eggs, salt, black pepper
ground red pepper
1 cup hot water

1. Slice the onion finely and saute it a little in oil. Add 2 tablespoons of water and continue to cook. Add the meat, stir and cook. Add the tomato paste and cook a little more.

2. Add the rest of the hot water, a little salt and the red and black pepper. Cover and cook. When almost done, crack the eggs on top. Cover and cook two more minutes before removing from the stove. Serve hot.

DIYARBAKIR STUFFED RIBS (KABURGA)

Ingredients:

2 kilogram (4 lb) rack of lamb
2 cups rice
black pepper, red pepper flakes
basil, salt
1/2 bunch parsley
2 tablespoons oil
1 tablespoon tomato paste

1. Heat the tomato paste in a little oil, add the rice and saute 5-10 minutes. Add 3 cups boiling water. When it returns to a boil cook on low flame until the water reduces.

2. Before the rice is completely done remove from heat and stuff it in the lamb ribs. Bind the rack of ribs together.

3. In a large pot heat a little more tomato paste in oil and place the rack of lamb on top, saute all sides in the sauce. Add boiling water and cook until done on a slow flame.

4. Remove the cooked ribs from the water and place in an oven pan. Heat until sizzling and serve hot.

Note: *Goes well with ayran (cool yoghurt drink), grated radish and turnip salad, or shepherd's salad.*

KEBAB WITH YOGHURT ON PITTA BREAD

Ingredients:

1 kilogram (2 lb) boneless lamb
2 onions
3 tomatoes
3 tablespoons oil
flat bread
2 cups yoghurt
salt, black pepper

1. Grate the onion and strain off the juice into a bowl. Allow the meat to marinate in the onion juice overnight or at least 2-3 hours.

2. Saute the marinated meat cubes a little in a tablespoon of oil. Add grated tomatoes, salt and black pepper and

saute 2-3 minutes more. Cover with hot water and cook until the meat is tender (allow most of the water to evaporate but leave some of the broth and oil mixture.)

3.Cut the flat bread in tiny pieces, moisten a little and spread on the serving platter. Drizzle the remaining broth from the pan over the bread.

4. Beat the yoghurt until it is creamy and pour over the bread. Then place the meat cubes on top and serve.

Note: *If a mixed platter is desired, add some grilled meatballs or shish kebab on top.*

ANTALYA CLAYPOT KEBAB

Ingredients:

500 grams (1 lb) spring lamb
3-4 finely chopped onions or equivalent in pearl onions
4-5 garlic cloves
3 medium sized eggplants
4-5 small green peppers
2-3 potatoes
2 tablespoons oil, salt
black pepper, oregano

1. Cube the eggplants and potatoes and chop the peppers about half an inch long. Chop the garlic. Mix all together with the chopped onions or pearl onions, meat, salt, pepper and oregano.

2. Place mixture in a large clay cooking pot, add the oil and cover the pot.

3. Seal the top tightly all around with a layer of dough. Place in a medium oven or on an open flame and cook very slowly.

Notes: *1. To achieve the best flavor, if possible prepare outdoors on hot coals*

2. Peas and cubed carrots may be added to this dish if desired.

STEAMED KEBAB

Ingredients:

1 kilogram (2 lb) boneless mutton
3 handfuls pearl onions
2 tablespoons oil
1/3 teaspoon oregano
1/3 teaspoon black pepper
1 garlic clove
2-3 bay leaves
salt

1. Peel and wash the onions and place in a pan with the meat.

2. Add the garlic, oil (if meat is fatty oil may be omitted), black pepper, garlic and salt. Mix once and without adding water cook covered on high heat until the meat is tender. Goes well with a pilaf and salad.

LAMB SHISH KEBAB

Ingredients:

*1 kilogram (2 lb) mutton or lamb
cubes*
3 tomatoes
4 small green peppers
1 teaspoon oregano, salt, pepper
juice of 1 lemon
1/4 cup olive oil
1 red onion
1 bunch parsley

1. Prepare a marinade mixture of the salt, pepper, oregano, lemon juice and olive oil.

2. Mix the meat by hand into the marinade and leave in a cool place over night or at least 3-4 hours.

3. Cut the tomatoes and pepper into pieces about the size of the meat cubes. Dip the pieces in oil and alternate placing the tomato, meat and pepper pieces on skewers. Turn on an electric grill or over an open flame until well browned all around.

4. Serve with a salad of red onions and parsley. Goes well with ayran, a pilaf with carrots and peas and flatbread.

Notes: *1. If the meat appears to be drying out brush on a little oil.*

2. The kebab may be done with meat only.

FOREST KEBAB

Ingredients:

*1 kilogram (2 lb) boneless
mutton cubes
3 tablespoons oil
2 onions (or 3 handfuls pearl
onions)
2 1/2 tablespoons tomato
paste
1/2 tablespoon pepper sauce
1 cup peas, 3 potatoes
3 carrots, 3/4 teaspoon
oregano, salt, black pepper*

1. Peel, wash and chop the onions (if pearl onions use whole). Saute a little with the meat. Add the tomato paste and cook a little more. Add 2-3 cups of hot water and cook on slow flame until the meat is tender.

2. Peel potatoes, scrape carrots, wash both and cut in cubes. Add to the cooking meat and cover. When the vegetables are done, add canned peas and salt and cook five more minutes. Add pepper and oregano and remove from heat.

SAC (GRIDDLE) KEBAB

Ingredients:

*500 grams (1 lb) meat pieces
3-4 small green peppers
1 kilogram (2 lb) tomatoes
red pepper flakes, black pepper,
salt
1/3 cup oil
1 onion*

1. Boil the meat in very little water for 10 minutes and drain.

2. Pour oil in the sac (a round slightly convex pan made of sheet metal) or in a teflon frying pan or stainless steel double boiler. Add finely chopped peppers,

grated onion and tomatoes and salt. Saute lightly and add meat and spices. Stir once and cover. Cook on low heat until done.

Note: *Goes well with flat bread or pitta.*

STOVE-TOP KEBAB

Ingredients:

500 grams (1 lb) boneless lamb
2 onions
2 tablespoons tomato paste
salt, black pepper
a little cumin
2 tablespoons oil
2 cups rice
3-4 cups water

1. Cut the lamb into small cubes and mix together well with thinly sliced onions, tomato paste, salt, pepper, cumin and oil. Press mixture into a pot, then place a tray on top and flip over. Place a weight, such as a teapot full of water, on top of the overturned pot to keep it from moving.

2. Put 3 cups water in the tray and cook on a slow flame about an hour or until the meat is done. The meat will first absorb the water and then give it out as broth.

3. Sort the rice and soak 20 minutes in salt water. Strain and wash 2-3 times and place in the broth in the tray (spread evenly around the pot). After the rice has absorbed all the water turn off the flame and let it set before serving.

Goes well with a cold cucumber-yoghurt drink (cacık), ayran or cold salads.

URFA TRAY KEBAB

Ingredients:

1 kilogram (2 lb) eggplants (not too thin, not too fat)
750 grams (1 1/2 lb) ground meat
salt, black pepper
3-4 tablespoons oil
5-6 medium sized tomatoes

1. Cut off the tops from the eggplants and set aside. Cut the eggplants crossways in 2-3 finger wide pieces not quite all the way through so they remain intact at the bottom side.

2. Work the salt and pepper into the ground meat. Stuff all except a spoonful of the meat between the eggplant slices. Then hold both ends of each eggplant and squeeze.

3. Place them on an oiled flat pan. Start from the edge of the pan and roll them into place them so that they are touching. Place a bit of the remaining meat on each of the tops and press them firmly back onto the eggplants. Arrange all in the middle of the pan. (If the pan selected is big enough the appearance of the dish will not be upset.) Pour the oil over the eggplants and place in the oven. Do not add water.

4. Meanwhile, remove the hard stem area from each tomato. Cut the tomatoes in half from the top and place them cut sides up on an oiled flat pan. Add a little salt and place in the oven. When the bottoms of the tomatoes have browned a little remove the pan from the oven, turn the tomatoes over and return to the oven until the other size is cooked and the juice begins to come out. Place them on the service platter next to the eggplants. The tomatoes add flavor and sauce to the dish.

This Urfa specialty goes well with pitta, bread or flat bread and can also be served with a pilaf and ayran.

WEDDING KEBAB

Ingredients:

1 kilogram (2 lb) sliced tender lamb cubes
3 tablespoons margarine
4 large onions
1 teaspoon tomato paste
1 teaspoon salt
pinch of black pepper
4 cups water

1. Melt the margarine in a pan and saute the meat 3-4 minutes. Add thinly sliced onions and continue to cook until lightly browned. Add the tomato paste and cook 1-2 minutes longer.

2. Add salt, pepper and 4 cups hot water and cook on a slow flame for 1 1/2 hours. Serve with a pilaf.

OVEN STEAK

Ingredients:

500 grams (1 lb) steak
oil, salt, pepper, oregano

Cut pieces according to the number of servings and allow to remain for at least 3-4 hours in a marinade of oil, salt, pepper and oregano. Roll the pieces in fine breadcrumbs and either bake uncovered in the oven or fry in oil. Goes well with mashed or fried potatoes; a mayonnaise or other sauce; and a pilaf.

DONER

1. Mix a marinade of salt, pepper and oregano in oil and pour over steak. Wrap and place in freezer. About a half-hour before cooking remove. Before it has thawed slice very thin on a board.

2. Place in a teflon pan or sac, cover and cook on a slow flame.

3. First the juice will come out and later it will cook in its own fat. After the juice comes out and only the fat remains it is necessary to stir.

4. When it begins to cook in its own fat, peppers and tomatoes (that have had their juice squeezed out) may be added to the pan.

It may be served in flat bread or pitta. Goes well with pilaf and ayran.

PEPPER VEAL STEW

Ingredients:
500 grams (1 lb) veal pieces
500 grams small green peppers
1/2 cup water
oil
2 bay leaves
salt, black pepper
red pepper flakes

1. Cover the veal pieces in water and cook on a slow flame until the water is evaporated. Slice the peppers coarsely. Add peppers, oil and bay leaves to the meat. Cook on low flame 20-25 minutes, stirring occasionally.

2. When the stew looks almost done add salt and spices. Serve hot.

Goes well with bulgur pilaf and shepherd's salad.

Eggplant kebab

EGGPLANT KEBAB

Ingredients:

1 kilogram (2 lb) medium sized eggplants (not too thin and not too fat)
750 grams (1 1/2 lb) fatty ground meat, salt

1. Slice the eggplants crossways into 4 or 5 pieces not quite all the way through so they remain intact at the bottom side Keep them together and place them one by one to the side.

2. Mix salt well into the ground meat. Form into meatballs that can be stuffed in between the eggplant slices. After the meatballs are in place, squeeze the eggplants a little at both ends. Place on skewers. Cook over a grill or under a broiler.

3. For this kebab turning type skewers are used. After it has cooked a little on one side turn slightly and continue in this way until done. Place in hot in pitta or flat bread. Goes well with pilaf and ayran.

KEBAB ON SKEWERS

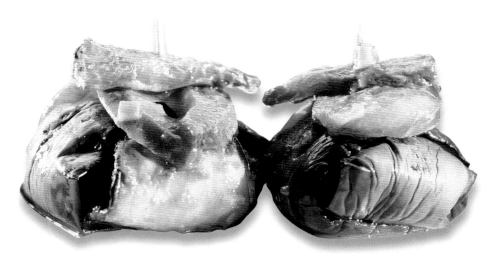

Ingredients:

500 grams (1 lb) lean ground veal
1 slice stale bread, crusts removed
1/2 bunch parsley
1 large onion, 2 tomatoes
4-5 small green peppers
1 1/2 tablespoons tomato paste
4-5 eggplants, 1/4 teaspoon black pepper
1 teaspoon cumin
salt, frying oil

1. Cut the eggplants in thin slices lengthwise and soak in salted water for a half-hour. Wash, drain and dry.

2. Fry the eggplant slices in hot oil. Lay on a plate in 2's, one crosswise on top of the other.

3. Grate the onion; moisten the bread in water and squeeze out excess. Mix together well the ground veal, grated onion, bread, salt, finely chopped parsley, cumin and black pepper. Form walnut-sized balls and flatten into patties. Place each one on top of the eggplant slices in the middle and fold over the 4 ends so that the patties are closed inside. Spread finely sliced tomatoes on top and on top of that one or one-half of a pepper. Pierce each kebab with a stick and place on a flat oven pan.

4. Mix the tomato paste with the salt and a little water and pour on top of kebabs. Bake until done.

Goes well with pilaf and cold yoghurt soup (cacık).

ROLLED ROAST

Ingredients:

Half of a mutton butt
2 tablespoons margarine
1 tablespoon tomato paste, salt

1. Remove the bones and roll meat tightly with string. Salt the meat and rub on the margarine. Place on an oven pan in a hot oven. Turning occasionally, continue until the surface of the meat is lightly browned.

2. Pour the juice from the pan into a bowl. Spread the tomato paste on the meat and leave in the oven 5 more minutes.

3. Served with a pilaf, vegetables and salad.

STEAK AND POTATOES

Ingredients:

5-6 pieces veal steak
5-6 potatoes
3-4 onions
1/2 cup water
1/2 bunch parsley, salt
black pepper, sweet red pepper
1 1/2 tablespoons vinegar

1. Prepare a marinade with vinegar, salt, black pepper and red pepper. Marinate the meat 2-3 hours, turning the meat in the marinade every half hour.

2. Slice the potatoes in rounds a little over 1/4 inch thick. Peel and cut the onions in half from the top, then slice thinly from top to bottom by placing the face of each half on a board. Cook potatoes and onions in a pan with the water until it starts to boil. Immediately empty the contents onto an oiled flat pan.

3. The meat may be grilled as is or can be dipped in flour and egg and fried. Then place on top of the potatoes and cook in the oven until brown.

LAMB CHOPS

Ingredients:

15 thin lamb chops
3 eggs
1/2 cup flour
1 cup crumbled stale bread or fine breadcrumbs
1 1/2 tablespoons water
3 tablespoons margarine
salt, black pepper

Sprinkle the chops with salt and pepper. Mix flour with the egg and add 1 1/2 tablespoon water, then the breadcrumbs. Dip the chops in the mixture and fry in margarine on both sides. Goes well with macaroni, tomato sauce and any kind of salad.

ROAST LEG OF LAMB

Ingredients:

1 leg of lamb (upper)
2 tablespoons oil or margarine
1 1/2 tablespoons potato starch
1 cup water, salt

1. Place lamb on an oven pan and sprinkle with salt. Spread oil or melted margarine over it and place uncovered in the middle of the oven. Turn over from time to time and baste in its juices two or three times during cooking.

2. When the meat is well done remove from oven and slice in the pan. Lay slices on a serving platter.

3. Pour the juices from the pan into a smaller pan and add 1 cup of water. Bring to a boil. Mix the potato starch in a little cold water and slowly add to the boiling broth stirring constantly. Return to a boil and simmer a little longer. Pour over the meat on the platter or serve in a separate dish.

Goes well with Russian salad and pilaf.

GARDENER'S VEAL CUTLETS

Ingredients:

1 kilogram (2 lb) (more or less) veal cutlets
400 grams (13 oz) thin fresh carrots
400 grams (13 oz) fresh green beans
250 grams (1/2 lb) green asparagus
2 tablespoons butter
1/3 teaspoon black pepper
1 teaspoon salt
1/8 teaspoon sugar
1 cup vinegar
400 grams (13 oz) peas

1. Saute the cutlets in butter until the color changes. Add pepper. Place in a flat pan and continue cooking uncovered in the oven until done.

2. Sort and wash vegetables. Cut in pieces about the same size. Boil or steam each one separately and drain. Combine and saute in butter. Add salt and sugar.

3. Place meat on a serving platter and arrange vegetables around it. Mix meat juices from the pan with vinegar and pour over the meat.

SCHNITZEL

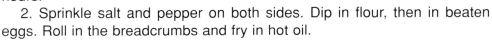

Ingredients:
1 kilogram (2 lb) steak (pounded thin)
2 onions
6 tablespoons fine bread-crumbs
4 1/2 tablespoons flour
3 eggs
frying oil
salt, black pepper

1. Grate onions and squeeze out water through a cloth into a bowl. Put the steak in the onion juice and set aside over night or at least 2-3 hours.

2. Sprinkle salt and pepper on both sides. Dip in flour, then in beaten eggs. Roll in the breadcrumbs and fry in hot oil.

Goes well with mashed potatoes, Russian salad or shepherd's salad.

Notes: *1. For an even tastier result the meat can be rolled in grated kashar cheese instead of flour. (cheese + egg + breadcrumbs).*

2. The meat can be rolled in rolled oat flakes instead of breadcrumbs (flour + egg + oat flakes).

Rolled Roast

LIVER STEW

Ingredients:

1 sheep's liver
1-2 garlic cloves
1 bayleaf
1 bunch parsley
salt, black pepper
500 grams (1 lb) pearl
onions
2 tomatoes
1 tablespoon tomato paste
2 tablespoons oil

1. Wash and cut liver in tiny bite-size pieces. Put in water with the oil and cook until it steams.

2. Add the peeled onions and garlic, bay leaf, salt and pepper and cook stirring for 5 minutes.

3. Remove skins from tomatoes and chop small. Add to stew. Mix a little water with the tomato paste and add, cooking 1-2 more minutes. Pour on enough hot water to cover and bring to a high boil, then turn down very low and cook until done. Remove to a serving plate and add parsley.

Albanian liver

ALBANIAN LIVER

Ingredients:

1 sheep's liver
flour, salt
frying oil

1. Heat oil in a frying pan.
2. Cut liver in cubes, salt and roll in flour. Fry in hot oil.
3. Remove with a slotted spoon to a serving plate. Arrange parsley and thin-sliced onions around it. Goes well with bread and ayran.

FRIED BRAIN

Ingredients:

5 lamb brains
1 onion
1 bay leaf
1/2 bunch parsley stems
1 tablespoon grated kashar cheese
3 eggs
salt, black pepper
1/2 cup flour
8 tablespoons margarine

1. Cover the brains in ice water and set aside for 10-15 minutes. Drain off water and remove the membrane.
2. Place in a pot with salt, onion, bay leaf and parsley stems and a little water. Bring to a boil and cook 5-6 minutes. (If veal brains are used, cook 10 minutes.) Remove from water and allow to cool.
3. Beat eggs with a fork and mix in flour.
4. Cut the brains into small pieces of equal size. Add salt and pepper. Mix into the grated cheese. Put the pieces one by one in the egg-flour mixture and fry in hot oil.

STEWED BRAIN

Ingredients:

4-6 sheep brains (or 2 veal brains)
1 carrot
1 onion
1 celery root
a few springs parsley
3-4 small green peppers
salt

1. Place brains in cold water and remove membrane.
2. Cube the onion, carrot and celery root and chop the parsley and peppers. Add to the brains.
3. Cook on medium flame 20-25 minutes in its own water. Before the pieces fall apart, drain and remove to a serving plate. Garnish with leaf lettuce.

Note: A brain salad is made by preparing boiled brain as in above recipe. Place on a platter with boiled potatoes, romaine leaves, sliced tomatoes and a lemon dressing.

KIDNEY SAUTE WITH MUSHROOMS

Ingredients:

15 slices of veal kidney (1 cm thick)
8 tablespoons flour
6 tablespoonbs margarine
1 medium onion
100 grams (1/4 lb) mushrooms
1/2 bunch parsley
salt, black pepper

1. Mix salt, black pepper and sifted flour. Dip kidneys in the flour on all sides.

2. Fry in half of the oil, stirring occasionally, for five minutes. Drain and place in a bowl.

3. Cut the onions in half and slice lengthwise on a board with the face down. Wash, dry, and slice the mushrooms. Put the rest of the oil in the pan and heat. Fry the onions. Stir a little. When softened add mushrooms. Cook until the juice has evaporated.

4. Add the fried kidneys and cook together a minute longer. Remove to a serving plate. Chop the parsley and sprinkle on top.

URFA FRIED LIVER

Ingredients:

1 kilogram liver
2 tablespoons tomato paste
1 onion
2 tablespoons oil
1 bunch parsley
2- green and red peppers
salt, black pepper
red pepper flakes

1. Cut liver into small pieces. Place in a frying pan.

2. Cook on a low flame until the juices come out. Slice the onions and peppers finely. Add to liver. Add salt, black pepper and red pepper. Cook until lightly browned.

3. Goes well with a pilaf. In Urfa it is eaten in flat bread.

4. If in flat bread add chopped green onions and finely chopped parsley.

CHICKEN DISHES

CONTENTS

TO IMPROVE THE FLAVOR OF CHICKEN:

Ingredients for marinade:

1/3 teaspoon oregano
1/3 teaspoon red pepper flakes or ground red pepper
1/3 teaspoon mustard
1/3 teaspoon cumin
3-4 cloves crushed garlic
6 tablespoons oil
1 1/2 tablespoons yoghurt
6 tablespoons lemon juice
3-4 bayleaves

Before baking chicken or chicken parts, mix all ingredients together in a bowl. Put the chicken in the marinade and allow to set in the refrigerator for 1-2 hours. If the chicken is to be fried, remove bowl from refrigerator, roll the pieces in fine bread crumbs and fry in hot oil. Note that the given proportions for the marinade are more suitable for oven chicken.

BOILED CHICKEN

Ingredients:

1 chicken
salt, pepper

1. Cut chicken into pieces, wash and drain.

2. Singe each piece over a flame. (To avoid burning the hand, use either a skewer or a long fork to hold the piece or hold it with tongs.)

3. After singeing the chicken rinse once more, place in a large pot and add just enough water to cover. (Cold water may be used but use hot water to better bring out the flavor of the chicken.) When the pot begins to boil, remove foam from the top, cover and cook on low flame. When almost done

add salt and pepper.

4. The chicken may also be cooked without water. In this case, after the singed pieces have been rinsed again, place in a pan without water, preferable heavy steel with a tight cover. The flame must be very low and the cooking takes longer than with water.

Notes: *1. The foam that forms as the chicken boils should be removed. If not the broth may be bitter and dark in color.*

2. The broth may be used to make a soup or a pilaf.

CHICKEN STEAK

Ingredients:

4 chicken steaks
2 eggs, salt
black pepper
fine breadcrumbs
frying oil

1. Wash and drain the chicken; sprinkle thoroughly with salt and pepper.

2. Beat the eggs. Dip the chicken in the egg, roll it in the breadcrumbs and fry in hot oil.

3. As the steaks are done, drain on paper towels to remove excess oil before serving.

Goes well with a pilaf and sliced cucumbers.

STUFFED CHICKEN STEAK

Ingredients:

4 chicken steaks
2 eggs, salt, black pepper
red pepper flakes
fine breadcrumbs

Stuffing:

1 tablespoon butter
1/2 bunch parsley
salt, black pepper
ground red pepper

1. Mix into a pasty consistency the butter, black pepper, red pepper and finely chopped parsley (using a food processor if possible).

2. Spoon some of the mixture onto the center of each steak and roll it. Dip each one in beaten egg, roll in breadcrumbs and fry in hot oil.

BAKED CHICKEN AND VEGETABLES

Ingredients:
1 kilogram (2 lb) chicken pieces
4 tomatoes
4 small green peppers
2 onions
4 potatoes
1 cup peas
1 head garlic
2 tablespoons yoghurt
1 tablespoon tomato paste
1/3 cup olive oil
salt, black pepper

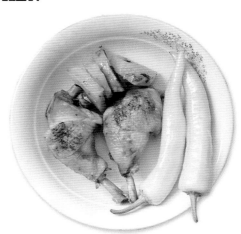

1. Crush half of the garlic and mix in a bowl with yoghurt, tomato paste and olive oil. Dip the chicken pieces in the mixture being sure all surfaces are coated and place them on an oven pan.

2. On top lay sliced potatoes, finely sliced peppers and onions, peas, skinned and cubed tomatoes and the rest of the garlic. Spinkle on salt and pepper and bake in a hot oven.

FRIED CHICKEN

Ingredients:
6 whole legs of a young chicken
2 tablespoons corn meal
salt, frying oil

1. Wash and remove all or most of the skin from chicken legs.

2. Pierce the pieces lightly and sprinkle on salt.

3. Roll in corn meal and fry in hot oil.

CHICKEN AUX GRATINS

Ingredients:
1 chicken
2 tablespoons margarine
2 tablespoons flour
2 eggs
1/2 liter milk
about 1/3 cup grated kashar
cheese
salt, black pepper

1. Wash and singe the chicken. Again wash and boil. Drain and place in a bowl.

Chicken buryani

2. When cooled cut into small chunks.

3. To make a bechamel sauce, brown flour lightly in margarine and gradually add the milk stirring constantly until it reaches a smooth pudding-like consistency.

4. After the sauce has cooled down a little blend in the eggs and half of the cheese.

5. Spread half of the sauce in a pan and place the chicken pieces on top. Pour the remaining sauce over the chicken and bake in the oven until light brown.

Stuffed chicken

STUFFED CHICKEN

Ingredients:

1 young chicken
1 1/2 cups rice
3 tablespoons pine nuts
1 tablespoon currants
1/3 teaspoon stuffing spice
salt, margarine

1. Clean the chicken thoroughly. Remove all inner parts except the liver. Singe and wash again.

2. Salt the bird inside and out and let it set for at least 2-3 hours. If left over night, drain off the water under the bird in the morning.

3. Soak the rice in hot salted water for at least 1 hour. Drain and rinse 2-3 times.

4. Put pine nuts in oil in a pan and saute until nuts are light brown. Add currants and stir once or twice. Add drained rice and saute together for 5 minutes. Add 2 cups hot water and salt. Bring to a boil and turn down flame. Cook until all water has evaporated.

5. After the cooked rice has set for awhile stir in the spice.

6. Stuff the bird with the mixture and sew up the opening. Place the bird in a cooking bag and close tightly. Bake in oven until done. Remove bag and transfer chicken to an oval serving platter. If some of the filling remained arrange it around the chicken. Serve with green salad and ayran (yoghurt drink) or other drink as desired.

CHICKEN AND RICE BURYANI

Ingredients:

5 chicken legs with thighs
3 cups rice
1 onion
2-3 tablespoons margarine
1 teaspoon tomato paste
salt

1. Clean and wash the chicken and cook in plenty of boiling water. Remove from the water.

2. Saute finely sliced onion in margarine. Stir in tomato paste.

3. Wash rice 2-3 times, drain and place in a deep baking pan. Add the onions.

4. Add 5 cups of the chicken broth and salt. Stir. Place the chicken in the middle of the pan and place in a pre-heated oven. Remove from oven when the water has evaporated.

CRETAN CHICKEN

Ingredients:

a 1-1/2 kilogram (3 lb) chicken
1 cup raisins
3 tablespoons butter
3 small green peppers
2-3 tomatoes
20 green or black olives
2 onions, 2 garlic cloves
1/4 cup vinegar, salt
1/3 teaspoon black pepper
1/4 teaspoon saffron
1/2 teaspoon curry powder

1. Bring raisins to a boil, remove from heat and allow them to soak in the water.

2. Cut the chicken into pieces and brown lightly on both sides in a large pan using half of the butter. Remove the chicken.

3. Put the remainder of the butter in the pan and fry the finely sliced onion and garlic.

4. Skin the tomatoes and cut in 4's. Remove the seeds from the peppers and cut small. Add the tomatoes, peppers, salt and pepper to the frying pan. Cover and cook on low flame a few minutes more.

5. Strain the raisins and dry on a towel. Cut the olives in half and remove the pits. Ad the olives and raisins to the pan. Add the chicken pieces and vinegar.

6. Add more salt if needed and black pepper, saffron and curry. Cover the pan and cook about 1 1/2 hours.

Note: *If a spicier dish is desired use more curry powder.*

CHICKEN AND MUSHROOM SAUTE

Ingredients:

500 grams (1 lb) mushrooms
2 chicken breasts
2 carrots
2 onions, 2 tomatoes
1 tablespoon tomato paste
curry powder
black pepper, salt, red pepper flakes

1. Cut the chicken in bite-size pieces and boil, or cut after boiling.

2. Wash and cut the mushroom in cubes.

3. Cook the carrots in a little water or chicken broth and cut in cubes.

4. Place the chicken and carrots in a pan. Add finely sliced onion. Skin and cube the tomatoes and add. Add the tomato paste, curry, black pepper and red pepper. Cook a minute or two longer, remove from heat and serve. Goes well with pilaf.

Note: *If desired, bechamel sauce and grated kashar cheese may be put on top of the cooked saute and the dish placed in the oven until the cheese is light brown.*

FISH

CONTENTS

HELPFUL HINTS ABOUT FISH

1. Pay attention to the following when shopping for fresh fish:

- The eyes look alive and shining.

- The flesh looks firm and fresh.

- The gills are bright red.

- The tail cannot be moved from side to side.

- The scales do not come off easily.

- The fish still carry the smell of the sea.

2. Fish should be cleaned and cooked soon after purchase. If not cooked immediately, do not keep for more than one day.

3. If fish with scales, such as grey mullet, red mullet and bass, are put in cold water for 5-10 minutes and then washed, the scales do not stick when they are scraped off.

4. Cooking time ranges from 15 to 40 minutes, depending on the type of fish.

5. All varieties of fish go well with a big green salad or carrot and radish salad.

Boiled:

6. When boiling fish with vegetables the vegetables tend to take on the fish taste. This is reduced by leaving the pan cover slightly open.

Steamed:

7. A special pan is used for steaming fish. Otherwise, put some water in a pan along with vegetables as desired. Place a grate over the top and lay the fish on the grate. Cover and steam.

Fried:

8. Fry in plenty of oil in a deep pan. This method is very tasty but hard to digest. Fish should be coated before frying. Flour, egg, fine breadcrumbs or a combination of flour and egg are used.

9. When frying the fish add a little lemon juice and black pepper to enhance the flavor.

Broiled or grilled:

10. Oily varieties of fish are best grilled over an open flame or broiled under the flame. Wash the fish and sprinkle with salt and pepper. The fish's own fat will come out in the cooking.

11. When preparing fish for either grilling or frying, if the fish is very large it is recommended to cut the **fillet:** Split fish lengthwise along the spine. Remove bones and skin. Cut each half into two or three pieces.

BONITO (PALAMUT) FILLETS

Ingredients:

1 kilogram (2 lb) bonito fillets
1 celery root
1 carrot
2 bay leaves
salt, black pepper
lemon juice

1. Wash the celery and carrot and cut into large chunks. Place in a wide pan and put the fillets on top. Sprinkle salt, pepper and lemon juice on top and add bay leaves.

2. Add just enough water to cover and cook on top of stove for 20-25 minutes.

3. Remove fillets from the water and drain. Serve with salads or macaroni.

4. A sauce of almond or lemon may be spread on top.

BONITO WITH RUSSIAN SALAD

Ingredients:

1 kilogram (2 lb) bonito
1 onion, 2-3 bay leaves
salt, dry mint, black pepper
Salad:
2 potatoes, 1 carrot
1/2 cup peas
10 fresh pickling cucumbers
1/3 teaspoon mustard
5 tablespoons mayonnaise
juice of 1 lemon, salt

1. Clean and wash the fish. Place large pieces in hot water and bring to a boil. Remove the foam from the surface.

2. Cut the onion in large chunks. Add to the fish along with salt, mint, pepper and bay leaves. Boil 15-20 minutes. Let the fish cool in its broth. When cooled remove and cut into smaller pieces.

Fish with tomatoes

3. Meanwhile boil the carrot and potatoes in another pan, cool and cut into small cubes. Drain the canned peas or, if fresh, boil, drain and add to the other vegetables. Slice cucumbers in thin rings and a add.

4. Mix mayonnaise, mustard, salt and lemon juice together and add to the vegetables. Mix well.

5. Place the fish on a serving platter and spoon the salad on top. Add parsley sprigs as garniture if desired before serving.

STEAMED FISH

Ingredients:

750 grams (1 1/2 lb) fish, any variety
1/3 cup water
1/3 cup olive oil
1 lemon
1/2 bunch fresh dill
1/2 bunch parsley

1. Clean and wash the fish and place in a flat oven pan. Put the olive oil, water, salt, minced dill and parsley, and lemon slices on top.

2. Steam covered in the oven or on top of the stove for 7-8 minutes. Serve after cooling.

Note: *In place of olive oil, 2 tablespoons butter may be used.*

FISH WITH TOMATOES

Ingredients:

750 grams fish (1 1/2 lb) (such as large red sea-bream, large grey mullet or red mullet)
1 cup olive oil
3-4 ripe tomatoes or 4 tablespoons tomato paste
1/2 cup water
1/2 bunch parsley
salt, black pepper

1. If using tomatoes, remove skins and chop very small. Mix tomatoes or tomato paste with salt, pepper and olive oil and cook into a smooth puree.

2. Add water. De-bone and slice the fish thin. Place into the sauce and cook 15-20 minutes. When slightly cooled add chopped parsley.

FISH WITH ONIONS AND TOMATOES

Ingredients:

750 grams (1 1/2 lb) fish of choice
3-4 tomatoes
2 onions
1/3 cup olive oil
1 small lemon
2 bay leaves
parsley, salt
black pepper

1. Clean and wash the fish well and place in a pan.

2. Slice the onions in half-moons and saute a little in oil. Peel and cube the tomatoes, add to onions and cook a little longer. Put the vegetables on top of the fish.

3. Add salt, pepper, bay leaves and lemon slices. Cook 15-20 minutes. When placing the fish on the platter add parsley sprigs.

FRIED MACKEREL

Ingredients:

1 kilogram (2 lb) mackerel
frying oil
1 handful flour, salt
1 lemon
1/2 bunch parsley
black pepper

1. Clean, wash and drain the fish.

2. Just before mealtime sprinkle on salt and pepper. Roll in flour and fry in hot oil.

3. Place fish on a serving platter and arrange lemon slices and parsley springs around them.

GRILLED WHITING

Ingredients:

1 kilogram (2 lb) whiting
1/3 cup olive oil
juice of 1 lemon
parsley, salt, black pepper

1. Clean, wash and drain the fish.

2. Just before mealtime sprinkle salt and pepper and oil on the fish (to prevent grilled fish from sticking, oil it thoroughly). Place fish on the grill and cook until done. Add lemon juice to the remaining oil and beat until light in color. Add pepper and chopped parsley.

3. Place the fish on a serving platter and pour the sauce over it. Goes well with sliced onion.

Note: *Other fish that may be substituted in this recipe include red snapper, bass, mackerel and fresh-water trout.*

TRABZON SARDINE CASSEROLE

Ingredients:

500 grams (1 lb) fresh sardines
4 onions, 4 potatoes
2-3 tomatoes or tomato paste
3 tablespoons olive oil
1/2 bunch parsley
1/3 cup water, salt, black pepper

1. Clean, wash and drain the sardines.

2. Slice onions thinly and slice the potatoes in rounds.

3. Mix together finely chopped parsley, half the oil, salt and pepper. Add the onions and mix well.

4. In a pan place half of the potatoes, then half of the onion mixture, then the sardines, the remaining onions and on top the remaining potatoes.

5. Pour the remaining oil and the water on top and bake in the oven. Serve hot.

BLACK SEA SARDINE OMELETTE

Ingredients:

15 salted sardines
3 tablespoons wheat flour
1 tablespoon corn meal
1 bunch parsley
1/3 cup milk
5 eggs
1 cup oil, salt

1. Wash the sardines to eliminate the salt. Remove the spines and cut into small pieces.

2. Mix milk, eggs, salt and add the flour. Mix well. Add finely chopped parsley. Dip the sardine pieces in this mixture and stir. Fry the pieces in hot oil.

3. Serve with boiled or mashed potatoes. Also goes well with macaroni.

BONITO (PALAMUT) IN OLIVE OIL

Ingredients:

1 kilogram (2 lb) bonito
1/2 cup olive oil
1/2 cup water
3 potatoes
2 carrots, 2 onions
1 celery root
2 bay leaves
1 bunch parsley
4-5 garlic cloves
1 tablespoon tomato paste
1 lemon, salt, black pepper

1. Clean and wash the fish and cut in slices. Sprinkle a little salt and pepper on the fish and place in a pan.

2. Wash, peel and cut in cubes the potatoes, carrots and celery root. Cut the onions in rounds and finely chop the garlic and parsley. In another pan saute the vegetables in oil.

3. Add the tomato paste, a little salt and pepper. Spread the vegetables over the fish. Add bay leaves and lemon slices. Pour 1/2 cup water on top. Begin cooking on high flame, then turn down and cook until the fish is done.

Notes: *1. If desired place half of the sauteed vegetables in the pan first, then the fish and then the remaining vegetables.*

2. Other fish that may be substituted in this recipe are fresh tuna or fresh sardines.

CHOPPED SARDINE BALLS

Ingredients:

1 kilogram (2 lb) fresh sardines
1 large onion, 1 bunch parsley
salt, black pepper, 2 tablespoons flour

1. Clean and wash the sardines, remove the spines and cut into very small pieces.

2. Chop the onions and parsley very fine and mix well with the flour, salt and pepper and then mix in the sardines.

3. Drop spoonfuls of the mixture into hot oil. Use a slotted spoon to remove the pieces as they are fried.

RICE PILAFS

CONTENTS

ABOUT RICE PILAFS

1. Be sure the rice is not damp or mouldy.

2. The best quality varieties of rice take twice as much water as rice in the cooking.

3. There are two basic approaches to rice: either to wash it before cooking or not to do so:

Technique of washing the rice:

a. Gently rinse the rice 2-3 times. Heat water to the point one can still place one's hand in it. Soak the rice in the water for at least 20 minutes. It is not necessary to rinse the rice again. Strain and it is ready for cooking. The strained water may be used in making soup.

b. Before the rinsing, soak the rice for one to three hours in salt water. Just before cooking, gently rinse the rice 2-3 times.

A cup of rice that has been rinsed and soaked usually requires 1-1/2 cups of water for cooking and when cooked yields 2 cups.

Technique of cooking when the rice is not washed:

In some recipes and areas, particularly in the southeastern part of Turkey, rice is place in boiling water without rinsing it first. 1 cup of rice cooked this way usually requires 2 cups of water.

4. While rice is cooking it is important not to stir it. If it is stirred it will become mushy, especially white rice. Brown rice does not easily become mushy.

5. Rice is first brought to a boil and cooked over a high flame for the first five minutes, then on medium flame until the water has been absorbed, and then on a very low flame until it is done (until the bottom of the pan sizzles).

6. Butter or margarine make the pilaf tastier, although harder to digest. It is suggested to use half butter or margarine and half oil in the cooking.

7. If the rice is to be cooked without first frying it in oil, it is best to heat the oil or butter before adding it.

8. After the pilaf is cooked, place a clean cloth or paper towel over the pan and then a tightly fitting lid. Allow to set for at least a half-hour.

9. When ready to serve the pilaf, gently stir it once to release the steam.

10. If very white and dry rice is desired, add 1/3 teaspoon sugar and one or two drops of lemon juice to the pan at the point in the cooking when the water has been absorbed.

11. To add a nice aroma and flavor to the rice, add one or two bay leaves about a minute or two after the rice comes to a boil.

12. Various types of meat patties can be added to leftover rice. Small meatballs can be made with a mixture of ground meat, grated onion, minced parsley, meatball spice, salt and pepper that is fried on hot oil. If oily meatballs are not desired, cooked ground meat can be mixed with the other ingredients and served as garniture.

To re-heat leftover pilaf: Boil some water in a wide pan and place the bowl containing the rice in the pan. This avoids any sticking.

PLAIN RICE

Ingredients:
2 cups rice
3 cups water or broth
3 tablespoons oil or butter, salt

1. Sort the rice. Soak in salt water at least an hour.
2. Place the water or broth in the pot the rice will be cooked in, add salt and bring to a boil.
3. Strain the soaked rice and gently rinse 2-3 times. Add the rice to the boiling water or broth. More salt may be added. Stir the boiling rice once.
4. Boil 5 minutes on high flame, 5 minutes on medium flame, then continue to cook on very low flame until the pan sizzles. Remove from heat.
5. Add hot oil or butter to the pan.
6. Place a clean cloth or paper towel over the pan and close the lid. All to set at least a half-hour. When ready to serve stir once.

RICE WITH VERMICELLI

Liver pilaf

Ingredients:
2 cups rice
1/3 cup vermicelli
4 cups water or broth
4 tablespoons oil, salt

1. Sort the rice and rinse until the water is no longer starchy.
2. Saute the vermicelli in the oil until light brown. Add the water and salt and bring to a boil.

3. Add the rice. Boil 5 minutes on high flame, 5 minutes on medium flame, then continue to cook on very low flame until the pan sizzles. Remove from heat.

4. Place a clean cloth or paper towel over the pan and close the lid. All to set at least a half-hour. When ready to serve stir once and sprinkle on some black pepper if desired.

RICE WITH CHICK PEAS

Ingredients:
2 cups rice
1 cup chick peas
2-1/2 to 3 cups water or broth
3 tablespoons oil, salt

1. Put chick peas to soak in cold water the night before. Strain and put in water to boil until soft. Drain and set aside.

2. Sort and wash the rice. Heat (to the point one can place one's hand in) enough water to cover the rice and allow rice to soak for a half-hour. Strain the rice.

3. Place the water or broth in a pan and add the cooked chick peas. Bring to a boil and add the rice and salt. Stir once.

4. Boil 5 minutes on high flame, 5 minutes on medium flame, then continue to cook on very low flame

5. When the pan sizzles, remove from heat. Heat the oil or butter in a small pan and pour over the rice.

6. Place a clean cloth or paper towel over the pan and close the lid. All to set at least a half-hour. When ready to serve stir once and sprinkle on some black pepper if desired.

Note: *If desired, the rice may be sauteed in the oil or butter before adding the it to the boiling water. If this is done, add the chick peas after that.*

hicken pilaf

UZBEK PILAF

Ingredients:

2 cups rice
2 tablespoons oil
3 cups water or broth, salt
meat ingredients:
250 grams (1/2 lb) lamb cubes
1 onion, 1 carrot
2 tomatoes
1/2 cup peas
3 tablespoons oil
1-1/2 cups water, salt
black pepper, oregano

1. Sort rice. Heat (to the point one can place one's hand in) enough water to cover the rice and allow to soak for a half-hour. Strain and rinse 2-3 times.

2. Heat 2 tablespoons oil in a pan. Add the rice and cook on high flame 6-7 minutes. Add 3 cups hot water. Bring to a boil and cook 5 minutes on medium flame, then cook on low until the water has been absorbed.

3. Put a clean cloth over the pan and the pan lid and set aside.

4. Meanwhile grate the onion and saute in 3 tablespoons oil. Add the meat and cook 5 minutes. Cut the carrots in cubes and skin and chop the tomatoes. Add them to the meat and 1-1/2 cups water. Cook 15-20 minutes.

5. Strain the peas and add. Boil a few minutes longer, remove from heat and set aside.

6. Stir the rice once gently and turn onto a serving platter. Arrange the meat stew around the pilaf or in the center of the platter. Serve hot.

Note: *This dish goes well with shepherd's salad or yoghurt soup.*

CHESTNUT PILAF

Ingredients:

2 cups rice
250 grams (1/2 lb) chestnuts
4 cups water or broth
3 tablespoons oil, salt

1. Boil the chestnuts until soft but not so much that they fall apart. Remove the outer layers and cut in 4's.

2. Sort the rice.

3. Boil the water in a pan, add the rice and salt. Boil 5 minutes on high flame, then 5 minutes on medium flame. While cooking add the chestnuts and stir once. Cook until the water has been absorbed. Heat the oil or butter in a small pan and pour over the rice.

4. Place a clean cloth or paper towel over the pan and place its lid on top. All to set at least a half-hour. When ready to serve stir once.

Note: *If desired saute the rice in the oil before putting in the boiling water.*

IZMIR PILAF

Ingredients:

2cups rice
3 tablespoons oil
3 cups water or broth
1 medium onion
3 tablespoons pine nuts
3 tablespoons currants
3 dried apricots
3 tablespoons finely chopped walnuts
1/4 teaspoon cinnamon
1/4 teaspoon sugar, salt

1. Sort rice. Heat (to the point one can place one's hand in) enough water to cover the rice and allow to soak for a half-hour. Strain and rinse 2-3 times.

2. Grate onion and saute until light brown in oil. Add pine nuts and continue cooking a little longer. Add the water or broth and put to a boil.

3. Add the currants, walnuts, cinnamon, sugar and salt and stir once.

4. After boiling on high flame for 5 minutes turn low and cook until the water is absorbed.

5. Place a clean cloth or paper towel over the pan and place its lid on top. Allow to set at least a half-hour. When ready to serve stir once.

EGGPLANT PILAF (ME'LUBE)

Ingredients:

2 cups rice
300 grams (5 oz) boneless lamb
3 large eggplants
1 tablespoon oil
cooking oil
3 cups water
salt, black pepper

1. Sort rice. Heat (to the point one can place one's hand in) enough water to cover the rice and allow to soak for a half-hour. Strain and rinse 2-3 times.

2. Trim the skins off the eggplants top to bottom in alternating strips. Chop in cubes. To eliminate bitterness soak at least a half-hour in salt water. Wash well and drain. Roll the cubes in a kitchen towel or paper towels to take out the water. Fry the cubes in hot oil, remove to a bowl.

3. Place the meat in a deep pot of water and bring to a boil. Remove the foam with a slotted spoon. Cover the pot and cook on low flame until done. Use a slotted spoon to transfer the meat to a bowl.

4. Place a tablespoon of oil in a pan (one that has a tight cover) and saute the meat a little. Add salt and pepper. Turn off the flame. Put the eggplant cubes on top and the strained rice over it. Add 3 cups of the meat broth by pouring it in slowly around the edges of the pan so as not to disturb the ingredients.

Eggplant pilaf

5. Turn on flame. When the broth begins to simmer, cover tightly enough so that, holding the pot with both hands, it may be flipped 360 degrees. Return to the stove or place in the oven. Cook until the water is absorbed. Remove from heat and allow to set covered 15-20 minutes. When ready to serve carefully slide the contents out from the edges of the pan so that the appearance of the dish is not disturbed.

TOMATO PILAF

Ingredients:
2 cups rice
2-3 tomatoes
3 cups water or broth
3 tablespoons oil, salt

1. Sort rice. Heat (to the point one can place one's hand in) enough water to cover the rice and allow to soak for at least one hour. Strain and rinse 2-3 times.

2. Skin the tomatoes and chop into very smal pieces. Saute a little in the oil. Add the water or broth. When it comes to a boil add the rice and salt.

3. Cook on high for 5 minutes, then on medium flame for 5 minutes. Then turn on low and cook until the the pan sizzles. Remove from heat.

4. Place a clean cloth or paper towel over the pan and place its lid on top. Allow to set at least a half-hour. When ready to serve stir once.

Note: *This pilaf goes well with a grilled meat dish or vegetable saute. If you don't want the tomato pieces to show, grate or pass them through a sieve. Or, squeeze the juice out of them before chopping and sauteeing in oil.*

BUHARA PILAF

Ingredients

2 cups rice

250 grams (1/2 lb) boneless lamb

3 medium carrots

1 tablespoon pine nuts

1 tablespoon currants

3 tablespoons oil

3-1/2 cups water or broth

salt, black pepper

1. Sort rice. Heat (to the point one can place one's hand in) enough water to cover the rice and allow to soak for at least a half-hour. Strain and rinse 2-3 times.

2. Cut the meat in bite-size pieces and place in a pan on low flame until its own juice comes out. Remove from flame and strain the juice into a bowl.

3. Scrape and wash the carrots, cut in half lengthwise and slice in half-rounds. Heat the oil or butter in a pan and saute the carrots a little. Add the pine nuts and continue to cook until light brown. Add the meat and cook a little longer. Add the currants that have been washed and drained.

4. Add the water or broth, salt and pepper. Bring to a boil and add the rice. Stir once and cook on low flame until the water is absorbed and the pan sizzles. Remove from heat and allow to set for 15-20 minutes before serving.

Goes well with shepherd's salad or cold cucumber-yoghurt soup.

SULTAN RESHAT PILAF

Ingredients:

2 cups rice
2 tomatoes
3 tablespoons oil
3 cups water or broth
200 grams (3 oz) lean ground beef
1 onion, 1 slice stale bread
2 tablespoons oil, salt, pepper

1. Sort rice. Heat (to the point one can place one's hand in) enough water to cover the rice and allow to soak for at least a half-hour. Strain and rinse 2-3 times.

2. Heat the oil in a pan and saute the rice on high flame for 6-7 minutes. Add the water or broth and bring to a boil. Cook on hot flame for 5 minutes then continue on low until the water is completely absorbed.

3. Place a clean cloth or paper towel over the pan and place its lid on top. Set aside.

4. Meanwhile, grate the onions. Remove the crusts from bread slice, moisten it, then squeeze out excess water. Mix together well the onions, bread, ground meat, salt and pepper. Divide the mixture into hazelnut sized balls and fry in hot oil. Remove meatballs from oil with a slotted spoon.

5. Skin tomatoes and cut in small cubes. Saute a little in the oil remaining in the pan. Add the meatballs and 1/4 cup water. Simmer 10 minutes.

6. Gently spoon the rice into the tube of a tube cake pan (such as is used for sponge cakes). Place a serving plate over the opening and turn upside down so that the pilaf stands high in the middle. Around it arrange the meatballs and sauce.

Note: *Serve this pilaf with shepherd's salad, a green salad or grated carrot and radish.*

LIVER PILAF

Ingredients:

2 cups rice
3-1/2 cups water or broth
3 tablespoons oil
1/2 a lamb's liver (or use turkey or chicken livers)
1-1/2 tablespoons pine nuts
1-1/2 tablespoons currants
2 medium tomatoes or, 1-1/2 tablespoons tomato paste, salt, pepper

1. Sort rice. Heat (to the point one can place one's hand in) enough water to cover the rice and allow to soak for at least a half-hour. Strain and rinse 2-3 times.

2. Skin tomatoes and cut in small cubes. Cook lightly in 2 tablespoons oil. Add the water or broth, salt and pepper and bring to a boil.

3. Sort, wash and dry the pine nuts. Cut the liver into tiny pieces. In a separate pan saute the nuts until light brown, add the liver and cook a little more. Add the currants and the boiling tomato broth.

4. When the pot comes to a boil add the rice and salt. Cook 5 minutes on high flame, turn down and cook until all the water is absorbed.

5. Place a clean cloth or paper towel over the pan and place its lid on top. Allow to set at least a half-hour. Serve hot.

Note: *Goes well with a vegetable dish, salad or cold cucumber-yoghurt soup.*

IRAN PILAF

Ingredients:

2 cups long-grain American rice
500 grams (1 lb) boneless veal cubes
3 potatoes
3 medium carrots
1c up peas
frying oil
75 grams (1.5 oz) margarine
3 tablespoons tomato paste
1/3 cup oil
juice of 1 lemon, salt

1. Boil rice in plenty of salt water (salt prevents the rice from becoming mushy). Strain, rinse gently once in cold water and strain.

2. Peel potatoes and cut in rounds. Pour the oil around the edges of a pan (one that has a good lid) and place the potatoes in the oil leaving space in the middle of the pan. Put rice in the middle.

3. Cut the margarine into tiny bits and place on top of the rice. Spread a clean cloth over the pan and cover tightly with the lid. Cook on high flame until it starts to sizzle, then turn flame very low and cook for one hour.

4. Place the meat in a pan and cook on high flame until it gives out its juices, then simmer covered on very low flame so as not to add water. Avoid stirring meat while cooking. Instead shake the pan a little and turn upside to help distribute the juices.

5. Wash and scrape carrots and cut in rounds. Saute a little in oil, drain.

6. Strain the peas (either canned or fresh cooked). Put cooked meat, carrots and peas in a bowl. Mix tomato paste and lemon juice together well. If too thick add several tablespoons water. Pour on the meat and vegetable mixture. Gently stir.

7. Spoon about half of the rice onto a serving platter. Add a layer of half of the vegetable-meat mixture, then the remaining rice and remaining vegetables. Then arrange the potatoes around the sides.

Note: *Any type of salad or yoghurt drink may be served with this pilaf.*

CYPRUS PILAF

Ingredients:
2 cups rice
3 cups water or broth
3 tablespoons oil, salt
1/3 cup peas
2 medium carrots
2 medium potatotes
1/2 bunch fresh dill

1. Sort rice. Heat (to the point one can place one's hand in) enough salted water to cover the rice and allow to soak for at least an hour. Strain and rinse 2-3 times.

2. Boil the vegetables. Cut the potatoes and carrots sugar-cube size.

3. Bring water or broth and oil to a boil. Add rice and salt and cook on high flame for 5 minutes, then turn flame low and cook until the water is absorbed.

4. Place a clean cloth over the pan and cover with a tight lid. Set aside.

5. Chop the dill very fine. Combine with the potatoes, carrots and peas. When the rice has set for awhile gently mix with the vegetables. Chill before serving.

Note: *This recipe by Ms. Inci Akyar won first prize in a cooking competition in Istanbul.*

Carrot pilaf

PILAF WITH KEBAB

Ingredients:

2 cups rice

300 grams (5 oz) mutton cubes

1 onion

1-2 tomatoes or 1/2 tablespoon

tomato paste

3 cups water

2 tablespoons oil

salt, black pepper

1. Sort rice. Heat (to the point one can place one's hand in) enough salted water to cover the rice and allow to soak for at least an hour. Strain and rinse 2-3 times.

2. Saute the finely sliced onion with the meat in oil and cook until the meat is soft. If the meat's own juice is not sufficient add a little hot water.

3. Remove the meat from the pan with a slotted spoon and place in a heavy bowl that can take the fire. Flip the bowl placing it upside down in the center of the pot for cooking the rice.

4. Using the pan the meat was cooked in, pour 3 cups water on the hot oil that remains. Bring to a boil, adding pepper and salt.

5. Slowly pour the boiling liquid on top of the upside down bowl. To prevent the bowl from moving, a heavy weight may be placed on top of it.

6. Place the rice in the simmering liquid and remove the weight. Cover the pan well. Cook on high, then turn very low and continue cooking until the broth is absorbed. Remove from heat and allow to set 15-20 minutes.

When ready to serve remove the bowl carefully in order to keep the shape.

LATTICE PILAF

Ingredients:

2 cups rice
3 cups water or broth
3 tablespoons oil
1/3 cup peas
50 grams (1-1/2 oz) pistachios or almonds
1/2 a lamb's liver (or use chicken livers)
salt

Dough:
1 cup flour, 1 egg
salt and water

1. If fresh peas are used, boil a little, drain and saute a little in a tablespoon of oil. If canned are used, drain and saute a little in a tablespoon of oil. Cut liver in small pieces. Add to the saute and cook.

2. Sort rice. Heat (to the point one can place one's hand in) enough salted water to cover the rice and allow to soak for at least an hour. Strain.

3. Put the water or broth to boil in a pan. Add the rice, peas and liver. Add salt and stir once.

4. Cook 5 minutes on high flame, then 5 minutes on medium, then cook until done on very low flame.

5. When the pan sizzles remove from heat. Heat the oil in a small pan and pour it over the cooked rice.

6. Place a clean cloth over the pan and cover with a tight lid. Set aside.

7. Make a dough with the egg, salt and water. Roll about a half cm thick. Cut into 1-cm wide strips.

8. Oil a round pan. Press the cut strips criss-crossing to form a lattice on the bottom of the pan and place the nuts in the openings. Put the pilaf on top. Turn the pan onto a oven pan and bake until the dough is cooked. (If desired do not turn before placing in oven.) When done turn upside down onto a serving platter.

Note: *Goes well with green salad, shepherd's salad or yoghurt drink.*

BURSA PILAF STUFFED IN FAT

Ingredients:

2 cups rice
rendered fat (lamb or mutton)
200 grams (3 oz) lamb liver
1 onion
1-1/2 tablespoon each of currants
and pine nuts
2 tablespoons oil
2 egg whites, salt, pepper

1. Put the lard in warm water until the remaining ingredients are ready. Sort rice and soak 1/2 hour in salt water.

2. Slice onion thinly and saute in oil with the pine nuts. Cut the liver in cubes. Add liver, currants, pepper and salt to the onions. Add 2 cups hot water and put to a boil. Rinse and drain the rice 2-3 times. Add to boiling pot. Cook on low flame until all the water is absorbed.

4. Spread the softened fat at the bottom and sides of a deep pot and place the pilaf in the pan. Cover the pilaf with the fat. Turn the pot upside down on an oven pan, remove the pot and place in a hot oven for 5 minutes.

5. Beat the egg whites. Remove the pilaf from the oven. Spread the egg whites over the pilaf and return to the oven. When lightly browned remove and serve hot.

SARDINE PILAF

Ingredients:

2 cups rice
1 kilogram (2 lb) fresh sardines
1/4 cup oil
3-4 onions
1-1/2 tablespoons each of currants
and pine nuts
2/3 cup olive oil
1 bunch each parsley, dill and mint
1 teaspoon sugar
2 lemons, salt, black pepper, dolma
spice

1. Sort rice and soak 1/2 hour in salt water. Saute finely sliced onions and pine nuts in some of the olive oil until lightly browned.

2. Rinse and drain the rice 2-3 times and add to the onions. Saute together a little.

3. Add enough water to cover and add the (washed) currants, salt and sugar. Cover and cook on high flame until all the water is absorbed. Remove from heat and add the finely chopped parsley, dill and mint, dolma spice, and juice of 1 lemon. Stir.

4. Clean the sardines and wash one at a time in 2-3 waters. Holding the head, remove the spine and tail of each fish. Drain. Spread 1/3 cup oil over an oven dish. Lay some of the sardines in the dish touching so that no spaces between remain, if possible.

5. Place a border of sardines end to end all around the pan. Gently cover the sardines with the pilaf and cover completely with the remaining sardines, as on the bottom, touching with no spaces. Pour remaining oil over the fish and a little salt and pepper. Arrange thin lemon slices and parsley sprigs on top and place in oven.

6. When the sardines are sizzling, remove from oven. Discard lemon slices, arrange fresh lemon slices and parsley sprigs on top, and serve hot.

PEAS PILAF

Ingredients:

2 cups rice
1/3 cup peas
3 cups water or broth
3 tablespoons oil, salt

1. If canned peas are used, drain and saute in 1 tablespoon oil. (Sauteeing them keeps them from being crushed in the pilaf.) If the peas are fresh, boil a little before sauteeing.

2. Sort rice and soak at least one hour in salt water. Drain off the water.

3. Boil the water or broth. Add the rice, peas and salt. Stir once.

4. Cook 5 minutes on high flame, 5 minutes on medium flame, then cook on low flame until all water is absorbed.

5. When the pan sizzles remove from heat. Heat the oil in a small pan and pour over the pilaf.

Curtain pilaf

6. Place a clean cloth or paper towel over the pan and close tightly with the lid. Allow to set at least a half-hour. When ready to serve stir once and add black pepper if desired.

Note: *If desired the rice may also be sauteed before adding to the water.*

Vegetable pilaf

VEGETABLES PILAF

Ingredients:

2 cups rice
1 bunch kale (spinach or leeks may be substituted)
1 coil of sausage (or 3-4 table-spoons cooked ground meat)
2 carrots
1 onion
3 tablespoons oil
2-1/2 cups water
salt, black pepper

1. Sort rice. Heat (to the point one can place one's hand in) enough salted water to cover the rice and allow to soak 20-25 minutes. Strain.

2. Cut the onions in cubes and the carrots in tiny cubes. Saute these in oil until light brown.

3. Wash the kale 3-4 times and boil lightly in very little water. Drain off the water and chop finely. Add to the saute and stir. Chop the sausage in tiny pieces and add. Add salt and pepper. Add ground meat at this stage if used instead of sausage (or, if meat is raw it can be sauteed with the onions). After the vegetables are cooked, make an opening in the center of the pan and place the rice there. Gently add from the edges sufficient water to cover vegetables. Bring to a boil and cook on low flame until all water is absorbed. Cover and allow to set for 20 minutes before serving.

Goes well with yoghurt drink.

CURTAIN PILAV

Ingredients:

2 cups rice
4 cups chicken broth
2 tablespoons oil or butter, salt
Stuffing ingredients:
1 chicken
1-1/2 tablespoons each currants and pine nuts
3 tablespoons almonds
black pepper, salt
Dough ingredients:
1/2 packet lard
2 eggs
2 cups water
flour
1-1/2 tablespoons butter

1. Clean chicken and singe over a flame. Cut in large pieces and boil. When almost done add salt. Remove chicken from water. When cooled remove skin and bones, cut into small pieces and place in a bowl.

2. Saute the nuts in the oil until lightly browned. Set aside. Strain chicken broth to remove any froth or tiny bones and pour 4 cups into the pan to be used for the pilaf. Bring to a boil.

3. Sort and wash the rice 3-4 times until all of the starch is gone from the water. Drain. Add to the boiling broth.

Add the currants. Add salt to taste and stir once.

4. Cook 5 minutes on high flame, then cook on low flame until done.

5. Remove from heat when the pan sizzles.

6. Place a clean cloth or paper towel over the pan and close tightly with the lid. Allow to set at least a half-hour.

7. Mix the egg, margarine, water and salt, keeping in mind the salt in the pilaf. Keep adding enough flour to make a stiff dough. ow dough to set 5-10 minutes and roll out 1 cm thick.

8. Grease well the bottom of a round pan. Arrange the almonds on the bottom. Fit the dough to cover the bottom and sides of the pan, overlapping the edges slightly. Place the pilaf on another pan and mix with the chicken pieces and black pepper. Put the chicken and rice on top of the dough and enclose it with the dough. If there is too much dough cut it off. (it can be used to make noodles).

9. Place the pan in a pre-heated medium oven for 5-10 minutes. Dot the top with a little butter and return to the oven until the dough is cooked through.

10. Remove pan from oven, place a serving platter upside down on top and turn all at once so that the almonds appear on top. Slice and serve.

Goes well with green salad and yoghurt drink.

PERSIAN PILAF WITH CARROTS

Ingredients:

2 cups rice
2-3 medium carrots
2-3 onions
1 tablespoon tomato paste
3 tablespoons oil
3-1/2 cups water or broth
salt, pepper

1. Sort rice. Heat (to the point one can place one's hand in) enough water to cover the rice and allow to soak for at least one hour. Strain and rinse 2-3 times.

2. Slice onions thinly. Scrape carrots and cut in large chunks (matchbox size). Place vegetables in a pan, add oil and saute until the onions are lightly browned. Add tomato paste and cook a little more.

3. Add the rice and saute 5 more minutes, add water or broth and salt. Boil 5 minutes on high flame, then on low flame until all the water is absorbed.

4. Remove from heat and add black pepper. Place a clean cloth or paper towel over the pan and cover tightly with the lid. Allow to set at least a half-hour. When ready to serve stir once.

MACARONI AND RAVIOLI

CONTENTS (MACARONI-NOODLES-RAVIOLI)

TIPS FOR COOKING MACARONI

1. Macaroni is boiled on high flame in salted water. To avoid it from becoming sticky, immediately upon adding it to the boiling water add a cup of cold water and a tablespoon olive oil to the water.

2. It is possible to know if the macaroni is cooked by the smell. If the starchy smell is gone it is cooked. If this method is not preferred, take a bit of the macaroni out of the boiling water with a spoon and chew it. If it sticks to the teeth it is not done.

3. After removing a boiling pan of macaroni from the flame immediately add a cup of cold water and allow to set 5-10 minutes, then drain in a colander. The water can be used in soups. It is best to use the minimum amount of water possible when boiling macaroni. Macaroni can be cooked until the water is absorbed, as with rice.

THE COOKING UNTIL ALL WATER IS ABSORBED METHOD

MACARONI WITH GROUND MEAT

Ingredients:

500 grams (1 lb) macaroni

200 grams (3 oz)

2 tablespoons oil

2 tomatoes

1 teaspoon tomato paste

5 cups water

salt, black pepper, cumin

1. Grate the tomatoes. Saute in the oil until the juice is evaporated. Add the tomato paste and ground meat and saute a little more. Add 5 cups hot water, salt, black pepper and cumin. When it comes to a boil add the macaroni.

2. Cook uncovered on medium flame until the water is absorbed. Remove from heat and cover. Allow to set for 5-10 minutes.

MACARONI WITH VEGETABLES

Ingredients:

500 grams (1 lb) macaroni

1 onion

2 tomatoes

2 small green peppers

200 grams (3 oz) mushrooms

3 tablespoons oil

7 cups water

salt, black pepper

1. Slice the onion very finely. Remove the tomato skins. Chop tomatoes, peppers and mushrooms into tiny pieces and mix with the onions. Saute all of this together.

2. Add 7 cups water. When the water comes to a boil add the macaroni and cook uncovered on medium flame until all the water is absorbed. Remove from heat and cover. Allow to set for 5-10 minutes.

Sayings about eating

"When the food is ready the spoon is on duty."

"Food's gone, wedding's over."

"When the food boils over the ladle isn't important." (When there is plenty, nobody measures how much each one gets.)

THE RAPID
BOILING METHOD

BAKED MACARONI AND CHEESE

Ingredients:
500 grams (1 lb) no. 4-5 spaghetti
200 grams (3 oz) kashar cheese
5 eggs
1 cup milk
3 tablespoons butter or
margarine
salt, black pepper

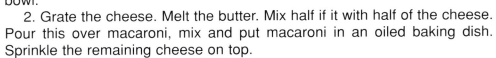

1. Put sufficient water in a large pot to boil and add the salt. When rapidly boiling add the spaghetti. Immediately add a cup of cold water and a tablespoon of olive oil to prevent sticking. Boil 15-20 minutes. Remove from heat and add 1 glass cold water. Allow to set 5 minutes, drain and put in a bowl.

2. Grate the cheese. Melt the butter. Mix half if it with half of the cheese. Pour this over macaroni, mix and put macaroni in an oiled baking dish. Sprinkle the remaining cheese on top.

3. Beat the eggs a little with a fork. Mix in milk, salt and pepper. Pour so that it covers the individual portions when ready to serve.

MACARONI AND CHEESE

Ingredients:

500 grams (1 lb) macaroni

3 tablespoons oil

1/3 cup grated kashar cheese

salt, black pepper

1. Put sufficient water in a large pot to boil and add the salt. When rapidly boiling add the macaroni. Immediately add a cup of cold water and a table-spoon of olive oil to prevent sticking. Boil 15-20 minutes. Remove from heat and add 1 glass cold water. Allow to set 5 minutes. Drain.

2. Add the oil and grated cheese and stir. (If tomato sauce is also added it is called **Tomato Sauce Macaroni.**)

MACARONI IN DOUGH

Ingredients:
250 grams (1/2 lb)
macaroni
4 leaves of phyllo pastry
(milfoy pastry or home-
made dough may be sub-
stituted)
150 grams (about 2-1/2
oz) lean ground beef
1 tablespoon tomato
paste or 2 tomatoes
1/3 cup peas
2 tablespoons oil or
margarine
100 grams (1-1/2 oz)
kashar cheese
salt, black pepper
1 egg yolk

1. Bring a pot of water to a high boil and add salt, then the macaroni. Add 1 cup cold water and 1 tablespoon olive oil (to keep it from sticking). Boil 15-20 minutes. Remove from flame, add 1 cup cold water and allow to set 5 minutes before draining.

2. Saute the ground meat in the oil until the juices come out. If using tomato paste mix it with 1/4 cup water; if using fresh tomatoes, skin and chop. Add tomato paste or tomatoes and saute a little longer. Add salt and pepper and stir.

3. Drain the cooked or canned peas and grate the cheese. Mix these with the macaroni. If homemade dough is used, roll out to a half-cm thick and place all ingredients on top, then close dough over it with three or four corners, as desired. If phyllo is used oil 2 leaves on 1 side and place half the ingredients between the oiled sides. Close as desired and place in an oiled oven pan. Or, oil 4 leaves on 1 side and place 2 leaves (oiled sides facing) on the bottom and the same on the top. Mix an egg yolk with a little oil and drizzle over the top before placing in the oven. Bake until browned.

MACARONI WITH SESAME SAUCE

Ingredients:

500 grams (1 lb) macaroni
Sesame sauce (see recipe in Cold Dishes chapter)
2 chicken thighs or 1 breast
olive oil
2-3 cups chicken broth
200 grams green beans
2 cucumbers, 2 carrots
3-4 fresh onions
salt, black pepper

1. Wash and boil the chicken and cut in thin slices.

2. Bring a pot of water to a high boil and add salt, then the macaroni. Add 1 cup cold water and 1 tablespoon olive oil (to keep it from sticking). Boil 15-20 minutes). Boil 15-20 minutes. Remove from flame, add 1 cup cold water and allow to set 5 minutes before draining. Place in a deep bowl.

3. Mix a half tablespoon of the chicken broth with the sesame sauce.

4. Scrape carrots, peel cucumbers, trim beans and slice all thin. Cut the onions in halves or fourths, then cut crosswise in 4-5 cm pieces.

5. Boil the carrots and beans in salted water until soft; drain and saute them in very little oil in a teflon pan. Turn off heat and mix in the cucumbers and onions.

6. Pour 1/3 of the sesame sauce on the macaroni, add the vegetables, add 1/3 of the sesame sauce, then the chicken slices and the remaining sauce on top.

MACARONI WITH BECHAMEL SAUCE

Ingredients:

500 grams spaghetti
3 chunks (matchbox size) kashar cheese
2 cups milk
3 tablespoons flour
1 tablespoon margarine
4 finger length of sausage
salt, black pepper

1. Bring a pot of water to a high boil and add salt, then the macaroni. Add 1 cup cold water and 1 tablespoon olive oil (to keep it from sticking). Boil 15-20 minutes. Remove from flame, add 1 cup cold water and allow to set 5 minutes before draining. Place in a deep bowl.

2. Brown flour lightly in the oil; turn flame low while very gradually stirring in the milk until smooth and add salt and pepper. Stir once more and remove from heat. Grate the cheese and add half of it. Stir again and pour over spaghetti. Slice sausage very thin and stir into the spaghetti. Empty the mixture into a baking dish.

3. Spread remaining cheese over the top and place in the oven. Bake until lightly browned on top.

MACARONI WITH GROUND MEAT

Ingredients:

500 grams (1 lb) spaghetti
200 grams (3-1/2 oz) lean ground beef
1 onion
1-1/2 cups yoghurt
2 tablespoons oil
3 cloves garlic, salt, black pepper ground red pepper

1. Bring a pot of water to a high boil and add salt, then the macaroni. Add 1 cup cold water and 1 tablespoon olive oil (to keep it from sticking). Boil 15-20 minutes. Remove from flame, add 1 cup cold water and allow to set 5 minutes before draining. Place in a deep bowl.

2. Saute the meat in 1 tablespoon oil until the juices come out. Add salt and pepper and cook a little longer.

3. Oil a baking pan and alternate layers of spaghetti and meat. Crush the garlic and mix with the yoghurt. Put on top of the spaghetti. Heat red pepper in a tablespoon of oil and drizzle over the top.

HOMEMADE EGG NOODLES

Ingredients:

500 grams (1 lb) flour
3 eggs
1/3 cup milk, salt

1. Sift the flour and place in a bowl. Break the eggs into the middle of the flour. Add salt and milk and work into a stiff dough.

2. Place a damp cloth over the bowl and allow to set 15-20 minutes. Roll out dough into a very thin (3 millimetre) large round on a floured board. Dough should be dry. Allow it to air before proceeding. Cut the dough into half circles. Stack one on top of the other, add flour and cut crosswise, again add flour and cut again repeating until the desired width for the noodles is reached. Stack them and cut to the desired length. If the noodles are to be stored for winter, lay out a large clean cloth in a cool place and place each noodle on separately to dry.

Note: Noodles are cooked like macaroni.

Flavored noodles:

- **Yellow noodles:** 500 grams flour, 5 eggs, 1 teaspoon salt, 1-1/2 tablespoons oil

- **Green noodles:** 500 grams flour, 2 eggs, 200 grams (3-1/2 oz) cooked and finely chopped spinach leaves, 1/3 teaspoon salt, 1-1/2 tablespoons oil

- **Red noodles:** 500 grams flour, 100 grams tomato paste, 2 eggs, 1/3 teaspoon salt, 1-1/2 tablespoons oil

All three types can be made in separate bowls, each by mixing all ingredients into a stiff dough. Place a damp cloth over reach bowl and allow to set 15-20 minutes. Proceed with the cutting. A little cornstarch or other starch can help separate the small pieces. Dry them on a clean cloth or pastry board in a cool place. When ready to cook, place in boiling water for 10 minutes, drain and add sauce or other ingredients as desired.

Ravioli macaroni

MACARONI WITH LIVER

Ingredients:
500 grams (1 lb) macaroni
2 tablespoons oil
1/4 lamb liver
3 tomatoes
50 grams (1-1/2 oz) grated kashar cheese
salt, black pepper

1. Bring a pot of water to a high boil and add salt, then the macaroni. Add 1 cup cold water and 1 tablespoon olive oil (to keep it from sticking). Boil 15-20 minutes. Remove from flame, add 1 cup cold water and allow to set 5 minutes. Drain off the water and add 1 tablespoon oil. Holding the pan in both hands toss lightly without using a spoon.

2. Cut tomatoes in large chunks and simmer until soft. Pass through a sieve.

3. Cut liver in thin slices about 2 cm long and saute in 1 tablespoon oil. Add tomatoes and when almost done add a little salt (keeping in mind the salt in the macaroni) and pepper.

4. Transfer macaroni to a serving platter and sprinkle with the grated cheese. Serve with the liver on top.

Mock ravioli

MOCK RAVIOLI

Ingredients:

250 grams (1/2 lb) macaroni
200 grams (6-1/2 oz) lean ground
beef
2 tablespoons oil
1 onion
2 cups yoghurt
3 cloves garlic
salt, black pepper
ground red pepper

1. Fill a pot with water and put to boil. When about to boil add salt. When boiling add macaroni, meat, thin-sliced onion and black pepper. Boil without covering. Whjen done remove from heat. Cover the pan 5-10 minutes.

2. Crush garlic and mix well with yoghurt. Place macaroni on a serving platter and spread the garlic yoghurt over it. Fry red pepper in a little oil, drizzle over the top and serve.

RAVIOLI

Dough ingredients:
500 grams (1 lb) flour
1 egg, salt
Sauce ingredients:
2 cups yoghurt
2-3 cloves garlic
2 tablespoons butter
ground red pepper
Filling ingredients:
250 grams (1/2 lb) lean
ground beef
1 onion
1/2 bunch parsley
salt, black pepper
(In Kayseri, the herb rey-
han, a type of basil, is
also added.)

1. Spread the flour on a board add the egg, salt and enough water to form a hard dough. Place in a bowl and cover with a damp cloth for a half-hour.

2. Slice the onion very fine. Mix with finely minced parsley, ground beef, salt and pepper.

3. Flour the board and roll the dough about 3 millimetres thick. Cut into 3 cm squares. Place a dot of the filling in the middle of each square and close. (If more meat is desired in each piece make the square a little bigger.)

There are two methods of cooking the ravioli:

Method 1: Boil water in a big pot and add a little salt (remembering the salt put in the dough). Drop raviolis into the boiling water and cook over a medium flame until floury smell goes away. Remove with a slotted spoon to a serving platter or individual plates. Fry some red pepper in oil. Spoon garlic yoghurt on top of the ravioli and drizzle the oil over it.

Method 2: Put the ravioli in an oiled oven pan. Place in a medium oven until it has fried a little. Remove from oven and pour 5-6 cups hot water or hot meat broth. Return to oven and cook until the water has evaporated. If the ravioli are not completely cooked add a little more boiling water and continue cooking in the oven until done. Remove with a slotted spoon to a serving platter or individual plates. Fry some red pepper in oil. Spoon garlic yoghurt on top of the ravioli and drizzle the oil over it.

RAVIOLI MACARONI

Ingredients:
250 grams (1/2 lb) macaroni
200 grams 6-1/2 oz) lean ground beef
2 tablespoons oil, 5 cups water
1 onion, salt, black pepper

1. Bring a pot of water to a high boil and add salt, then the macaroni. Add 1 cup cold water and 1 tablespoon olive oil (to keep it from sticking). Boil 15-20 minutes. Remove from flame, add 1 cup cold water and allow to set 5 minutes before draining.

2. Grate the onion and mix with meat. Mix in the salt and pepper and form tiny balls.

3. Fry the meatballs a little in oil. Add 5 cups water and a little salt and bring to a boil. Add the cooked macaroni and cook uncovered until done.

AMASYA CHEESE RAVIOLI

Ingredients:
500 grams (1 lb) flour, 1 egg, salt
Filling:
250 grams (1/2 lb) white cheese

1. Place flour on a board, Add egg, salt and enough water to make a stiff dough. Place in a bowl covered with a damp cloth for a half-hour.

2. Roll the dough on a floured board 3 millimeters thick. Cut in 4-5 cm squares. Add a bit of cheese to the center of each square and close in 3's.

3. Boil water in a big pot and add a little salt. When boiling, add the ravioli and cook on medium flame until the floury smell goes away.

4. Drain and place on a serving platter. İn Amasya, this ravioli is eaten with yoghurt drink.

Note: *If desired, garlic yoghurt or another sauce may be put on top.*

CHICKEN RAVIOLI

Ingredients:

1 whole chicken
1/3 cup rice
1-1/2 tablespoon tomato paste
3 onions
2 tablespoons oil
Dough ingredients:
flour, 1 cup water, salt

1. Cut off the chicken breast and slice thin.. Sort and wash the rice. Saute in oil the chicken slices with one of the onions that has been thinly sliced. Add rice and cook part way. Set the pan aside to cool.

2. Make a stiff dough with 1 cup water, salt and as much flour as is needed. Place a damp cloth over the bowl and set aside for 5-10 minutes. Roll out dough 3 millimeters thick and cut in 4-5 cm squares. Place dots of the chicken mixture in the middle of each square and close. Place the ravioli on an oiled backing dish and cook in the oven.

3. Meanwhile, cut the remaining chicken into large pieces and the remaining onions into large chunks. Place in a pan with the tomato paste, salt and pepper and cover with water. Boil 5-10 minutes.

4. Put the cooked chicken on top of the ravioli and return to the oven. Cook until all water is absorbed and serve hot.

BOSNIAN RAVIOLI

Ingredients:

1 kilogram (2 lb) flour, salt
500 grams ground beef
2-3 onions
2 tablespoons oil
1 teaspoon black pepper
ground red pepper
margarine, butter

1. Make a bread dough with the flour, salt and warm water. Allow to set 15 minutes. Knead again and wait 5 minutes. Repeat twice more. Cover with a damp cloth and set aside for a half-hour.

2. Filling: Mix well together chopped onion and raw ground beef. Add black pepper, salt, red pepper and oil.

3. Divide the dough into 25 or 30 sections. Roll each one into 15 cm diameter circles. Dip each piece in a mixture of melted margarine and butter. Lay each one on the board and holding the edges pull the circle wider. When finished put all the pieces in piles.

4. Cut into each pile, making 2-3 cm wide strips, then crossways to make 2-3 meter wide squares. Put a hazelnut-sized bit of the filling onto the middle of each square and close by bringing together opposite corners. Oil a baking pan and line up the raviolis so that they touch. Brush the tops with melted butter and bake in a hot oven.

5. (If desired: Mix a few crushed garlic cloves with a container of yoghurt and let it sit in a warm - not hot - oven for a little while, then spread it on top of the ravioli.) Immediately after removing the ravioli from the oven, place a paper (e.g. newspaper) over the pan, then another pan and a large cloth. This collects some steam and softens them. Serve hot.

ÇANAKKALE RAVIOLI

Ingredients:
500 grams (1 lb) flour
1 egg, salt
Filling:
1 cup chick peas
2-3 garlic cloves
2 cups yoghurt
3 onions
1 cup rice
2 tablespoons oil
1/2 cup cracked wheat
100 grams (3-1/2 oz) ground meat
1/3 teaspoon black pepper, salt

1. Put chick peas to soak the night before. Boil until done.

2. Make a stiff dough with egg, salt, flour and water. Allow to set for a half-hour.

3. Saute the thin-sliced onions a little in oil. Continue cooking adding the meat, rice and bulgur. Stir in 1 cup boiling water. Turn flame low and cook until the water is evaporated. Add salt and pepper and remove from stove and set aside until the dough is ready.

4. Divide the dough into three parts. Roll out to a half-centimeter thickness. Cut in 2 cm square, add a little of the meat mixture to the center of each and close. Arrange on a baking dish and place in oven until they sizzle.

Bosnian ravioli

5. Add the cooked chick peas and salt. Add enough hot water or broth to almost cover. Return to oven and cook until all water is absorbed.

6. When ready to eat, put garlic yoghurt on top. If desired fry a little ground red pepper in oil and drizzle it over the ravioli.

Note: *Chicken may be used by eliminating the ground meat in this recipe. Slice the cooked chicken and add before the chick peas. Use chicken broth.*

WHEAT DISHES

CONTENTS

Notes:

1: The names of many recipes in this section begin with the name of the region of Turkey where they originated. The type of wheat used differs according to size. They are translated as three types: whole wheat (aşurelik) which is used for keshkek dishes, cracked wheat (bulgur) which is used mainly for pilaf, and ground wheat (köftelik), which is used mainly for mixing with ground meat.

* 2: "Keshkek" (keşkek) is a traditional eastern dish of boiled whole wheat and meat.

GAZIANTEP KESHKEK WITH CHICK PEAS

Ingredients:

500 grams (1 lb) boneless lamb
1 cup chick peas
1 onion
1 cup whole wheat
2-3 tablespoons butter
salt, ground red pepper
cumin, black pepper

1. Put chick peas and whole wheat to soak separately the night before. Cook the chick peas with the meat. Remove meat and cut in small pieces.

2. Add the wheat and finely chopped onion to the broth with cumin, red pepper and salt. Bring to a boil and cook until water is evaporated. Fry the butter and pour over it.

3. Transfer to a serving dish and place the sliced meat on top. Sprinkle black pepper over the dish.

ÇORUM KESHKEK

Ingredients:

1/2 chicken breast
250 grams (1/2 lb) mutton on the bone
1-1/2 cups whole wheat
6 cups water
1 large onion
3 tablespoons butter
salt, red pepper flakes

1. Place wheat, meat, chicken breast and water in a deep pot. Chop onion in cubes and add with salt and pepper and 2 tablespoons butter. Bring to a boil and cook on high flame for 2 hours.

2. Remove from heat. Discard the bones from the chicken and mutton, slice thin and beat well with a wooden spoon. Put the cooked wheat on top and beat together well to a pasty consistency.

3. Transfer to a serving platter. Fry 1 tablespoon butter and drizzle over the top.

TOKAT KESHKEK WITH MARROW BONES

Ingredients:
1 kilogram (2 lb) meat with marrow bones
2 cups whole wheat
1 cup chick peas
2 tablespoons fat
3 heaping tablespoons cumin
salt

1. Soak chick peas over night. Drain.
2. Put fat in a pressure cooker and add cumin; stir a little but do not cook.. Add wheat and chick peas and stir.
3. Stir in the meat and cover 1-1/2 times with water. (If not using a pressure cooker cover 2 times with water and add more if needed.) Cover, bring to a boil and when boiling starts turn very low and cook for 1 hour (without the pressure cooker, up to 2 hours).
4. Transfer the keshkek to a copper pan or other baking pan and bake until browned on top.

DENIZLI KESHKEK WITH MUTTON

Ingredients:
500 grams (1 lb) mutton cubes
100 grams (3-1/2 oz) mutton tail fat
500 grams (1 lb) whole wheat
3 cups water
2 tablespoons oil, salt
ground red pepper, black pepper

1. Sort and wash the wheat and place in a pot with the meat and tail fat. Fill the pot with water and bring to a boil, cooking on high flame until the wheat is soft. Add boiling water if needed.
2. Remove the tail. Add salt to taste and put in food processor until consistency of a thick pudding with the meat remaining in slivers.
3. Transfer to serving platter and sprinkle on black pepper. If desired, fry red pepper in oil and drizzle over the top.
Note: *Excellent with shepherd's salad or assorted pickles.*

TUTTI PILAF

Ingredients:
2 cups whole wheat
2 cups cabbage pickle juice
2 cups water
3 tablespoons butter
3 tablespoons tomato paste
1 teaspoon red pepper, flakes or
ground type

1. Place the wheat, water and pickle juice in a pot and cook until soft on high flame. Add hot water as needed.

2. Mix butter and tomato paste in a small pan and saute; add red pepper and saute a little more. Add to the boiling wheat when it is almost done. Boil 1-2 minutes longer and serve.

Note: *Goes well with boiled meat dishes.*

CRACKED WHEAT PILAF

Ingredients:
2 cups cracked wheat
2-3 tablespoons butter
2 tablespoons vermicelli
4 cups water or broth, salt

In a pan saute vermicelli until light brown. Add cracked wheat and saute a little more. Add 4 cups hot water. Bring to a boil, turn down and cook until the water is absorbed.

CRACKED WHEAT TOMATO PILAF

Ingredients.
2 cups cracked wheat
2-3 tablespoons butter
1 tablespoon tomato paste (or a mixture of tomato and pepper sauce or 2-3 tomatoes)
4 cups water or meat broth
salt

Melt butter in a large pan and add tomato paste (or grated tomatoes). Saute a little. Add 4 cups hot water. When the water boils stir in the cracked wheat and cook until the water is absorbed.

CRACKED WHEAT PILAF AND LENTILS

Ingredients:
2 cups cracked wheat
2 cups lentils, 4 cups water
3 tablespoons butter
salt, black pepper
red pepper flakes

Prepares as for rice pilafs.

CRACKED WHEAT PILAF AND CHICK PEAS

Ingredients:
2 cups cracked wheat
2 cups chick peas, 4 cups water
3 tablespoons butter
salt, black pepper
red pepper flakes

Soak chick peas overnight. Bring a pot of water to boil and add chick peas.

Prepare as for a rice pilaf.

STUFFED POTATO-WHEAT BALLS

Ingredients:
4 potatoes
1-1/2 cups cracked wheat
2 eggs
250 grams (1/2 lb) ground meat
1 onion
2 tablespoons butter
1/2 bunch parsley
black pepper, salt, frying oil

1. Saute chopped onion in butter. Add the ground beef and continue to cook. Add finely minced parsley, salt and pepper. Stir. Remove from flame and set aside to cool.
2. Boil potatoes, peel and mash.
3. Moisten the cracked wheat with hot water. Add mashed potatoes, egg and salt and mix well. Divide into egg-sized pieces. Open each "egg", place a spoonful of the meat mixture inside and close. Fry in hot oil.

MARAŞ STUFFED MEATBALLS

Ingredients:
250 grams (1/2 lb) very lean ground
meat
250 grams (1/2 lb) ground wheat, salt
Filling:
250 grams (1/2 lb) ground meat
50 grams (1-1/2 oz) tail fat (mutton)
5 onions, 1 bunch parsley
1/2 tablespoon tomato paste
2 tablespoons butter, black pepper
1/2 cup walnut pieces

1. **Filling:** Saute chopped onion in butter. Add ground meat and tail fat and continue cooking. Add tomato paste, salt, pepper and finely minced parsley. Mix and remove from heat. Add walnuts and stir. Set aside to cool.

2. Meanwhile, mix together well the lean ground meat, ground wheat and salt. Add water off and on with the hands and continue kneading until no more water is taken in and it becomes like a dough.

3. Wet the hands and form walnut-sized pieces. Open each one in the middle and place a bit of the filling inside. Close to form small "eggs."

4. Drop them in salted boiling water until done, or roll each one in beaten egg and fry in hot oil.

BITLIS STUFFED MEATBALLS

Ingredients:

1 kilogram (2 lb) ground wheat (called "içli köftelik yarma" in Southeastern Turkey)
500 grams very lean ground meat
1 large onion
150 grams (2-1/2 oz) margarine
1/2 bunch parsley
1/3 cup rice
black pepper, red pepper flakes
salt, reyhan (a type of basil)

1. Prepare a dough-like mixture with the ground wheat, water and salt. Add a handful of water off and on and continue kneading until no more water is taken in and it becomes like a dough.

2. Mix ground meat, minced onion and parsley, black pepper, red pepper flakes, salt, basil and margarine.

3. Wash rice. Cook in 2/3 cup water until sticky. If excess water remains, strain it a little. Add rice to ground meat mixture.

4. Form the wheat mixture into balls. Open each one, put a bit of the filling inside and close.

Boil in a deep pot of water. Continue cooking according to the instructions in the recipe for Mardin stuffed meatballs in this chapter.

Note: *Goes well with the spinach soup recipe in the Soups chapter.*

GAZIANTEP STUFFED MEATBALLS

Ingredients:

250 grams (1/2 lb) lean ground meat
1 kilogram (2 lb) ground wheat
2 boiled potatoes
1 onion
1 cup flour, 1 cup semolina
salt, black pepper
Filling:
750 grams (1-1/2 lb) lean ground meat, 4 onions
1 cup finely chopped walnuts
salt, black pepper

1. Thoroughly moisten wheat in hot water so it swells. Peel boiled potatoes. Mix together wheat, grated onion, meat, potatoes, farina, flour, salt and pepper and knead to a doughlike consistency.

2. **Filling:** Chop onions and saute with the meat. Mix in black pepper and walnuts.

3. Divide the wheat mixture into egg-size pieces. Roll each one in the hands and press an opening to stuff in a small amount of the filling, but not too much. Close the opening and fry in hot oil.

Note: *If a bread kneading machine is available it can be used in making the wheat mixture.*

Gaziantep stuffed meatballs

URFA STUFFED MEATBALLS

Ingredients:

500 grams (1 lb) lean ground meat
3 medium onions
black pepper, salt
ground red pepper
1 tablespoon tomato paste
3 tablespoons butter

Dough:
1 kilogram (2 lb) ground wheat
1 onion
black pepper, salt
ground red pepper
6-7 cups water

1. Soak wheat in water for 15 minutes. Drain. Cut 1 onion into 4 pieces and place on top of the wheat. Add salt, black pepper and red pepper. Press the onion into the wheat and continue working it in for 15 minutes. Remove any pieces of the onion not mixed in. Knead the mixture until it becomes a dough. If too stiff take some water in the hand and knead a little more.

2. **Filling:** Mince onions and mix with the meat, salt, red pepper, black pepper, and half the tomato paste.

3. Divide the dough into pieces the size of two walnuts. Make an opening in each one, insert a bit of the filling and close. Roll into egg shapes.

4. In a deep pot, saute the butter and remaining tomato paste a little. Add 6-7 cups water and bring to a boil. Put the meatballs in the boiling water and continue cooking uncovered. After water returns to a boil place continue cooking partially covered on a medium flame. Cooks in 25-30 minutes. Serve hot with onion salad.

MARDIN STUFFED MEATBALLS

Ingredients:
*250 grams (1/2 lb) very lean
ground meat
250 grams (1/2 lb) ground wheat
250 grams (1/2 lb) ground meat
50 grams tail fat
5 onions
1 bunch parsley
1/2 cup walnuts
1/2 tablespoon tomato paste
black pepper*

1. Moisten wheat in warm water and allow to set 1-1/2 to 2 hours.

2. Mince onions and saute in butter until light brown. Add all the meat and tomato paste and continue to saute. When the meat juices come out and the meat is slightly browned remove from heat. Mix in salt, black pepper and minced parsley. Set in refrigerator.

3. Knead the wheat into a dough, divide into egg-size pieces and make an opening in each one.

4. Remove meat mixture from refrigerator and stir a little. Put a spoonful into each ball and close it up. Form into the desired shape (oval, round, etc.).

5. Select a deep pot so as not to crowd the meatballs and fill with water. Bring to a boil and add salt (or a dash of citric acid — this helps to stop the meatballs from opening while boiling). When the water is at a high boil add the meatballs slowly. Use a slotted spoon to turn the ones underneath before adding more.

6. When the meatballs begin to come to the surface, cook about 5 more minutes and remove with a slotted spoon. Place one at a time side by side on a serving platter.

Note: *In Southeastern Turkey, local (homemade) ground wheat called "yarma" is used. If the yarma is not finely ground enough, add 3 tablespoons flour.*

SIIRT LIVER PATTIES

Ingredients:
1 whole mutton or lamb liver
2 cups ground wheat
2 tablespoons flour
1 large onion
1 bunch fresh dill
3 tablespoons butter, salt
red pepper flakes
1/3 teaspoon citric acid

1. Salt ground wheat and moisten well with warm water. Allow to set 10-15 minutes.

2. Put liver through a meat grinder. Add wheat, grated onion, flour and minced dill. Knead until a dough-like consistency. Divide into egg-size pieces. Flatten each one a little in the hands to make round patties. Poke a hole in the middle of each with a finger.

3. Fill over half of a deep pan with water. Add salt and citric acid and bring to a boil. When boiling gently add the liver patties. When the patties come to the surface cook about 5 more minutes and remove carefully with a slotted spoon. Place on a serving platter with the hole facing up. Melt butter and mix in a generous amount of red pepper flakes. Drizzle over the patties so that a little butter falls in each hole. Goes well with yoghurt drink and shepherd's salad.

Note: *Onion and dill are not used in this dish in the Muş region of Turkey and, after boiling, the patties are fried.*

GROUND WHEAT BALLS

Ingredients:
500 grams (1 lb) ground veal
6 tablespoons ground wheat
1 egg
1 large onion
1/2 bunch fresh dill
1/3 teaspoon black pepper
1-1/2 tablespoons tomato paste
1-1/2 cups water
frying oil
1/3 teaspoon cumin, salt

1. Grate the onion. Mix together into a dough veal, egg, onion, salt, black pepper, cumin and wheat. Form into balls of desired shape and fry in hot oil. Remove with a slotted spoon and place on a baking pan.

2. Mix tomato paste with the water and pour over the meatballs. Cover well. Place in a medium high oven until it sizzles.

HARPUT CRACKED WHEAT BALLS

Ingredients:

500 grams (1 lb) lean twice-ground meat
Heaping cup ground wheat
1 medium onion, salt
reyhan (a type of basil)
red pepper flakes
1/2 bunch parsley
2 tablespoons tomato paste
2 tablespoons oil

1. Grate onion and mince parsley. Mix these together with meat, salt, red pepper and basil. Add wheat and mix. Gradually form a dough adding as much water as needed. Divide into pieces smaller than a walnut. Roll in the hands and flatten a little with the thumb.

2. Mix tomato paste with butter and saute a little. Place sufficient water in a pot so that it will just cover the meatballs and put the water to boil. When boiling add the meatballs. If more water is needed to cover, add boiling water.

3. When done remove meatballs and some of the broth to a serving dish.

ELAZIĞ GRILLED MEAT RINGS

Ingredients:

500 grams (1 lb) ground meat
Heaping cup ground wheat
1 onion
1/2 bunch parsley
salt
pepper
reyhan (basil)

1. Soak wheat in warm water for awhile. Mix with ground meat, finely chopped onion and parsley. Add salt, black pepper and basil and mix well.

2. Form into rings and place on skewers. Cook on an electric or fire rotisserie.

LADY'S MEATBALLS

Ingredients:

500 grams (1 lb) lean twice-ground meat
2 cups ground wheat
1 medium onion
1/2 bunch parsley
salt
reyhan (basil)
red pepper flakes

1. Combine all ingredients and knead, adding water as needed to form a dough.

2. Separate into patties. Fry on both sides using very little oil in a teflon pan on low flame partially covered. Serve hot.

ELAZIĞ LENTIL PATTIES

Ingredients:
Heaping cup red lentils
Scant cup ground wheat
1/2 tablespoon pepper sauce
1 tablespoon tomato paste
1 tablespoon butter or margarine
2 medium onions
6-7 green onions
1/2 bunch parsley
Urfa style red pepper flakes (isot)
salt
1/3 cup oil

1. Place lentils in a pan and add water to a level 2 fingers higher than the lentils, cook lentils to consistency of pudding. At that point add red pepper and turn off flame.

2. After the red pepper has given its color and flavor to the lentils, add ground wheat and salt. Allow to set until the wheat grains swell up.

3. Mince the onions. Heat butter in a pan and saute onions until light brown. Add pepper sauce and tomato paste and cook a few more minutes. Add this sauce to the lentils and wheat mixture and knead all together well. Mince the green onions and parsley and work into the mixture. Divide into small pieces and press into the desired shape.

URFA RAW MEATBALLS

Ingredients:
(This recipe serves 5)
1-1/3 cups ground wheat
1-1/3 cups ground meat
300 grams (5 oz) Urfa style red pepper (isot)
1 small onion
3-4 garlic cloves, salt
1/3 teaspoon cinnamon
1 teaspoon tomato paste
black pepper

Greens:
4-5 fresh pearl onions
1/2 bunch parsley
4-5 sprigs fresh mint (or dried mint)
1 small green pepper
1/2 small fresh red pepper
3-4 tomatoes
1 bunch parsley

1. Mince onion and garlic and combine with meat, isot, salt, black pepper and cinnamon. Continue to mix and press with the hands for 5 minutes.

2. Gradually add small amounts of the wheat continuing to knead with the hands. When all the wheat has been added in this way continue to knead for 15 more minutes.

3. Crush 5-6 ice cubes and place on top of the mixture. As it melts and the mixture softens, continue to knead.

4. Add tomato paste and knead 3 minutes more.

5. **Greens:** Meanwhile, mince 1/2 bunch parsley and cut onions, mint and peppers in thin slices. Place on top of the meat. Mix lightly without crushing the vegetables. Serve fingers of the mixture bedded in romaine leaves. Garnish with tomatoes and parsley.

POTATO-WHEAT PATTIES

Ingredients:

1 cup ground wheat
1 bunch green onions
1 bunch parsley
3-4 small green peppers
4-5 potatoes
1/2 teaspoon cumin
1/2 teaspoon ground red pepper
olive oil - 1 cup, or to taste
juice of half a lemon, salt

1. Wash and boil potatoes and mash by hand or in blender.

2. Place wheat in a pan or bowl with a lid and pour 1 cup boiling water over it. Cover tightly.

3. Chop onions, peppers and parsley very fine. When the wheat has swollen put all the ingredients on top and knead well.

4. Form into oblong patties and serve on romaine leaves; garnish with tomatoes, parsley etc. as desired.

URFA WHEAT PATTIES WITH EGG

Ingredients:
5 cups ground wheat
2 heaping tablespoons red pepper
flakes
1 heaping tablespoon tomato paste
1/2 tablespoon pepper sauce
1 small onion, garlic (to taste)
3 eggs, 3 tomatoes
4 tablespoons mixture of oil and
butter
Greens
4-5 green pearl onions
1/2 bunch parsley
4-5 sprig fresh mint (if not avail-
able use dried)
1 small green pepper
1/2 fresh red pepper
3-4 tomatoes, romaine
1 bunch parsley

1. Mix together lightly: thinly-sliced onion, tomato paste, pepper sauce, pepper flakes and chopped garlic (if desired). Skin and chop 3 tomatoes. Add tomatoes and wheat and knead a little. Gradually add water, working in with the hands until the consistency of a meatloaf mixture.

2. Beat eggs well, pour into in a wide pan of hot oil and butter and cook.

3. Slice the greens thin and put on top of the wheat mixture. Put the eggs on top. Gently stir everything together. Serve on romaine leaves with tomato slices.

TOKAT LENTILS AND GROUND WHEAT (BAT)

Ingredients:
2 cups green lentils
10 tablespoons ground wheat
1-1/2 tablespoons tomato paste
salt, black pepper, water
1 bunch parsley
1 bunch dill
1 bunch green onions
1 teaspoon mint
1 teaspoon reyhan (a kind of basil)
3 small green peppers
1/3 cup walnut pieces
3 tomatoes

1. Cook lentils in plenty of water so when done a little broth remains. While hot add wheat and allow to set until wheat softens.

2. Add tomato paste, salt, black pepper, mint and basil.

3. Slice/chop thinly: green onions, parsley, dill and green peppers. Skin tomatoes and chop small. Add vegetables to the lentils and wheat. Mix well.

4. Place on individual plates and sprinkle some walnuts on each one. Goes well wrapped in preserved grape leaves or a thin flatbread.

MALATYA WHEAT BALLS

Ingredients:

2 cups yarma (homemade ground wheat from Southeastern Turkey)
a little salt

Filling:

1 cup lentils
500 grams (1 lb) spinach
8 cups water, 1 onion
2 tablespoons oil
lemon, sumach, sour plum or pomegranate juice, salt

1. Sprinkle salt on the wheat and moisten well with hot water. Set aside one hour. Knead until a dough consistency.

2. Place 8 cups of water to boil and add lentils. Cut onion in thin slices and saute a little. Add to boiling lentils. Add salt.

3. Separate wheat into hazelnut size pieces and roll with the hands into balls. Add all at once to the boiling lentils. When almost cooked add finely chopped spinach, then the fruit juice. Cook 10 more minutes.

Notes: *1. Green beans or cabbage may be used in place of spinach. These need longer cooking and should be chopped and added to the boiling water right after the lentils.*

2. Eggplant may also be used but in this case eliminate the sour juice from the recipe.

MALATYA WHEAT BALLS IN SAUCE

Ingredients:

4 cups yarma (homemade ground wheat from Southeastern Turkey) and 1 cup ground wheat (or 5 cups ground wheat)
2 onions, fresh dill
ground red pepper, salt

Sauce:

2 onions
4 tablespoons ground meat
5-6 tomatoes or, in winter, 2-3 tablespoons tomato paste
3-4 small green peppers, reyhan (a type of basil), mint
1 bunch parsley

1. Chop the onions and dill finely. Mix together onions, dill, a little salt, red pepper and wheat. Gradually add water kneading with the hands into a dough-like consistency.

2. Divide into hazelnut size pieces and roll into balls. Press the tops a little with the thumb.

3. Put a deep pot full of water to boil. When boiling add the wheat balls and cook partially covered on high flame 5-10 minutes.

4. **Sauce:** Slice onions thinly and saute a little with the ground meat. Slice the pepper and skin and chop tomatoes if used. Add peppers and tomatoes or tomato paste to the saute. Add mint, basil and minced parsley. Stir once.

5. Drain wheat balls and put them in the sauce. Cook on high flame 10 minutes, stirring constantly. Serve with yoghurt drink.

CHICK PEAS AND GROUND WHEAT

Ingredients:
2 cups ground wheat
500 grams (1 lb) ground meat
4 tablespoons oil
1 cup chick peas
2 onions
3-4 small green peppers
2 tomatoes (or 2 tablespoons
tomato paste)
1 tablespoon tomato paste
1 tablespoon pepper sauce
black pepper, red pepper flakes,
mint, reyhan (a type of basil),
1/3 teaspoon citric acid

1. Put chick peas to soak the night before.

2. Shake a little salt on the wheat and moisten well with hot water. Allow to set at least 1-1/2 to 2 hours.

3. Knead the wheat gradually working in a little water until the consistency of a dough. Form tiny (bigger than chick peas) balls in the hand.

4. Fill a deep pot over half full of water, add salt and citric acid and bring to a boil. When boiling add the wheat balls all at once. Stir gently once and boil 10-15 minutes. Drain and set aside.

5. Drain the chick peas and add new water. Boil until soft, drain and transfer to a bowl.

6. Cut onions and peppers in thin slices. Saute onions with ground meat until light brown. Add peppers and saute a little more. Skin tomatoes if used and chop into tiny pieces. Add to the saute and cook until soft. Add tomato paste and pepper sauce and cook a little longer. Add chick peas and wheat balls and stir gently while cooking 5-6 more minutes. Add spices and herbs at the end. Transfer to a serving dish and serve hot.

This dish goes with boureks and sweets at a tea table. For a regular meal it should be served with yoghurt drink.

Note: *Spoon some garlic yoghurt on top, if desired.*

SIIRT CHICK PEAS AND GROUND WHEAT STEW

Ingredients:
*2 cups yarma (homemade
Southeastern Turkey style ground
wheat)
1 cup chick peas
1 lamb liver or mutton liver or 500
grams (1 lb) mutton meat
2 onions
3 small green peppers
2 tomatoes
1 tablespoon tomato paste
1/2 cup oil
red pepper flakes
ground sumach
1 tablespoon reyhan (a type of
basil), salt
7-8 cups hot water*

1. Soak chick peas in water the night before and boil the next day.
2. Moisten wheat well and set aside for 1-1/2 to 2 hours.
3. Slice onions and peppers finely. Saute in a large pan in 1/2 cup oil.
4. Cook the liver or meat in a pot and cut in bite-size pieces.
5. Add chopped tomatoes and tomato paste to the onions and peppers. Add the cooked meat and chick peas. Add salt, pepper flakes, sumach. Add boiling water. Return to a boil.
6. Add salt to the wheat and knead. Form in tiny (chick pea sized) balls. When the stew returns to a boil add wheat balls and cook 10 minutes. Just before removing from the flame, add basil. Serve hot.

MALATYA PICNIC BALLS

Ingredients
*4 cups coarsely ground wheat
500 grams very lean ground meat
a little salt and water*

1. Knead the wheat and meat together well. Form in chick pea sized balls.
2. Fill a deep pot with water and put to the boil. Add salt. When boiling add wheat balls and boil. Drain. May be served at a picnic or at a tea table.

ADANA FALAFEL

Ingredients:

2 cups ground wheat
1 cup semolina
2 tablespoons flour
4-5 tablespoons oil
1 egg
4-5 tomatoes
1 tablespoon tomato paste
1 tablespoon pepper sauce
5-6 garlic cloves
red pepper flakes, black pepper
ground red pepper, salt

1. Mix wheat and semolina with a little salt. Moisten thoroughly in hot water and set aside for 10-15 minutes. Break the egg on top and knead until a dough consistency. Divide into hazelnut sized pieces and form into balls with the hands.

2. Bring a full pot of water to boil. When boiling add all the wheat balls. Stir once gently. Boil 10-15 minutes and drain.

3. Chop garlic and saute a little. Skin and cube tomatoes and add to garlic along with tomato paste and pepper sauce. Add spices. Add drained wheat balls and simmer, turning them in the sauce, for 5-6 more minutes. Transfer to serving platter.

May be served at tea table or as a meal with yoghurt drink.

MALATYA STUFFED MEATBALLS

Ingredients:

500 grams (1 lb) lean ground meat
3 cups cracked wheat, salt, water
Filling:
500 grams ground meat
8 medium sized onions, salt
red pepper flakes, black pepper
1/2 bunch parsley
Broth:
1 cup chick peas, 1 onion
2 tablespoons oil
2 tablespoons tomato paste
4 cups broth from boiled meat bones

1. Put chick peas to soak the night before. Boil until soft.

2. Knead wheat, lean ground beef and a little salt adding water as needed to form a stiff dough.

3. **Filling:** Slice onions very thin. Saute in oil. Add a little salt and other ground meat. Saute a little longer. Add salt, black pepper, red pepper flakes and minced parsley. Mix and set aside to cool.

4. Divide wheat-meat mixture into egg-size pieces. Open each one a little, insert a bit of the filling and close up.

5. **Broth:** Slice the onion thinly and saute in oil in a pot. Add tomato paste and stir. Add broth and put to the boil. Strain cooked chick peas and add. Add stuffed meatballs to boiling broth and cook 5-10 minutes. Serve hot in the broth.

ROLLED LOAF

Ingredients:

250 grams (1/2 lb) ground meat
1 onion
2 cups ground wheat
1 egg
125 grams (1/4 lb) margarine
2 tablespoons flour
2 tablespoons tomato paste
black pepper, salt

1. Saute half of the ground meat in a little margarine. Slice onion thin, add and saute a little more. Add salt and black pepper. Stir and remove from flame.

2. Thoroughly moisten the wheat and allow to set 10-15 minutes. Mix with the remaining ground meat and knead a little. Break the egg on top. Add tomato paste, flour, salt and pepper. With wet hands continue to knead, using water as needed to form a dough like mass.

3. Divide the mixture in two. Flatten each one and shape so that the two look the same. Spoon the ground meat mixture onto one of them and place the other on top. Form a roll and place on a greased oven pan. Melt remaining margarine and pour over the top. Cover and place in the oven. When done, slice and serve.

This dish may be served at tea table or as a meal with yoghurt drink.

SIIRT FRIED MEAT PATTIES

Ingredients:

1 kilogram (2 lb) yarma
(Southeastern Turkey homemade ground wheat)
500 grams (1 lb) hand-chopped (or very coarsely ground) lamb
50 grams (1-1/2 oz) lamb tail fat
2 onions, 2 potatoes
1 tablespoon tomato paste
frying oil, black pepper, salt
red pepper flakes, reyhan (a type of basil)

1. Wash the (salted) meat and (if possible, 3-4 days before preparing this dish) beat by hand with a meat chopper until like ground meat. Put tail fat through a meat grinder. Chop onion very finely. Mix all together. Boil potatoes, mash and add.

2. Moisten wheat thoroughly and allow to set for a half-hour.

3. Add all remaining ingredients, mix and knead. Divide into parts of desired size and form patties 1 cm thick. Fry in hot oil.

GAZIANTEP MEATBALL SHISH KEBAB

Ingredients:

750 grams boneless mutton
2 cups ground wheat
2 onions
1 garlic head, salt, black pepper
ground red pepper, mint

1. Thoroughly moisten the wheat. Finely slice onion and along with the garlic and wheat, pass through the food processer. Add meat and put in processor again.

2. Add spices and knead in well. Form balls, place on oiled skewers and grill over a fire or under an oven broiler.

Note: If a food processor is not available, use ground meat and knead well.

GARLIC WHEAT PATTIES WITH STEWED LAMB

Ingredients:
2 cups yarma (Southeastern Turkey homemade ground wheat)
500 grams winter kavurma(*)
3-4 garlic cloves
red pepper flakes, black pepper
salt, 1/3 teaspoon citric acid

(*) Kavurma is a type of small boneless lamb cubes that are canned or preserved in packages. The meat solidifies into a hard block. Grocery shops sell the packages or open the cans and sell by weight. The recipe for Meat saute in the "Meat dishes" chapter may be substituted, eliminating the spices.

1. Salt the wheat and moisten thoroughly. Allow to set at least a half-hour. Knead until consistency of dough. Divide into egg-size pieces and form thin patties.
2. Fill a pot over half full of water, add a little salt and the citric acid to keep the patties from falling apart.
3. When the water is boiling add all the patties. Gently insert a slotted spoon from the edges of the pot and lift the patties toward the top to prevent them from sticking to the bottom.
4. After boiling for a while the patties will start to rise to the top. From that point on cook 10 more minutes, drain and place in a bowl.
5. Put the cooked meat on a serving platter. Add minced garlic and red pepper. With a ladle transfer some of the boiling water from the patties onto the meat (or, if meat was freshly cooked, use its own juices).

Notes: 1. If desired, put the boiled patties into the meat dish before serving . If this is done, the patties should be made smaller.

2. The stew can be ladled like soup into individual serving dishes and the patties added in the amount desired, then eaten together with a spoon.

WHEAT BALLS IN GARLIC YOGHURT

Ingredients:
*2 cups yarma (Southeastern
Turkey homemade ground
wheat)
2 cups yoghurt
3-4 garlic cloves
3 tablespoons butter
red pepper flakes, ground red
pepper, salt*

1. Salt the wheat and moisten thoroughly. Allow to set for at least a half-hour. With wet hands knead, using water as needed, to form a dough-like mass. Divide into hazelnut size pieces (or as desired). Squeeze and form round patties. Press the middle of each with the thumb.

2. Put a pot of water to boil. When it boils add salt. Return to a boil and add the patties. After it returns to a boil cook 10 minutes. Drain and transfer to a serving dish. Put garlic yoghurt on top. Melt butter and fry red pepper. Drizzle over the dish. Serve hot!

URFA MEATBALLS AND CHICK PEA STEW

Ingredients.
*500 grams (1 lb) ground wheat
250 grams (1/2 lb) twice-ground
meat
1/2 tablespoon red pepper flakes
1 onion, frying oil*
Stew:
*1 cup chick peas
250 gram (1/2 lb) meat pieces
1/ kilogram (1 lb) kale
1 small onion
1/2 tablespoon tomato paste*

1. Put the chick peas to soak the night before.

2. Slice onions finely and mix well with ground wheat, ground meat, red pepper and black pepper. Knead and divide into hazelnut size pieces. Fry in hot oil.

3. To make the stew, cut onion in thin slices and fry with the meat in a little oil. Chop the kale and add. Add tomato paste and 6 cups water. When it comes to a boil, drain the soaked chick peas and add. Cook well.

4. When ready to serve, place some of the meatballs in each dish and add a ladle of the chick pea stew.

MUŞ MEATBALLS

Ingredients:

*500 grams (1 lb) boneless lamb
cubes*
300 grams lean ground veal
1 cup chick peas
500 grams (1 lb) ground wheat
500 grams fresh yarpuz*
1 tablespoon tomato paste
2-3 tablespoons butter
2-3 garlic cloves
ground red pepper, salt
500 grams (1 lb) yoghurt

1. Put chick peas to soak the night before. In a large pan, saute the lamb cubes lightly in some of the butter. Add tomato paste and cook a little more. Add soaked and drained chick peas. Cover with hot water and put to the boil. Cook until done.

2. Moisten wheat and allow to set 15 minutes. Mix with ground veal and a little salt. Knead well until consistency of dough. Divide into hazelnut size pieces and form into balls.

3. Wash and chop the yarpuz. When the chick peas are soft, add to the boiling water and cook 2-3 minutes more. Add wheat balls and cook 10 minutes more.

4. Do not drain. Transfer to a serving dish and put garlic yoghurt on top. Fry red pepper in the remaining butter and drizzle over the yoghurt. Eat with pickles.

Since this dish is served in the broth, an excessive amount of liquid should not be remaining at the end of the cooking.

Note: *Yarpuz* is a Turkish herb similar to mint. Fresh mint may be substituted in this recipe.*

GAZIANTEP MEATBALLS IN YOGHURT-CHICKPEA SAUCE

Ingredients:
Meatballs:
500 grams ground wheat
100 grams ground meat
1 onion
1/3 cup flour
ground red pepper, salt
Stew:
500 grams (1 lb) lamb on the bone
1 cup chick peas
1/3 cup rice, 1 egg
2 cups yoghurt
1/4 cup flour, mint, salt

1. Put chick peas to soak over night. Drain. Put to boil in water with the lamb meat. When almost done add rice and continue to cook until rice is done.

2. Beat together well the yoghurt, egg and flour. Slowly add to the stew stirring constantly. When it returns to a boil add salt and a generous amount of dried mint.

3. Moisten the wheat and allow to set for 15 minutes. Grate the onion. Mix together well with ground meat, flour, red pepper and salt. Knead until dough-like. Divide into pieces (hazelnut size or larger) and form into balls. Add all the balls to the boiling stew and boil 15 minutes longer. Serve hot.

Goes well with small green peppers and sliced onions.

ADANA MOTHER-DAUGHTER MEAL

Ingredients:

500 grams (1 lb) ground wheat
2-3 handfuls flour
1 tablespoon tomato paste
1 egg
250 grams (1/2 lb) ground meat
1 cup chick peas, 2 onions
3-4 garlic cloves
2 lemons
3 tablespoons butter or margarine
oil
mint, salt, black pepper

1. Moisten wheat in hot water until soft. Add egg, flour, salt. Knead well.

2. Slice one of the onions very thin and fry in 1 tablespoon butter. Add a little salt and black pepper. Stir and set aside to cool.

3. Split the wheat mixture in two. Divide one part into egg-size pieces (mothers) and the other part into hazelnut size pieces (little girls).

4. Slice the other onion very thin and saute in a large pot in 1 tablespoon butter. Add tomato paste and cook a little more. Add 6 cups water and bring to the boil. Add chick peas (that have been soaked and drained). When the chick peas are soft, add all the wheat balls to the boiling stew and cook 10-15 minutes longer. When about done add minced garlic and the juice of 2 lemons. Fry the mint in oil and drizzle on top. Serve hot.

RICE MEATBALLS

Ingredients:

1 kilogram (2 lb) rice
3 eggs
6 tablespoons oil, salt
Filling:
1 tablespoon butter or margarine
1 kilogram (2 lb) ground meat
1 onion
1 bunch parsley
red pepper flakes, black pepper
salt, frying oil

1. Slice onion thin. Saute onion and meat in oil. When the meat juices come out, add salt, black pepper and red pepper. Add minced parsley. Remove from heat and set aside to chill.

2. The rice should be moistened thoroughly with warm water and allowed to set 2-3 hours before preparation.

3. When the rice is softened place in a bowl and open in the middle. Add 1 egg, 3 tablespoons oil and salt. Knead thoroughly to a dough-like consistency. Use the other 3 tablespoons of oil on the hands to work the rice into walnut-sized pieces. Open each one and insert 1 tablespoon of the chilled meat mixture. Close.

4. Beat 2 eggs. Dip the meatballs in the egg and fry in hot oil. Drain and transfer to a serving platter.

GROUND WHEAT SALAD

Ingredients:

2 cups ground wheat
1/2 bunch parsley
1 bunch green onions
3 small green peppers
4 tomatoes
1 tablespoon tomato paste
1 tablespoon pepper sauce
juice of 1 lemon or 2 table-
spoons pomegranate juice
mint, cumin
red pepper flakes, salt
1/2 cup olive oil

1. Moisten wheat in hot water. Set 10-15 minutes. Add tomato paste, lemon or pomegranate juice, salt and spices. Knead until mixed very well.

2. Trim, wash and chop the raw vegetables and place on top of the wheat mixture. Add oil, mix together well and serve.

ADANA WHEAT BALLS IN CHICK PEA STEW

Ingredients:

500 grams (1 lb) ground wheat
2-3 handfuls flour
1 egg
1 tablespoon tomato paste
1 cup chick peas
250 grams meat on the bones
oil
mint, salt
2 lemons
4-5 garlic cloves

1. Put chick peas to soak overnight. Cook with the meat until done.

2. Moisten wheat thoroughly with hot water until soft. Break an egg over the wheat. Add salt, flour and tomato paste. Knead and form hazelnut size balls.

3. When the chickpeas and meat are about done, add wheat balls and cook 10-15 minutes. Add chopped garlic and lemon juice at the end. Fry mint in oil and drizzle over the top just before removing from the fire. Serve hot.

STUFFED
VEGETABLES

CONTENTS

STUFFING FON VEGETABLES
IN OLIVE OIL*

Ingredients:

2 cups rice
750 grams (1-1/2 lb) onions
3 tablespoons pine nuts
3 tablespoons currants
1-1/2 cups olive oil
1 bunch fresh dill
1 bunch parsley
1 bunch fresh mint
1 teaspoon sugar
2 lemons
salt, black pepper, allspice

1. Saute thin-sliced onions and pine nuts until light brown. Soak rice in hot water for 1/2 hour. Wash and drain. Add to onions and saute a little more. Add hot water (1-1/2 to 2 cups), currants, salt and sugar. Cover and cook on high flame until the water is absorbed.

2. Remove from heat. Stir in minced herbs, spice and juice of lemon (slice the second lemon to be spread on top of the prepared stuffed vegetable).

*** Note:** Dishes prepared in olive oil are generally not eaten hot but rather are allowed to cool to room temperature first, or are served slightly chilled.*

STUFFED EGGPLANTS IN OLIVE OIL

Ingredients:
1 kilogram (2 lb) eggplants
(aubergines)
2-1/2 cups rice
1 cup olive oil
5 onions, 3 tomatoes
1-1/2 tablespoons pine nuts
1-1/2 tablespoons currants
1 teaspoon sugar
2 lemons, 1 bunch parsley
1 bunch mint, 1 bunch dill, salt
black pepper, allspice

1. Saute thin-sliced onions and pine nuts until light brown. Soak rice in hot water for a half-hour. Wash and drain. Add to onions and saute a little more. Wash currants and add with salt and sugar to the onions.

2. Skin 2 of the tomatoes and chop small. Add to rice saute. Cover with water, cook covered on high flame until the water is absorbed.

3. Remove from heat and stir in minced herbs, spice and juice of 1 lemon.

4. Cut eggplants in half lengthwise and scoop out the centers. Fill with the stuffing and place in a pan. Cut the remaining tomato in round slices and use to cover eggplants. Add 2 cups water and cook on a medium flame until done. When cooled, transfer to a serving platter and garnish with lemon slices and parsley sprigs.

STUFFED CABBAGE IN OLIVE OIL

Ingredients:
1 medium sized head of cabbage
2 cups rice
1 cup olive oil
5 onions
1-1/2 tablespoons pine nuts
1-1/2 tablespoons currants
1 teaspoon sugar
2 lemons, 1 bunch parsley
1 bunch mint, 1 bunch dill, salt
black pepper, allspice

1. Prepare the stuffing as per the instructions in the "Stuffing for vegetables in olive oil" recipe.

2. Arrange parsley and mint sprigs in the bottom of a pot for cooking the stuffed vegetables. Remove outer damaged leaves from cabbage head and wash it. Either put the entire head in water, cover and boil until soft, or separate the leaves first and then boil them.

3. After the boiled cabbage is cooled, cut the larger leaves in two if too large for rolling. Fill each leaf with the stuffing, roll up and place on top of the parsley and mint. Add 2 cups hot water and cook on a medium flame until done. When cooled, transfer to a serving platter and garnish with lemon slices and parsley sprigs.

Note: *In place of pine nuts and currants, grate and lightly saute a carrot and add it to the stuffing.*

STUFFED PEPPERS IN OLIVE OIL

1. Saute thin-sliced onions and pine nuts until light brown. Soak rice in hot water for a half-hour. Wash and drain. Add rice to onions and saute a little more.

2. Skin two of the tomatoes and chop small. Add to rice saute. Cover

Ingredients:

1/2 kilogram (1 lb) small bell peppers

2-1/2 cups rice

1 cup olive oil

5 onions

3 tomatoes

1-1/2 tablespoons pine nuts

1-1/2 tablespoons currants

1 teaspoon sugar

2 lemons

1 bunch parsley

1 bunch mint

1 bunch dill

salt, black pepper

allspice

Pine nuts

with water, cook covered on high flame until the water is absorbed.

3. Remove from heat and stir in minced herbs, spice and juice of 1 lemon.

4. Cut out a circle from the tops of the peppers. Remove seeds and wash. Drain well. Place the peppers in a cooking pot. Cut a tomato in large slices and place a slice on top of each pepper. Add 2 cups water and cook on medium high flame until done. When cooled, transfer to a serving platter and garnish with lemon slices and parsley sprigs.

CELERY ROOT IN OLIVE OIL

Ingredients:

1 kilogram (2 lb) celery roots
1/2 cup rice
1 carrot
1 onion
1 cup olive oil
1 teaspoon sugar
2 lemons
1 bunch dill
salt, black pepper
allspice

1. Peel celery roots and scoop out pulp in center. Soak in salt water until ready to stuff. (If this is not done the vegetable will turn dark. If desired, the pulp may also be soaked in salt water and used in another recipe.)

2. Slice onion very thin. Cut carrot in small cubes. Saute onion and carrot in a little oil. Soak rice in hot water for 1/2 hour. Drain. Add rice to saute and cook a little more. Add 1/2 cup

water, salt, pepper and sugar. Cook on high flame until water is absorbed. Remove from flame and add minced dill spices.

3. Remove celery roots from water (one at a time so they will not turn dark) and stuff with filling. Place them touching next to each other in a pan (do not stack). Add juice of 1 lemon and 1 cup water. Cook on high flame.

4. When done remove to a serving platter. Serve with lemon juice or garlic yoghurt.

Note: *This recipe may be used to prepare stuffed artichokes as well. Add 1 tablespoon flour to the salt water for soaking the vegetable. Instructions for cleaning and trimming artichokes are given in the "Stuffed artichokes" recipe in this chapter.*

STUFFED LEAVES IN OLIVE OIL
(Grape leaves, kale or black cabbage)

Ingredients:

1/2 kilogram (1 lb) leaves

1-1/2 cups rice

5-6 onions

1 cup olive

2 lemons

1 bunch each of dill, parsley and mint

1-1/2 tablespoon currants

1-1/2 tablespoon pine nuts

1 teaspoon sugar

1/3 teaspoon allspice

salt, black pepper

1. Drop each grape leaf in a pot of boiling salted water (containing lemon juice). Boil 1-2 minutes, drain and set aside to cool.

2. Slice onions thin. Saute with pine nuts in olive oil until light brown. Soak rice in hot water 20 minutes. Drain and add to saute. Add salt, sugar, currants and 1 cup water. Stir once. Cook on high flame until water is absorbed. Remove from flame and add spices and minced herbs.

3. Lay out each leaf with the fuzzy side up, put filling on top and gently roll up. Place close together in a pot and add 1 cup water. Cover and cook on high flame.

Note: *If preserved grape leaves are used, wash and soak in hot water for a half-hour. Drain them. They are ready to use without boiling first.*

MEAT STUFFING FOR VEGETABLES

Ingredients:

250 grams (1/2 lb) ground meat
1/3 cup rice
1 onion
2 tablespoons oil
2 tomatoes or 1 tablespoon tomato paste
1/2 bunch each of parsley and dill
salt, black pepper

Mix thin-sliced onion with meat. Sort and wash rice and add. Skin and chop tomatoes. Mince parsley and dill. Mix all ingredients together well, adding 1/3 cup water. Stuff the vegetable(s).

STUFFED ZUCCHINI

Ingredients:

1 kilogram (2 lb) zucchini squashes (courgettes)
1/3 cup rice
1 onion
1 tablespoon oil
2 tomatoes or 1 tomato and 1 tablespoon tomato paste
1/2 bunch each of parsley and dill
salt, black pepper

1. Wash zucchinis. Cut off one end and scoop out the pulp. Be sure they are well drained.

2. Mix thin-sliced onion with meat. Sort and wash rice and add. Skin and chop 1 tomato, if used. Mince parsley and dill. Mix together well the onion, meat, rice, tomato or tomato paste, herbs, adding 1/3 cup water.

3. Stuff mixture into zucchinis but not too tightly, and lay them in a pot. Slice 1 tomato in rounds and use to cover the opening at the top of each one. Add water, almost covering. Or, if desired mix a little water with some tomato paste and pour over the zucchinis before adding the water. Cook over a medium flame until soft.

Note: The pulp is useful in recipes found in the Diet Dishes chapter.

STUFFED DRIED SWEET PEPPERS

Ingredients:

1/2 kilogram (2 lb) dried sweet peppers (medium sized, soft and not crooked)
1/3 cup rice
250 grams (1/2 lb) ground meat

1 onion
2 tomatoes
1 tablespoon tomato paste
2 tablespoons oil
1/2 bunch each of parsley and dill
salt, black pepper

1. Wash peppers, cut out a circle from the tops and remove insides. Drain well.

2. Mix thinly sliced onion with meat. Sort and wash rice and add. Skin and chop 1 tomato, if used. Mince parsley and dill. Mix together well the onion, meat, rice, tomato and herbs, adding 1/3 cup water.

3. Stuff mixture into peppers but not too tightly, and set them touching side by side in a cooking pan. Slice remaining tomato in rounds and use to cover the opening at the top of each pepper.

4. Add a little water to some tomato paste and pour over the peppers along with enough water to almost cover. Cook over a medium flame until done.

Notes: *1. If desired mix in 1 tablespoon oil and some ground red pepper to the diluted tomato paste in the bottom of the pot before placing the peppers. Then add the water and cook.*

2. This recipe can be made with fresh sweet peppers, any color. Also it may be cooked in the oven.

STUFFED DRIED EGGPLANTS

Ingredients:
1 kilogram (2 lb) dried egg-plants (aubergbines)
1/3 cup rice
300 grams (10 oz) ground meat
2 onions
2 tomatoes
1 tablespoon tomato paste
1 tablespoon oil
1/2 bunch each of parsley and dill
salt, black pepper

1. Wash eggplants, cut off tops and slice length-wise in alternating strips. Save half the tops. Cut in

large pieces as desired. Scoop out the pulp.

2. Mix thinly sliced onion with meat. Sort and wash rice and add. Skin and chop 1 tomato. Mince parsley and dill. Mix together well the onion, meat, rice, tomato and herbs, adding 1/3 cup water.

3. Stuff mixture into eggplants but not too tightly, and lay them in a pot. Slice 1 tomato in rounds and use to cover the tops of half the eggplant pieces. Use eggplant tops for the other half.

4. Mix a little water with some tomato paste and pour over the eggplants along with enough water to almost cover. Cook over a medium flame until done.

Note: *The scooped-out insides are useful in some other eggplant recipes in this book, including in the Diet Dishes chapter.*

STUFFED RED AND GREEN TOMATOES

Prepare as for stuffed eggplants.

STUFFED POTATOES

Prepare as for stuffed eggplants, except: Cook and peel potatoes, wash and dry well, and scoop out the insides. Then fry the potato skins all over in hot oil before filling them.

STUFFED ARTICHOKES

Ingredients:
1 kilogram (2 lb) arti-chokes
1/4 cup rice
150 grams (5 oz) ground meat
1 small onion
2 lemons
2 tablespoons oil
1/2 bunch dill
1-1/2 tablespoons flour
salt
Sauce:
2 egg yolks
juice of 1 lemon
3 tablespoons water

1. Break off ends of outer leaves close to the stem. Cut off the stem leaving about 1 cm, and cut a little off the very top. Use a knife to scrape out the hair-like portion in the center. Rub each one with a half a lemon. Then place them in a mixture of lemon juice, salt, flour and water and set aside. (Just before filling wash them well again.)

2. Mix thinly sliced onion with meat. Sort and wash rice and add. Skin and chop 1 tomato. Mince dill. Mix together well the onion, meat, rice, tomato and dill, adding 1/3 cup water.

3. Stuff mixture into artichokes, but not too tightly.

4. Lay the artichokes side by side in a cooking pan. Place a cover such as oiled paper tightly over them and then the pan lid. Cook on high flame. When almost done, mix egg yolks, juice of 1 lemon and 3 tablespoons water. Remove covers from artichokes and pour mixture on top. Continue cooking 1-2 minutes and remove from stove.

STUFFED GRAPE LEAVES

Ingredients:

300 grams (10 oz) grape leaves
1/3 cup rice
1/2 kilogram (1 lb) ground meat
2 onions
2 tomatoes or 1 tablespoon tomato paste
1 tablespoon tomato paste
2 tablespoons oil
1/2 bunch each of parsley and dill
salt, black pepper

1. Separate the fresh leaves. Boil 1-2 minutes in salted water with lemon.

2. Mix thinly sliced onion with meat. Sort and wash rice and add. Skin and chop tomatoes. Mince parsley and dill. Mix together well the onion, meat, rice, tomatoes or tomato paste, herbs, adding 1/3 cup water.

3. Lay leaves fuzzy side up and place portions of the mixture on each one. Roll up and place in a pan. Mix 1 tablespoon oil, tomato paste and a little water and pour over the leaves. Add 2-3 cups water and cook on high flame.

Note: *If preserved leaves are used, wash and allow to set in hot water for a half-hour. Drain. Do not boil.*

STUFFED CELERY ROOT

Ingredients:

1 kilogram (2 lb) celery roots
(celeriac)
1/3 cup rice
150 grams (5 oz) ground meat
2 onions
2 tomatoes
1 tablespoon tomato paste
2 tablespoons oil
1/2 bunch dill
salt, black pepper

1. Peel celery roots and scoop out centers. Place roots and scooped-out insides together in salted water and set aside.

2. Slice 1 onion thin and mix with meat. Mince dill and add with a little salt and pepper.

3. Sort rice, place in hot water and parboil. Drain and add to meat mixture. Remove celery roots one at a time from water and stuff them. (If all are removed at once they can break.)

4. Meanwhile, slice the other onion thinly, skin and chop tomatoes very small. Saute onion llightly in the oil in the cooking pan. Add tomatoes and cook a little more. Place celery roots side by side in the pan. Add 1 cup hot water and cook on high flame.

Note: *The scooped-out insides may be mixed with mayonnaise for a salad.*

STUFFED CABBAGE LEAVES WITH LENTILS

Ingredients:

1 medium size cabbage
1 cup green lentils
1 cup ground wheat
1 onion
3 tablespoons oil
salt, black pepper, mint
reyhan (a type of basil)

1. Remove outer leaves of the cabbage. Wash and boil a little. Gently remove the leaves one by one. Place in a pot of boiling water. When soft, drain leaves and set aside.

2. Sort and wash lentils and put to soak the night before. Boil 1-2 minutes. Remove from heat and allow to set a little watery. Moisten ground wheat in hot water. Add thin-sliced onion, salt, pepper, mint, basil and oil. Mix all ingredients well with the lentils.

3. Place some of the mixture in each leaf and roll very thin. Place in a cooking pan and almost cover with water. Cook on high flame, then turn on low until done.

Note: *When ready to serve, if desired add garlic yoghurt and drizzle over the top a little ground red pepper fried in oil.*

STUFFED BLACK CABBAGE WITH CORN MEAL

Ingredients:
1 kilogram (2 lb) black cabbage
2 cups finely ground corn meal
500 grams (1 lb) meat pieces on the bone
2 onions
2 tablespoons tomato paste
1/3 cup rice or cracked wheat
3 tablespoons butter or margarine
salt, red pepper flakes

1. Wash and separate the leaves, boil, drain and set aside.
2. If corn is too coarse, pass through food processor or moisten the night before to soften. Drain.
3. Chop onions Remove from the bones as much meat as possible. Chop in small pieces. Saute a little with the onions and butter. Add tomato paste and saute a little more. Add corn meal and stir a few times. Add salt and red pepper. Add rice or cracked wheat. Cover with water and cook until water is absorbed. Remove from heat and set a side to cool.
4. Place meat bones in a pan. Roll the stuffing in the leaves (in fatter rolls than stuffed grape leaves) and place on top of the bones. Cover with hot water and bring to a boil. After cooking on high for awhile, turn low and simmer until done. Serve hot with yoghurt drink.
Note: *If desired add a little butter along with the cooking water.*

ERZURUM CHEESE-STUFFED PEPPERS

Ingredients*:*
1/2 kilogram (1 lb) small and thin bell peppers
1-1/2 cups low-fat soft white cheese (lor), 2 eggs
125 grams (1/4 lb) margarine
1/2 bunch dill, 2 tomatoes
salt, red pepper flakes

1. Cut out the tops and scrape out insides of the peppers, wash and drain well.
2. Mix finely minced dill, cheese, eggs, salt and red pepper. Fill the peppers. Place

Stuffed tomatoes

one thin slice of tomato over the top of each pepper.

3. Melt margarine. Place peppers in a pan and pour margarine over them. Add 1/3 cup water and cover. Cook on medium flame.

Note: *If desired, after placing peppers on serving plates drizzle over each serving a little red pepper fried in oil.*

CHEESE-STUFFED GREEN PEPPERS

Ingredients:
1 kilogram (2 lb) small and thin bell peppers
as many eggs as peppers
2 tablespoons oil
3-4 tomatoes
100 grams (3-1/2 oz) kashar cheese
salt, black pepper

1. Carefully cut out the tops of the peppers and set aside for later use. Scrape out insides of the peppers and sprinkle a little salt and pepper inside each one. Break an egg into each one. (If using fewer eggs, break eggs into a bowl, beat a little and add egg into each pepper with a spoon.)

2. Place thin slices of kashar cheese on top of each pepper and on top of that a slice of tomato. Place a pepper top over the tomato slice. Put 1/4 cup water in an oven pan and set the peppers side by side in the pan. Pour the oil over them and sprinkle on a little salt. Cover with oiled paper and and bake until done. When almost done remove the paper to allow peppers to brown slightly before removing from oven.

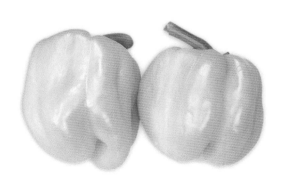

SIIRT SOUR STUFFED VEGETABLES

Ingredients:
250 grams (1/2 lb) small and thin bell peppers
250 grams medium sized eggplants
250 grams finely chopped meat
3 tablespoons oil
50 grams ground tail fat
1 cup rice, 1 onion
3 small green peppers, 2 tomatoes
1 tablespoon tomato paste
1/2 bunch parsley
1/3 cup sumach
salt, black pepper, red pepper flakes

1. Mix well with the hands the thinly chopped onion, salt and spices. Skin 1 tomato and chop small. Wash and drain rice. Slice small peppers thinly. Mince parsley. Mix onion, tomatoe, rice, ground tail fat, ground meat, sliced peppers, parsley and oil. Work until completely mixed.

2. Remove tops and insides of bell peppers and eggplants. Wash and drain well, stuff loosely and place side by side in a cooking pot. Place a slice of tomato over the top of each one.

3. Mix the sumach with 2 cups warm water and 1 teaspoon salt. Allow to set one hour. Strain and use the water to cover the stuffed vegetables. Put the lid on the pan and bring to a boil. Boil a little and reduce flame to low. Cook 1/2 hour. Remove from heat and allow to set for about 10 minutes before serving.

Notes: *1. If the meat is not finely chopped, pound it on a board before using.*

2. If dried peppers and dried eggplants are used, boil the eggplants until soft, then the peppers. Drain and allow to cool completely. In place of tomatoes and peppers the filling can take a lot more tomato paste. Use a little more water to cook. Place in the pan alternately one stuffed pepper, one eggplant etc.

3. Stuffed kale may be made using the same stuffing; however, with ground meat in the recipe, cabbage or grape leaves should not be used.

MALATYA STUFFED LEAVES IN YOGHURT

Ingredients:
250 grams grape leaves
2 cups whole wheat
1 cup finely ground wheat
5 cups yoghurt
2 tablespoons flour
3-4 onions
6 cups water
1 egg yolk
6 tablespoons butter
salt

1. Moisten whole and ground wheat in a little salt and hot water. Allow to set a half-hour. Knead into a soft dough-like consistency. Divide into hazelnut size pieces and place one on each of the grape leaves. Roll very tightly and line up in a wide pan. Add 1 cup hot water. Place a plate on top and weigh it down with a stone or other weight to

keep them from moving. Bring to a boil and turn flame on low to cook.

2. Mix in a deep pan the yoghurt, flour, egg yolk and 3 cups of water. Beat well. Stir over low flame until it bubbles. Add salt (keeping in mind the grape leaves have salt). During the last 20 minutes of cooking pour the mixture over the grape leaves.

3. Slice onions very thin and saute in butter. This may be added to the pan toward the end of the cooking or after the stuffed leaves are placed on a serving platter.

Note: *Various types of leaves may be used: grape, quince, sweet cherry, mulberry or hazelnut. If cherry, mulberry or hazelnut leaves are used, spoon off the foam when they come to a boil and then place them in cold water. This process eliminates any bitter taste.*

YOZGAT STUFFED LEAVES
WITH BROAD BEANS

Ingredients:

250 grams grape leaves
1/2 kilogram (1 lb) tender meat on the bone
2 cups broad beans
1 cup fine-ground wheat
2 onions
1/2 tablespoon tomato paste
1/3 cup oil
1/2 bunch each parsley and dill
salt, black pepper

1. Put beans to soak 1 day earlier. Peel and chop. (If the grape leaves are preserved, wash and soak in water to remove salt.)

2. Slice onions very thin and mince parsley and dill. Mix together with tomato paste, oil and wheat and beans. Add salt and pepper and mix well.

3. Place a tablespoon of filling on each leaf and roll them tightly.

4. Place meat pieces in a cooking pot and lay stuffed leaves on top. Press a cover tightly down on top of the leaves so they will not move in the cooking. Add water to cover and cook on high flame.If more water is needed add hot water. When cooked uncover and place serving platter over the pan. Turn upside down so that the meat is on top. Serve hot.

Note: *If desired, reserve one of the onions, slice and saute it in a tablespoon of butter. After the stuffed leaves and meat are on the platter, drizzle the buttered onions on top.*

STUFFED LAMB INTESTINES (BUMBAR)

Ingredients:
intestines of 1 lamb
1 kilogram (2 lb) rice
1/2 kilogram (1 lb) very lean
ground or chopped meat
2 onions
2 tablespoons butter or
margarine
1 tablespoon black pepper
red pepper flakes, salt

1. Wash rice and drain. Mix with meat, thin-sliced onions, butter, black pepper, red pepper and salt. Work into a doughlike consistency.

2. Cut the lamb intestines in 20-25 cm long pieces and wash in plenty of water 5-6 times. Salt well. Work the salt in for about 10 minutes and again wash 5-6 times, this time with soap. Wash 2-3 times more with plain water to remove any soap smell. Turn the intestines inside out. If the fat on the inside is clean, wash well once. If it does not look clean, completely remove the surface fat and wash 5-6 times. (If the amount is too much for one meal, cut some off and put in the freezer for another meal.)

3. Stuff the intestines. If desired, turn them right side out again before stuffing.

4. Place in a pan and add water to level of 4 fingers. Add 1 tablespoon salt and boil until well done.

Note: *The method of cleaning tripe (stomach) is identical to that of cleaning intestines. After the cleaning process cut it into pieces 20 cm long and 8 cm wide. These pieces are folded into two. One short side and one long side are stitched. Use same stuffing as for intestines. Then stitch remaining 2 sides. Cook the same way as for intestines. Serve hot, preferably along with raw meatballs and yoghurt drink.*

LEGUMES

CONTENTS

A FEW TIPS ON COOKING LEGUMES

1. Any of the dried legumes such as beans, chick peas and lentils must be stored in a dry place free of dampness and mold; it is useful to put some salt in the bottom of the container and to stir them from time to time. If put in warm water the evening before cooking, beans cook more easily.

2. To reduce excess gas, when ready to cook strain the soaked beans, cover with fresh water, bring just to a boil and drain.

3. Beans can be parboiled in advance, allowed to set for an hour and then drained and cooked. This is done often with fresh pintos or with dry beans that were not put to soak the night before.

4. If additional water is needed during cooking, add hot water.

5. Add the salt just before the beans are done.

6. When cooked beans set for awhile they continue to absorb liquid; therefore there should be some liquid remaining in the pot at the end of the cooking.

7. Bean dishes that are thoroughly cooked have greater food value.

8. Adding oregano to the legumes while cooking enhances the flavor and aroma.

WHITE BEANS WITH LAMB

Ingredients:

500 grams (1 lb) white beans
500 grams (1 lb) lamb on the bone or 400 grams (13 oz) boneless lamb cubes
2 onions
1 tablespoon tomato paste or 3 tomatoes
2-3 fresh or dried whole red peppers

1. Soak beans the night before. Drain and place in fresh hot water. Bring to a full boil and again drain and bring to a boil in fresh water. (This reduces the gas.)

2. Slice onions thin and sasute a little with the meat. When the meat juices come out add tomato paste and saute a little more. Add 5-6 cups hot water. When water boils add the beans. If peppers are fresh remove seeds, cut in large pieces and add to beans. If dry, cut stems off and wash well. Bring to boil in a little water, drain, cut in two or leave whole and add to the beans. When almost done add salt. Remove from heat while some of the water remains.

Allow to set awhile, then serve with pilaf and salad.

Note: *If ground meat is used instead of other meat, use 250 grams (1/2 lb).*

LENTILS WITH LAMB

Ingredients:

2 cups lentils
500 grams (1 lb) lamb cubes with bones or 250 gram (1/2 lb) ground lamb
2 tablespoons oil
3-4 onions
1 tablespoon tomato paste
1 tablespoon pepper sauce
salt
black pepper

1. Cut onions in half and slice in half-moons. Saute with meat in oil. When meat juices come out, add tomato paste and pepper sauce and saute a little more. Add 5-6 cups hot water.

2. Sort and wash lentils. Add to boiling liquid. When almost done add salt. Remove from heat while some of the liquid remains.

CHICK PEAS WITH LAMB

Ingredients:

500 grams (1 lb) chick peas
500 grams lamb on the bone or
400 grams (13 oz) boneless
2 onions
2 tablespoons oil
1 tablespoon tomato paste
1 tablespoon pepper sauce
salt
black pepper

1. Put chick peas to soak the night before. Drain off soaking water, add fresh water and bring to a full boil. Remove from flame and drain (this process eliminates excess gas).

2. Slice onions thinly and saute a little with the meat in oil. When the meat juices come out add tomato paste and peppe sauce. Saute a little more and add 5-6 cups hot water. When it comes to a boil add chick peas. Add salt when almost finished cooking. When soft remove from heat. Some of the liquid should remain.

Note: *In place of the meat 250 grams (1/2 lb) ground lamb may be used. (Goes well with plain pilaf and salad.)*

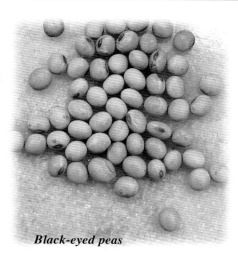

Black-eyed peas

PINTO BEANS WITH LAMB

Ingredients and instructions for "White beans with lamb" are the same for this dish.

BLACK-EYED PEAS WITH LAMB

Ingredients and instructions for "White beans with lamb" are the same for this dish.

DRIED OKRA WITH MEAT

Ingredients:
400 grams (13 oz) boneless meat
1 cup chick peas
250 grams (1/2 lb) dried okra
2 onions

2 tablespoons oil
1 tablespoon tomato paste or
3 tomatoes
lemon juice
salt, black pepper

1. Carefully wash the okra. Boil 5-6 cups water and add lemon juice and okra. When okra is soft remove from heat and drain. Put in cold water and drain.

2. Cut lamb in small pieces. Chop onion in cubes and saute with the meat. When meat juices come out add tomato paste and saute a little more. Add 5-6 cups hot water. When meat is almost cone add okra, salt and pepper. If a sour taste is desired add the juice of one lemon. Do not overcook okra and remove from heat before all the broth is evaporated.

(Goes well with pilaf.)

MIXED BEANS WITH LAMB

Ingredients:

2 kilogram (2 lb) fresh pinto beans
500 grams (1 lb) green beans
500 grams lamb pieces on the bone
2 onions
2 tablespoons oil
1 tablespoon tomato paste
1 tablespoon pepper sauce
salt, black pepper

1. Chop onions small and saute with meat a little in oil. When meat juices come out add tomato paste and pepper sauce. Saute a little more. Add 5-6 cups hot water and bring to a boil.

2. Shuck the fresh pinto beans and wash. Remove tips from green beans, wash well and cut to desired lengths. Add all the beans to the boiling pot. After it returns to a boil turn flame on low and cook until done. When almost done add salt and pepper. Remove from heat before all the broth has evaporated.

Note: *If desired add one or more dried or fresh whole red peppers during the cooking.*

PINTO BEANS IN OLIVE OIL

Ingredients and instructions for "White beans in olive oil" are the same for this dish.

WHITE BEANS IN OLIVE OIL

Ingredients:

500 grams beans
4-5 tablespoons olive oil
2-3 onions
1-2 carrots
3-4 garlic cloves
2 tablespoons tomato paste or 3-4 tomatoes
1/2 bunch parsley
1 teaspoon sugar
salt

1. Put beans to soak the night before. Drain. Cover with fresh water, bring to a boil and drain.

2. Chop onions small. Scrape and wash carrots and cut in rounds. Saute onions and carrots in oil. Add garlic, then tomato paste or chopped tdomatoes. Add 3-4 cups hot water and bring to a boil. Add beans and cook until soft. When almost done add salt and sugar. Remove from heat and transfer to serving bowl. Put minced parsley over the beans and allow to cool before serving.

Note: If desired wash and cut in pieces one or more dried whole red peppers and add during the cooking.

DRY BROAD BEANS IN OLIVE OIL

Ingredients:

500 grams (1 lb) broad beans
4-5 tablespoons olive oil
2-3 onions
1-2 carrots
3-4 garlic cloves
1/ 2 bunch parsley
1 lemon
1 teaspoon sugar
salt

1. Put beans to soak the night before and drain.

2. Chop onions in cubes and slice carrots in rounds. Saute onions and carrots a little in oil. Add garlic and tomato paste and saute a little more. Add 2-3 cups hot water. Bring to a boil and add beans. When almost done add salt and sugar. Remove from heat and transfer to a serving bowl. Garnish with parsley sprigs and lemon slices. Allow to cool before serving.

Pintos and lamb

White beans in olive oil

DIET DISHES

CONTENTS

ABOUT DIET FOODS

I have hypoglycemia. For their invaluable assistance in the preparation of this chapter, I wish to thank my dear friends Prof. Dr. Fatma Sevil Ozan, who has been my trusted doctor for many years, and Ms. Ayşe Özkarabulut, a dietician who has provided me with valuable dietary guidance and advice.

When thinking about the preparation of this chapter, I knew that it required expertise and that there were serious questions to resolve. My dietician emphasized that most diet products on the market are not very healthy. Through some investigating and research, it became clear that some products being marketed for dieters have no value for human health and are even harmful, and, for this reason, such products are banned in some Western countries.

As one seeking a diet that is truly beneficial, I placed importance on avoiding mistakes and thus received the support of the two above-mentioned ladies. In addition to their valuable ideas and advice they helped with the recipes as well. Many of the cooking instructions have come from my doctor and the practical information from my dietician. Again, I must thank them both for enabling me to produce a book under my own name that is useful for dietary patients.

A few moments of reflection will, I think, point to one important difference between dieting and eating normally. It is important not to put one's health at risk. Good health is both a joy of life and a gift of God. In the name of health, we must sacrifice the little pleasures of the palate. Yet, we should not reflect our dieting on our environment so as not to restrict the enjoyment of others as well as our own. Therefore, to come to terms with oneself and never complain, "I am dieting and can't eat what others can eat," is the first rule in the psychology of dieting.

Basically there is not a great difference between diet and normal foods.

PARTICULAR THINGS TO BE CAREFUL ABOUT REGARDING DIET FOODS

1. Whatever the category of the food, the ingredients must be fresh when preparing your portions each day, although with some dishes enough should be prepared for many meals.

2. Because fried foods are so oily and smoke up during the cooking, they are not very healthy. Therefore fried foods are to be avoided by anyone on a reducing diet.

3. When using meat and ground meat, no oil should be used or, if used, it should be in accordance with the total amount allowed in the daily diet.

4. When oil is called for in the preparation of any of the boiled, baked and broiled dishes in this book, the amount can be adjusted according to the diet. Therefore only a few examples are given in this chapter.

5. Diet yoghurt or milk can be used to add flavor to soups or boiled dishes.

6. Margarine should be avoided and butter used very sparingly.

7. Chicken and fish are recommended at least once a week, either boiled or baked.

8. When making boureks, mixtures of milk and egg or milk powder, water and egg can be substituted for the butter or margarine, and various boiled foods can be put in the bourek such as potatoes, leeks, spinach or lentils. If cheese is used it should be low-fat and, if necessary, low-salt as well.

9. White sauce can be made with very little or no fat (see recipe for bechamel sauce).

10. Sauces that have oil, vinegar, salt, pepper etc. in them can be prepared and stored well-covered in a glass container at room temperature for one week. If sweetener is to be added, wait until just before use. If added earlier the chemical balance could change.

11. Remember that mayonnaise is quite fattening (see recipe in this book) and should be used very sparingly. If put on a salad, do not also use oil.

12. Rice quickly turns to sugar in the body and therefore it is recommended to avoid it in favor of ground wheat and macaroni.

13. If macaroni is substituted for rice, use twice as much. That is, 2 spoonfuls of rice equals 4 of macaroni. One bowl of soup, 1 slice of bread, 2 tablespoons of pilaf or 4 tablespoons macaroni are about equal in calories.

14. In place of prepared fruit juices, prepare fresh juice at home. Instead of cola, make a delicious drink with sparkling mineral water, juice of half a lemon, some sweetener and, if desired, a few ice cubes.

SQUASH BOATS

Ingredients:
500 grams (1 lb) zucchini squash
2-3 tablespoons lean ground veal
1 onion
1/2 bunch parsley
1/2 cup water
grated kashar cheese
salt, black pepper

1. Scrape and wash zucchini and parboil. Open each one like a boat, scooping out some of the insides.

2. Saute onion and meat without oil. Add salt and pepper. Remove from heat. Chop the insides of the squashes and stir into the meat mixture. Add minced parsley and mix well.

3. Fill the squash boats. Oil an oven pan and place them in it. Sprinkle cheese on top of each one. Bake until the cheese melts and turns light brown.

Notes: *1. Bechamel sauce may be used.*
2. If a little oil is used in the saute it becomes a non-diet dish.
3. Eggplants may be prepared in the same way.

GRATED SQUASH
WITH MILK

Ingredients:

1 kilogram (2 lb) zucchini squash
1/3 cup fine ground wheat
1/3 cup water
1 cup milk
1/2 bunch fresh dill
salt, black pepper
red pepper flakes, if desired

Eggplant with milk

Meat with bouquet garni

1. Scrape, wash and grate squash and place in a stainless steel pan. Add ground wheat and 1/3 cup water and cook on high flame until water is absorbed.

2. Remove from heat and add milk, salt, black pepper and red pepper. Crush well with a fork, transfer to a serving dish and spread minced dill all over the top.

Note: *If milk is not pasteurized, boil before using.*

EGGPLANT WITH MILK

Ingredients:

500 grams (1 lb) eggplants
1 cup skim milk
3 tomatoes
2-3 garlic cloves
salt
black pepper

1. Peel eggplants and soak in salt water for a half-hour. After the bitterness is gone, rinse them once or twice and drain. Cut in cubes and place in a pan. Add milk and cook until soft. When almost done add salt. Remove from heat and mash with a fork. Transfer to a serving dish.

2. Skin and cut tomatoes in small cubes. Slice the garlic thinly. Combine these with a little salt and pepper and put on top of the eggplant.

Goes well with oven-baked chicken.

STEAMED LEEKS

Ingredients:

1 kilogram (2 lb) leeks
1/4 cup cracked wheat or rice
1 teaspoon red pepper flakes (or as desired)
1/2 cup water
olive oil (amount according to diet)
fresh dill
salt

1. Trim and wash leeks. Cut 3-4 cm long, then, to bring out as much of the flavor as possible, cut each piece into very thin slices (about the width of 2 matchsticks). Place in a pan (preferably a double boiler or teflon). Add wheat, then the red pepper, salt and oil. Add water and place on the stove.

2. Cover tightly and begin to cook slowly over a very low flame. Do not stir at all during the cooking.

3. After removing from heat transfer to a serving dish. Sprinkle minced dill over it. Serve hot . Can also be a garniture for grilled or baked chicken or meat.

Note: *Squash, cabbage, watercress, broccoli or (unsliced) brussel sprouts may be cooked in the same way.*

BOILED MEAT WITH BOUQUET GARNI

Ingredients:

*500 grams (1 lb) meat pieces on
the bone*
2 leeks
2 medium size carrots
2 potatoes
*1 onion or a handful of pearl
onions*
salt, black pepper, oregano

1. Put meat in a pan of cold water and set to boil. (Cold water is used to bring out the meat flavor which then passes to the vegetables. See the beginning of the "Meat dishes" chapter.)

2. Wash and trim the vegetables. Cut leeks into 4-5 cm long pieces. Split carrots lengthwise. When meat is almost done add all the vegetables. Add salt, pepper and oregano. When vegetables are done remove from heat.

Goes well with pilaf or macaroni.

Note: If additional water is needed, add hot water.

CAULIFLOWER WITH CHEESE

Ingredients:

1 small cauliflower
1/3 cup kashar cheese, salt
1 egg
*3 tablespoons powdered milk and
1/3 cup water, or 3 tablespoons
flour and 1 cup skim milk*

1. Separate all the flowerets and wash. Drain and place in a stainless steel pan. Add a little salt and, without adding water, cook on very low flame in its own juice. When soft, place on an oiled baking pan.

2. Mix together well the powdered milk and water well or the flour and skim milk. Pour over the cauliflower. Grate cheese and put on top. Bake until cheese melts and browns slightly.

Goes well with baked meat or chicken.

Salt: sodium chloride: These two elements both of which are combustible and explosive when separate, merge together to produce a very beneficial food.

"A meal requires salt and salt requires good proportion." Old saying

"To contribute a speck of salt to the soup." ... saying meaning "to contribute to a worthwhile effort."

"Oh brother, every meal tastes so good thanks to salt. The one who forgets easily those who offered him bread and salt is dropped from friendship." Old saying

DIET SWEETS

PARTICULAR THINGS TO BE CAREFUL ABOUT REGARDING DIET SWEETS

1. Of all the many brands of artificial sweeteners on the market, those that contain aspertane are most often recommended by dietary experts. Though other types are more heat resistant, their good or bad qualilties have not yet been established.

2. When artificial sweeteners are used in cooking, they can sometimes cause a metallic taste and sometimes lose their sweetening power. For this reason, for best results the sweetener is usually added after removing the pan from the flame or even after allowing the food to set a little.

3. The use of artificial sweeteners in cakes and tortes reduces their quality.

4. Some desserts can be stored in the refrigerator for a brief time. This is indicated in the recipes. However, ideally the quantity prepared is for one day, the reason being that the flavor of a dish containing artificial sweetener could deteriorate if it sets too long, just as some sweeteners alter the flavor if added during the cooking.

5. Keeping in mind the need for a low daily calorie count, the size of the portion is very important and the selection of foods given in the diet should not be changed. For example, one serving of rice pudding counts for 1 cup milk and either 2 tablespoons rice or 1 slice of bread.

6. Desserts are best prepared and kept in glass or porcelain dishes.

7. Because a diet given by a doctor or dietician necessarily prescribes a certain amount of fats and oils, the recipes in this book generally provide the exact amount to be used.

MEASUREMENT EQUIVALENTS FOR THE MOST COMMON GRANULATED OR TABLET SWEETENERS ON THE MARKET

1.5 packets Sweet'n Low = 1 large tablet Dulcaryl = 3 tablets containing aspertane (such as Canderel)

2 packets Sweet'n Low = 20 grams (1/3 oz) sugar

1 tablet Canderel = 1 sugar cube = 3 calories

1/3 teaspoon Spoonful Canderel = 1/3 teaspoon granulated sugar = 2 calories

PUMPKIN DESSERT

Ingredients:
2 slices pumpkin (balkabağı)
1/2 cup water
6 packets sweetener (Sweet'n Low or Spoonful Canderel)
1 tablespoon walnut pieces
diet portion equivalent:
1 vegetable portion + 1/2 of a fat allowance

1. Cut pumpkin into pieces of desired size and place in a glass pan. Add water and cook on low flame on the stove or in the oven.

2. When done remove from stove and add sweetener and walnuts. Chill before serving.

PUMPKIN IN BOUREK

Ingredients:
2 large phyllo pastry leaves
2 slices pumpkin, 1 egg
6 packets sweetener (Sweet'n Low or Spoonful Canderel, or 12 crushed tablets)
Pudding:
2 cups skim milk or water
1 tablspoon flour
1/2 packet (5 grams) dry vanilla (1/4 teaspoon liquid)
1 diet portion equivalent:
(3-4 slices) =
1 cup milk +
1 slice bread

Semolina banana pudding

1. Cut phyllo into squares for rolling. Boil pumpkin in a little water and mash with a fork. Put some of the pumpkin on the edge of a square and roll up starting from one corner. Place rolls on an oiled pan. Beat egg and pour over them. Bake in the oven.

2. Mix water or milk with vanilla and flour and cook until pudding consistency. Remove from heat, add the sweetener and mix.

3. When ready to serve, place the bourek rolls on a serving plate and spoon the pudding on top. Enjoy a low calorie dessert.

SEMOLINA BANANA PUDDING

Ingredients:
*500 grams (2 cups) milk (prefer-
ably skim)*
2 tablespoons semolina
*3-4 packets sweetener (Sweet'n
Low or 10 crushed Canderel
tablets)*
1 banana
1/4 cup hazelnut or walnut pieces
diet portion equivalent:
*1 serving pudding = 1 cup milk +
1 portion fruit + 1 slice bread*

1. Combine milk and semolina in a pan and stir while cooking until a pudding constitency. Remove from flame and immediately add sweetener. Blend well.

2. Transfer to a glass bowl and spread banana slices and nuts on top.

SEMOLINA MILK PUDDING
(8 servings)

Ingredients:
4 cups skim milk
1/2 cup water
1 cup semolina
*1 packet (5 gram) dry vanilla (1/4
teaspoon liquid)*
grated lemon rind
*15 packets Sweet'n Low or about
30 crushed Canderel tablets*
diet portion equivalent:
1/2 cup milk + 1 slice bread

1. Mix semolina, vanilla and grated lemon rind in a pan. Add milk and and stir while cooking until it reaches a pudding consistency.

2. Remove from heat and add sweetener. Transfer to individual serving dishes.

SEMOLINA CHEESE PUDDING

Ingredients:
1/3 cup semolina
2 tablespoons butter
1/3 cup skim milk
1/3 cup water
150 grams saltless low-fat cheese
*7-8 packets Sweet'n Low or about
15 crushed tablets*
**diet portion equivalent (makes
about 3 portions):**
*1 slice bread + 1 teaspoon fat +
1/2 cup milk*

1. Saute semolina in butter but do not brown. Mix water and milk and add. Stir while cooking until it reaches a thick pudding consistency. Remove from heat and add sweetener and cheese.

2. Mix until cheese blends in. Transfer to a bowl and press down with a spoon. Serve.

ULUDAĞ FROZEN CHOCOLATE DELIGHT
(Can set in freezer up to 12 hours)

Ingredients:
500 grams (2 cups) milk
2 tablespoons cocoa
6 packets sweetener or 12 crushed
tablets
2-3 small slices melba toast
2 apricots, 2 figs
1/4 cup hazelnut or walnut pieces
1 tablespoon raisins
diet portion equivalent:
1 slice Uludağ delight = 1 cup milk
+ 1 slice bread + 1 measure fat

1. Mix milk and cocoa in a pan and bring to a boil. Remove from heat and add sweetener.

2. Crush bread very finely and chop fruits and nuts. Mix together well and add the milk-cocoa mixture. Roll in foil and and put in deep freeze at least 3-4 hours. Slice and serve.

MOCK CHICKEN BREAST PUDDING
(8 portions)

Ingredients:
4 cups skim milk
1 scant cup whole wheat flour
2 tablespoons soft margarine
18 packets Sweet'n Low or
Spoonful Canderel (or 30-35
crushed tablets)
diet portion equivalent:
1/2 cup milk + 1 slice bread

1. Mix flour with cold milk and beat in a mixer. Cook on the stove, stirring until pudding consistency. When about done stir in margarine. Remove from heat and add sweetener. Whip in mixer for 15 minutes.

2. Rinse a glass bowl with water. Empty pudding into bowl and place in refrigerator 1-2 hours. Spoon into 8 serving dishes.

BAKED FRUIT

Ingredients:
500 grams (1 lb) quinces, apples or
pears
3 packets Sweet'n Low or Spoonful
Canderel (or 4-5 crushed tablets)
diet portion equivalent:
1 portion fruit

1. Peal fruit and place in an oven pan. Bake in its own juices until soft.

2. Remove from heat and add sweetener. Garnish with chopped nuts and cinnamon if desired.

Fruit salad

BREAD PUDDING (6 portions)

Ingredients:

2 cups skim milk
1/2 cup whole wheat flour
8 packets Sweet'n Low or Spoonful Canderel (or 16 crushed tablets)
8 small slices rush bread, preferably

whole wheat (melba toast or in Turkish, "Etimek")
2 cups water
10 packets Sweet 'n Low or Spoonful Canderel (or 20 crushed tablets)
diet portion equivalent:
1/2 cup milk + 1 slice bread

1. Put half the dry bread slices in each of two glass dishes.

2. Melt 10 sweetener packets in 2 cups hot water. Pour over the bread.

3. Mix flour and cold milk in a pan. Cook until pudding consistency, stirring constantly. Remove from heat and add 8 packets sweetener. Spread half the pudding over bread in one of the glass pans. Use a spatula to transfer the bread from the other pan on top of the pudding. Spread the remaining half of the pudding on top. Place in refrigerator for 2-3 hours. When ready to serve sprinkle cinammon on top if desired.

FROZEN FRUIT YOGHURT

Ingredients:

250 grams (1/2 lb) ripe fruit (apricots, bananas, peaches or strawberries)

1/4 teaspoon grated lemon rind

1/2 tablespoon lemon juice

2 tablespoons Spoonful Canderel

2 cups yoghurt

1 egg white

diet portion equivalent:

1 cup milk + 1 portion fruit

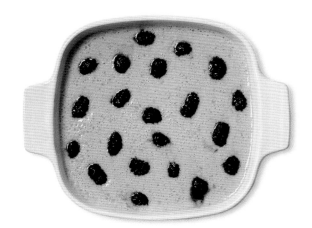

1. Puree the fruit in a food processor. Stir in grated lemon rind, lemon juice and sweetener.

2. Add fruit puree to yoghurt.

3. Whip egg white until frothy and add to mixture. Mix well and transfer to a glass bowl. Place in the freezer for 1-2 hours.

FRUIT SALAD

Ingredients:

500 grams (1 lb) mixture of apricots, bananas, peaches and/or strawberries

4 tablespoons Sweet'n Low or Spoonful Canderel

1 cup low-fat yoghurt

diet portion equivalent:

1 cup yoghurt + 1 portion fruit

1. Trim and wash fruit and cut as desired. Place in a serving dish.

2. Combine yoghurt and sweetener in a mixer. Cover fruit salad with yoghurt and serve.

FRUIT PUDDING
(6 portions)

Ingredients:

4 cups skim milk
3 medium sized pears (or apples quinces or bananas)
2 tablespoons cornstarch
2 tablespoons flour
1 egg yolk
1 packet (5 grams) dry vanilla (1/4 teaspoon liquid)
1 tablespoon margarine
15 packets Sweeet'n Low or Spoonful Canderel (or 30 crushed tablets)

diet portion equivalent:
1 slice bread + 1/2 cup milk

1. Peel and trim fruit and cut to desired size (for example cut pears in half lengthwise) and place in a glass pan on top of stove or in the oven. Allow to cook in its own juice. Remove from heat and set aside to cool.

2. Mix well together the starch, flour, egg yolk and some of the cold milk. Mix well. Then add remaining milk and place on the stove. Stir constantly, bringing the mixture to a pudding consistency.

3. Remove from stove and add margarine and sweetener. Rinse a serving bowl in water and transfer the pudding to the dish. Place pears on top of the pudding.

Note: *To serve, spoon into individual dishes including one piece of fruit in each serving.*

KADAYIF DESSERT

Ingredients:

100 grams tel kadayif *
2 tablespoons crushed walnuts
3 tablespoons soft margarine
1 cup skim milk
1/3 cup water
20 packets Sweet'n Low or Spoonful Canderel (or about 40 crushed tablets)

diet portion equivalent:
1 slice bread + 1 portion fat

1. Put half of the kadayif in an oven pan and sprinkle crushed walnuts over it. Melt margarine and pour on top. Brown in a medium oven.

2. Mix sweetener with warm milk and water. Remove kadayif from oven and pour warm milk over it. Serve immediately.

_____

* Tel kadayif is found in Turkish grocery stores, usually in 200 gram packages. It consists of very thin, wire-like dried wheat fiber formed in large flat rounds.

RICE PUDDING

Ingredients:

4 cups skim milk
1/3 cup rice
2 tablespoons cornstarch
1/2 cup water
12 packets Sweet'n Low or
Spoonful Candered (or 20-24
tablets – no need to crush them)
diet portion equivalent:
1/2 cup milk + 1 slice bread
(or 2 tablespoons cooked rice)

1. Boil rice in a little water.

2. Mix cornstarch in water until smooth. Bring milk to the boiling point and , stirring constantly, slowly add the cornstarch water. Add boiled rice and cook until pudding is done.

3. Remove from stove and mix in sweetener. Pour into individual serving cups and allow to cool.

Notes: 1. As an alternative to preparing the above diet rice pudding, when preparing the rice pudding recipe containing sugar in the "Milk-Based Desserts" chapter, take out a portion of the hot pudding before the sugar is added and mix sweetener into it.
2. The same can be done when making "Noah's pudding" in the "Desserts" chapter.

FRUIT COMPOTE

Ingredients:

5 small apples (or use peaches,
sour cherries, apricots or plums)
4 cups water
8-10 packets Sweet'n Low or
Spoonful Canderel (or 20 tablets)
diet portion equivalent:
1 fruit portion

1. Peel and trim apples and cut in cubes. Put water in a pan and add the apple chunks. Boil until apples are soft.

2. Remove from stove and mix in the sweetener.

PLAIN CAKE
(20 servings)

Ingredients:

2 eggs
1/2 cup granulated sweetener
3 tablespoons sugar
1 cup skim milk
1/2 cup olive oil
1/2 cup water
2 cups flour
vanilla, baking powder
diet portion equivalent:
1 slice = 1 cup milk + 1 slice bread
+ 1 teaspoon oil

1. Beat eggs in a bowl. Mix in sugar, vanilla, milk and sweetener.

2. Add oil and water and mix a little more. Mix baking powder with flour and add, blending into a dough.

3. Bake on oiled paper in a 180 C (350 F) oven 40-45 minutes.

OATMEAL COOKIES

Ingredients:
1 cup dry oatmeal
2 cups flour
3 tablespoons sugar
1/2 cup Sweet'n Low
1 packet (10 grams) baking powder
(4 teaspoons)
1 egg
1/3 cup olive oil
3 tablespoons low-fat yoghurt

1. Mix together in a deep bowl: oatmeal, flour, sugar and baking powder. Add egg, oil and yoghurt and form a dough.

2. Divide dough into walnut-size pieces and form rounds or ovals in the hands. Place on a teflon baking pan. Bake 20-25 minutes in a pre-heated 230 C (450 F) oven.

QUINCE PRESERVES

Ingredients:
2 medium sized quinces
1 cup water
4-5 teaspoons Sweet'n Low
1 teaspoon cinnamon
diet portion equivalent:
1 portion fruit

1. Peel, trim and wash quinces. Grate and put to boil in water until soft.

2. Add sweetener and cinnamon and cook 15 minutes longer. When it reaches the desired consistency, remove from heat, transfer preserves to a glass container, and allow to cool.

FRUIT DESSERTS

CONTENTS

FRUIT SALAD

Ingredients:

3 bananas
2-3 apples
2 oranges
3 tangerines
1/2 cup powdered sugar
1 packet dry whipping cream mix
1 cup milk
about 1/2 cup currants
1 handful pistachios

1. Wash, peel, chop each fruit in small pieces and stir them well.

2. Place some of the fruit in a glass bowl and put powdered sugar on top. Continue to layer all the fruit and sugar in this way.

3. Combine cream mix and milk and beat until stiff. Spoon on top of the fruit. Shell nuts and sprinkle nuts and currants on top.

CARROT-COOKIE DESSERT

Ingredients:

1-1/2 kilograms (3 lb) carrots
1 cup granulated sugar
125 grams (1/2 lb) margarine
1 cup coarsely chopped walnuts or pistachios
500 grams (1 lb) petit beurres (butter cookies)
1/3 cup water
1-1/2 tablespoons coconut

1. Scrape and grate carrots. Mix water and suger in a pan and cook carrots over a low flame until water is absorbed.

2. Crush cookies and pour hot carrots over it. Add margarine and walnuts. Mix well. Press aluminum foil into a mold and place mixture in it. Sprinkle

coconut over it and chill in refrigerator until it sets.

Note: This dessert keeps a long time in the refrigerator.

CARROT DESSERT WITH PUDDING

Ingredients:
6 carrots
scant cup sugar
3/4 cup flour
1 cup walnuts
1 kilogram (1 quart) milk
100 grams (3.2 oz) margarine
dash of cinnamon

1. Grate carrots and put in food processor. Transfer to a frying pan on the stove. Add 1/3 cup sugar and half the margarine. Cook, stirring frequently, until carrot is soft. Add walnuts and cinnamon and stir a little more. Transfer to a glass dish and set aside to cool.

2. Meanwhile, melt remaining margarine in a pan and stir in flour. Gradually add milk and remaining sugar and cook on high, stirring constantly until consistency of a pudding. Put on top of carrot dish and set aside to cool.

CHESTNUT DESSERT

Ingredients:
1 kilogram (2 lb) candied chestnuts
(see recipe in this chapter)
1 package dry whipping cream mix
(krem şanti)
4 cups milk
1/4 cup granulated sugar
1/4 cup cocoa
1-1/2 tablespoons flour
1-1/2 tablespoons cornstarch
1/4 cup crushed pistachios
1- 1/2 tablespoons orange garniture, fresh or candied (see p.374)

1. Mix 1 cup milk with krem şanti and whip. Place in refrigerator until ready to use.

2. Mix well together: flour, cornstarch, cocoa and sugar. Add 3 cups milk and cook, stirring constantly until thick and smooth. Add a tablespoon of orange garniture, boil a little more and remove from heat.

3. Place some candied chestnuts in a glass dish and some of the hot mixture over it, then remaining chestnuts and remaining mixture. Sprinkle pistachios over it and decorate the top with the whipped cream.

Notes: 1. If desired this dish can be pureed. 2. If desired, eliminate the hot ingredients and just layer the chestnuts with whipped cream.

PUMPKIN DESSERT

Ingredients:
1 kilogram (2 lb) pumpkin (bal kabağı)
1-1/2 cups sugar
1/3 cup walnuts or pistachios
1-1/2 tablespoon coconut

1. Trim wash the pumpkin and cut into 2 cm thick pieces. Either the night before or 2-3 hours before cooking, cover with the sugar and allow to set. Sugar brings out the juices.

2. Cook in its own juices until soft on high flame. If there is too much water in the bottom, let it boil, partially covered, and finish cooking in its steam. Transfer to a serving dish and sprinkle crushed walnuıts or pistachios and coconut on top.

Note: *2-3 whole cloves may be added during the cooking.*

BAKED QUINCE

Ingredients:

1 kilogram (2 lb) medium sized quinces
3 cups granulated sugar (or 10-12 tablespoons for each quince)
juice of half a lemon
3-4 whole cloves
whipped or clotted cream (or kaymak – water buffalo cream)

1. Wash and peel quinces. Remove seeds. Wash seeds and put with cloves in a small cheesecloth bag and tie tightly.

2. Split quinces lengthwise, place in a pot with just enough water to cover. Add cheesecloth bag. (This gives a reddish color to the dish and helps a gelatin to form.) Boil quinces until soft and remove from water.

3. Place in a baking dish. Put half of the sugar on top. Remove bag from water and put remaining sugar in the water. Boil until it thickens slightly. Pour over the fruit and bake in a medium oven until bubbling and the juice is absorbed and a gelatin forms. The more gelatinous the better the flavor. Add some crushed walnuts or hazelnuts to the gelatin if desired. Garnish each serving with a dollop of stiff whipped cream or kaymak.

Notes:

1. Eliminate cloves if desired. A chunk of traditional lohusa şekeri is usually added to the cheesecloth bag to make the quince red.

2. This dessert may be prepared over a very low flame on top of the stove instead of in the oven.

BAKED APPLE DESSERT

Ingredients:
6-7 apples
1-1/2 cups sugar
1 handful walnut, hazelnut or
almond pieces
2/3 teaspoon cinnamon
1 packet (5 grams) dry vanilla
(1/4 teaspoon liquid)
50 grams (1-1/2 oz) margarine

1. Remove the apple cores. Peel and wash apples.
2. Place in a pan with just enough water to cover. When apples are half-cooked, add sugar and boil just until sugar is melted.
3. Carefully set the whole apples upright in a baking dish in the juice. Mix together nuts, cinnamon and vanilla and spoon the mixture into the centers of the apples. Add a dot of margarine on top of the centers. Bake until lightly browned and set aside to cool before serving.

Notes: *1. Whipped cream or any type of milk pudding may be served with the apples.*
2. In place of granulated sugar, lohusa şekeri may be used.

PEARS AND CREAM

Ingredients:
10 medium sized pears
1 kilogram (2 lb) sugar
700 grams (about 2-3/4 cups) water
10 cloves
juice of half a lemon
whipped cream or kaymak (water
buffalo cream)

1. Wash pears, remove the cores and peel.
2. Mix in a pan: sugar, water, cloves and lemon juice. Put to boil and set pears in the pan. Cook until soft. Remove from heat and set aside to cool. Serve with a dollop of cream on top.

FIGS IN SYRUP

Ingredients:
1 kilogram (2 lb) dried figs
2 tablespoons sugar
1 cup walnut pieces
3 cups water or milk
2 cups sugar

1. Soak dried figs in warm water for 5 minutes. Cut stems and open each one. Put chopped walnuts in a bowl with 1 tablespoon sugar and mix well.
2. Fill each fig with 1/2 teaspoon walnuts, squeeze each one shut and place in a glass baking dish.
3. Bring to a boil the sugar and either water or milk and boil until syrup consistency. Pour over figs and place in the oven until bubbly.

DRIED APRICOTS IN SYRUP

Ingredients:

1/2 kilogram (1 lb) dried apricots
2-3 tablespoons butter
1 handful walnut pieces

1. Wash apricots a few times. Place in a pan with enough water to cover and cook until soft. If more water is needed to keep them covered, add hot water.

2. Set aside to cool. Melt butter and add, mixing in well. Or, place cooled apricots on a serving platter and pour butter over them. Sprinkle walnuts over them, allow to chill a little, then serve.

ORANGE DESSERT

Ingredients:

1/3 cup orange juice
2 eggs
7 tablespoons sugar
7 tablespoons flour
1 packet (10 grams) baking powder
(4 teaspoons)
grated rind of 1 orange
Syrup:
1 cup orange juice
1/2 cup water
1/2 cup sugar

1. **Syrup:** Mix sugar, water and orange juice in a pan and bring to a boil. Turn flame to medium low and boil 10 minutes. Set aside to cool. Chill.

2. Beat the sugar and eggs together. Add grated orange rind and orange juice.

3. Mix baking powder with flour and add. Stir until smooth. Transfer to a greased oven pan and bake in a medium oven. Remove and pour cold syrup over the top. Allow to cool, slice and serve.

CANDIED CHESTNUTS

Ingredients:

1 kilogram (2 lb) chestnuts
4 cups sugar
2-1/2 cups water
1 packet (5 grams) dry vanilla
(1/4 teaspoon liquid)

1. Remove outer layer from chestnuts, place in a pot with just enough water to cover. Boil until the insides can be separated from the next layer. Remove from heat, cool slightly and peel off that layer.

2. Mix the sugar, vanilla and water, bring to a boil and add chestnuts. Cook on high flame up to 2-1/2 hours. After removing from the stove allow to set 8-9 hours in its syrup. Transfer to a serving dish with a slotted spoon.

BANANAS AND HONEY

Ingredients:
1 kilogram (2 lb) bananas
1 cup walnut pieces honey

1. Peel bananas and cut in 1 cm thick slices. Place a layer in a glass dish.

2. Sprinkle on some of the walnuts and drizzle honey over them. Repeat this process in layers until all ingredients are added.

3. Place dish to chill in refrigerator before serving.

EGGPLANT DESSERT

Ingredients:
1 kilogram (2 lb) eggplants (aubergines)
1 cup walnuts or pistachios
2 eggs
2 tablespoons flour
1 cup frying oil

Syrup:
400 grams (about 13 oz) sugar
juice of 1 lemon, 2-3 cloves
2/3 teaspoon cinammon

1. Mix all syrup ingredients in a pan and boil until syrup consistency. Set aside to cool.

2. Cut off tops from eggplants and slice off skin in alternating strips lengthwise. Place eggplants in salt water for 1 hour. Wash them, squeeze tightly and drain well. Cut in 1 cm thick slices and lay on paper towels.

3. Beat eggs. Dip slices in the egg and fry in hot oil. As each piece is done, immediately transfer to the cooled syrup for 1-2 minutes. Remove from syrup and sprinkle chopped nuts on both sides. Place on a serving platter and when all slices are in place, sprinkle remaining nuts on top.

PUDDINGS AND CUSTARDS

CONTENTS

ABOUT COOKING WITH MILK

1. When milk is about to come to a boil, if it appears that it is about to curdle, add a little powdered sugar or soda.

2. A few drops of vinegar is useful in getting rid of the burnt smell from any milk that spills on the stove during cooking.

STRAWBERRY PUDDING

Ingredients:

1 scant cup flour

1 cup sugar

1 packet dry vanilla (1/4 teaspoon liquid)

100 grams (3.2 oz) butter

500 grams (1 lb) strawberries

1/3 cup sugar

1. Bring milk and 1 cup sugar to a boil. Add a little cold water to flour and mix until smooth. Add to the milk as it comes to a boil and stir well. Add vanilla. Cook until it reaches pudding consistency. Beat 5-10 minutes in a mixer. Transfer to individual serving dishes and chill.

2. Mix in a blender the strawberries and 1/3 cup sugar. Spoon on top of pudding dishes. Serve immediately or store in refrigerator up to 2 hours, if desired.

ORANGE PUDDING

Ingredients:

2/3 cup sugar

2 egg yolks

1-1/2 tablespoons flour

1-1/2 tablespoons rice starch

3 cups milk

juice of 1 orange

grated rind of 1 orange

1. Separate the yolks and whites. Put whites aside for another use.

2. Bring milk and sugar to a boil. Remove from eat and set aside to cool. Mix egg yolks, flour, starch and orange rind in a pan Add milk and stir, bringing to a boil.

3. When it reaches a pudding consistency remove from heat and stir in orange juice. Fill individual pudding dishes and allow to cool. If desired sprinkle coconut on top.

CRÉME CARAMEL

Ingredients:

1 liter (3-1/2 cups) milk

8 eggs

1-1/2 cups sugar

1 packet (5 grams) dry vanilla (1/4 teaspoon liquid)

1. Bring milk to a boil. Remove from heat and set aside until warm. Add 1 cup sugar and stir until it melts. Stir in vanilla.

2. Beat eggs in a mixer. Add milk mixture and stir.

3. Boil 1/2 cup sugar in a little water until brown. Without letting it get cool and hard, add to milk-egg mixture, stir and fill oven custard cups.

4. Put water in a baking pan and set the dishes in it so that the water level is the same as the pudding in the cups. Place in a hot oven for 15-20 minutes. Remove pan and allow to cool without removing the cups.

Note: When done the custard should be firm. Test for doneness, placing a clean, dry knife point in the center. It should come out clean. When ready to serve, scrape a thin knife around the edges of the cups and turn onto individual serving plates.

RICE PUDDING (SÜTLAÇ)

Ingredients:
4 cups milk
1 cup sugar
2/3 cup rice
a little butter
cinnamon

Boil rice in water until soft. Add sugar and milk and a little butter. Boil 2-3 minutes more and pour into individual serving dishes. Sprinkle cinnamon on top of each one.

*   **Note:** *One alternative is to use only 1/3 cup rice and add 1 tablespoon flour. However, for those with a weight problem, do not use this alternative and eliminate the butter.*

Chocolate pudding

OVEN RICE PUDDING

Ingredients:
1 liter milk
1 cup sugar
1/3 teaspoon
cornstarch
2 egg yolks, butter
1 packet (5 grams)
dry vanilla
(1/4 teaspoon liquid)
1/2 cup rice
2 cups water

1. Sort and wash the rice and cook in 1cup water. When water has evaporated add sugar and milk, then vanilla and butter. Mix cornstarch with egg yolks and 2-3 tablespoons water. When rice has returned to a boil, take 1 or 2 tablespoons from rice mixture and stir into egg mixture. Gradually blend this mixture back into the rice. Remove from stove.

2. Pour pudding into individual baking dishes. Put water in a baking pan and set the dishes into the water. Bake until browned on top.

3. If desired, the pudding may be eaten without putting in the oven and the egg yolks eliminated.

VANILLA-ALMOND PUDDING (KEŞKÜL)

Ingredients:
1 kilogram (1 liter, 3-1/2 cups)
milk
3 tablespoons rice starch
1-1/2 tablespoons cornstarch
1 cup sugar
1 handful almonds
dash of salt
pistachios or peanuts as garnish

1. Crush almonds in food processor with 2 tablespoons of the sugar.

2. Put remaining sugar in a pan with the milk and bring to a boil. Mix rice starch and cornstarch. Add a dash of salt and mix well with a little water. Slowly add to boiling milk and stir on a low flame until consistency of a smooth pudding.

3. Add almonds and cook 2-3 minutes longer. Remove from heat and fill individual bowls. Sprinkle crushed nuts on top.

COCOA CRÉME

Ingredients:

1 liter boiled milk

3 eggs

125 grams (1/4 lb) margarine

3 tablespoons cocoa

1 packet (5 grams) dry vanilla (1/4 teaspoon liquid)

1 heaping cup flour

1-1/2 cups sugar

Put milk, egg and sugar in a deep bowl and blend well with a mixer. When sugar is completely blended in add flour, vanilla and cocoa. Transfer to a pan and cook until pudding consistency. If the dish is to be eaten as a dessert by itself, add (unmelted) margarine. When done transfer to individual bowls and allow to set 1-2 hours in refrigerator. If the pudding is to be used as part of a cake, add margarine after cooking and beat 10 minutes with the mixer before using.

CHOCOLATE PUDDING (SUPANGLE)

Ingredients:

1 liter milk

1/2 cup sugar

1-1/2 tablespoons flour

1-1/2 tablespoons cornstarch

1 egg yolk

6 tablespoons cocoa

1 packet (5 grams) dry vanilla (1/4 teaspoon liquid)

1. Boil the milk and chill. Mix sugar, cocoa, flour, cornstarch and the egg yolk. Add a little of the milk and mix well. Add remaining milk.

2. Cook to a pudding consistency. When almost done add vanilla. Remove from heat and pour into individual bowls. Sprinkle coconut over them.

Note: *If glass bowls are used and a 2-color effect is desired, reserve 1/3 cup milk. Cook the pudding without the cocoa first, then divide into two. Mix 1/3 cup milk with the cocoa. Add to 1 part of the pudding. Mix well, then add the other half of the pudding. Cook them together for 2-3 minutes, then fill the bowls.*

CHOCOLATE SAUCE

2-1/2 cups milk
1 cup sugar
4-1/2 tablespoons cocoa
1-1/2 tablespoons cornstarch
2 egg yolks
1 packet (5 grams) dry vanilla
(1/4 teaspoon liquid)

1. Boil the milk and chill. Put cornstarch, cocoa, sugar and egg yolks in a pan. Add a little of the milk and stir. Add remaining milk and cook until thickened.

2. Remove from heat and add vanilla. Beat by hand or in a mixer. Chill. Use between cake layers or on top or with other desserts.

APPLE BALLS IN SAUCE

Ingredients:
400 grams (3/4 lb) petit beurre
(butter) cookies
1/2 cup sugar
4 medium sized apples
1 cup walnut pieces or pistachios
Sauce:
1/2 cup sugar
1 cup milk, 1 cup water
2 tablespoons cocoa
3 tablespoons cornstarch
coconut

1. Put cookies in food processor until like flour. Grate apples. Mix cookies, apples, sugar and walnuts and work with hands until like a dough.

2 . Wet the hands to form into walnut-size balls

3. **Sauce:** Mix together well: cold milk, water, sugar, cornstarch and cocoa. Cook on high flame, stirring constantly, until pudding consistency. Pour the sauce on top of the apple balls and sprinkle coconut over them. Set in refrigerator.

CHICKEN BREAST PUDDING

Ingredients:
125 grams (1/4 lb) butter or
margarine
1 cup flour
1 cup sugar
1 kilogram (1 liter, 3-1/2 cups) milk
1 packet (5 grams) dry vanilla (1/4
teaspoon liquid)

1. Mix together milk, flour, vanilla and sugar. Cook, stirring, until pudding consistency. Remove from heat and add butter.

2. When completely cooled, mix with a mixer for 10-15 minutes. While mixing slowly add margarine. Transfer to individual serving dishes and place in refrigerator for 1-2 hours.

Note: *If desired add some mastic during the cooking. Some recipes for this pudding do include bits of chicken breast.*

MOCK PROFITEROLES

Ingredients:
4 apples
1 cup walnut pieces
400 grams (3/4 lb) petit beurre
(butter) cookies
Sauce:
1/2 cup sugar
1/2 cup cocoa
2 eggs
100 grams (3.2 oz) butter

1. Grate apples. Bring cookies and walnuts to a flour consistency in a food processor. Add grated apple and knead with hands. Form walnut-size balls and place them in a glass pan.

2. **Sauce:** Meanwhile, break the eggs into a deep bowl and beat a little with a mixer. Add sugar and beat a little more. Melt butter. When cooled slightly, add to the bowl along with the cocoa and beat all together until creamy.

3. Pour the sauce on the apple balls. Sprinkle coconut on top, place in the refrigerator for 1-2 hours.

BOTTOM-OF THE-PAN PUDDING (KAZANDİBİ)

Ingredients:
4 cups milk
1/2 cup rice starch
1/4 cup potato starch or
wheat starch
1 cup granulated sugar
1 packet (5 grams) dry
vanilla (1/4 teaspoon liquid)
dash of salt
1/2 cup powdered sugar

1. Bring milk and granulated sugar to a boil.

2. In a bowl, mix rice starch and wheat starch together with a little water until smooth. Add a dash of salt (or, use a mixer to blend the starches) and then gradually blend into the milk and cook until a smooth pudding consistency. When almost ready to remove from stove, stir in the vanilla.

Starch wafer dessert

3. Put powdered sugar in a heavy oven pan and place over a flame on top of the stove. When it browns (carmelizes), remove and put granulated sugar on top, then the pudding. Place pan in the oven until browned on the bottom (or continue on top of the stove, holding the pan with both hands and turning it to be sure the bottom is browned all over.).

4. To make it easy to remove the pudding from the pan at serving time, place the pan in a larger pan of cold water and, when cooled, place pudding pan in refrigerator. When chilled, cut the pudding in 4x5 cm pieces and use a spatula to roll each piece out of the pan and onto individual serving plates.

STARCH WAFER DESSERT (GÜLLAÇ)

Ingredients:

1 400-gram (3/4 lb) package güllaç (starch wafers)

2 kilograms (2 liters) milk

1 packet (5 grams) dry vanilla (1/4 teaspoon liquid)

1 kilogram (2 lb) sugar

1-1/2 cups walnut pieces

cinnamon and rosewater, as desired

1. Boil milk 5-10 minutes and add sugar, rosewater and vanilla. Boil 1-2 minutes longer. Set aside until cooled enough to be held.

3. Place the leaves of starch waver one by one in a wide flat pan. Over each one pour one or two ladles of the milk mixture (enough to moisten well). When half of the leaves are done this way sprinkle on walnuts and continue to layer the remaining leaves with the ladles of milk. Spread remaining walnuts on top and sprinkle on cinnamon.

Note: *If rosewater is used vanilla is not necessary.*

MILK FONDANT

Ingredients:

2-1/2 cups sugar

2-1/2 cups milk

1/2 teaspoon lemon juice

2 cups walnut pieces

1. Add sugar to milk and boil until they coalesce well, stirring constantly. When thick, remove from heat and mix in lemon juice. Set aside

2. When cooled to a warm temperature, whip the mixture until it turns white. Set apart some of the walnuts for the top and add the remaining to the mixture. Mix well and form into little hazelnut size balls. Place on a serving platter and sprinkle walnuts over them.

CREAM & COOKIES DESSERT

Ingredients:

1 box (150 grams or 4.8 oz) dry whipping cream mix (krem şanti)
1-1/2 cups milk
200 grams (6.4 oz) petit beurres (butter cookies)
200 grams plain chocolate cookies
1 tablespoon powdered sugar
1cup crushed hazelnuts

1. Beat krem şanti with milk until creamy.

2. Break down cookies into chunks and mix with sugar and hazelnuts.

3. Combine two mixtures well. Press it into a container lined with a plastic bag. Close tightly and place in freezer. When ready to serve remove container from freezer and turn it upside down onto a board. Slice and serve.

Note: *Because it is frozen, the dessert is easily separated from the plastic.*

QUICK OVEN CUSTARD (TEZ PİŞTİ)

Ingredients:
1 liter milk
1 cup sugar
1/2 cup rice starch
2 eggs
1 packet (5 grams) dry vanilla (1/4 teaspoon liquid)

1. Boil milk and sugar together. Mix starch with a little cold water until smooth. Slowly add to boiling milk, stirring constantly. Bring to a smooth pudding consistency and remove from heat. Mix in the vanilla.

2. Put 1-1/2 ladles of the custard in a bowl and pour the remaining into individual baking cups. Set them asided to cool.

3. Separate egg yolks and whites. Mix the yolks with the custard in the bowl. Beat the whites until stiff and add to the bowl. Mix well.

4. Spoon some of this mixture on top of the custard in the baking cups. Put cups in the oven and bake until lightly browned on top.

"A good pot can produce bad food,
But bad pots can affect the food badly." Old saying
"The price for getting the pot to boil is to be proud when the steam carries the fragrance."
"May we avoid food prepared by the hand of degradation."
Sheikh Sadi

DESSERTS

CONTENTS

ABOUT DESSERTS

1. The information in the "About Breads" chapter are applicable to desserts.

2. A very small amount of salt added to floury desserts enhances the flavor.

3. Foods containing sugar, being in the carbohydrates category, give the body energy. Therefore since there are plenty of carbohydrates in the normal diet there is not much need for eating sweets. Eating sweets before a meal can be a cause of weight gain. Therefore, the time to have sweets is after a meal (after eating the foods the body needs).

4. All ingredients should be fresh and of good quality and the thickness of the syrup is especially important. If too watery the dessert will be too soft and if too thick it will not be properly absorbed.

5. If either the dessert or the syrup is hot, the other should be cold. The dish becomes mushy when both are hot.

6. In general, twice as much sugar as water is used in a syrup.

7. Stir the syrup as long as needed to completely melt the sugar. Stirring after the sugar melts can cause the syrup to become sugary again.

8. After removing the syrup from the stove adding a little lemon juice will prevent it from becoming sugary again.

9. Do not stir syrup with a metal spoon. If a wooden spoon is used be sure it does not pass any other food tastes into the syrup.

10. The consistency of the syrup depends on the dessert: For example, in the baklava and kadayif recipes, the syrup has arrived at the right thickness when, upon dipping in and lifting up a spoon, the drops from the spoon extend in threads.

NOAH'S PUDDING (AŞURE)

Ingredients:
500 grams (1 lb) whole wheat
1/3 cup rice
1/2 cup chick peas
1/2 cup white beans
1 handful raisins
5-6 figs
1 handful hazelnut pieces
1 handful peanuts
1 handful walnut pieces
cinnamon
1-1/2 kilogram (3 lb) sugar

1. Sort, wash and put whole wheat, chick peas and beans to soak in separate containers the night before.

2. Drain chick peas and beans and put to boil together until soft and drain.

3. Put the wheat to the boil in a large pot in its own soaking water and cook until soft. Remove from heat and place a thick cloth over the pot. Allow to set 1 hour (in order for the wheat pieces to completely open).

4. Add cooked chick peas and beans to the wheat pan.

5. Cook the rice separately and add to the pot.

6. Cook until consistency of a thick soup. If additional water is needed, be sure it is hot when added.

7. When the "soup" is done stir in the sugar. When melted, remove from heat.

8. Boil figs and raisins in water for 5 minutes. Cut figs in 4's. Add raisins, figs, hazelnuts and peanuts to the pot and bring to a boil once or twice. Pour into individual bowls and put walnut pieces and cinnamon on top. Set aside to cool and chill.

Note: *Rosewater and vanilla may be added after the sugar. Pomegranate seeds may be added along with the nuts.*

SAFFRON PUDDING (ZERDE)

Ingredients:

2 tablespoons + 2 teaspoons rice
3 cups water
1-1/2 cups granulated sugar
1 tablespoon cornstarch
small handful tumeric
small handful saffron
1/4 cup rosewater
1-1/2 tablespoons currants (or
cinnamon, coconut, pistachios or
hazelnuts)

1. Sort and wash rice and bring to a boil. Add sugar and continue to cook.

2. Put saffron, tumeric and cornstarch in 6 tablespoons warm water. Mix well and add to the boiling rice, stirring constantly. Bring to a boil once or twice more and add rosewater just before removing from heat.

3. Pour into individual serving bowls and sprinkle currants on top. Set aside to cool.

ERZURUM FLOUR SWEETMEATS

Ingredients:

1 cup sugar
2 cups flour
1cup butter or margarine

1. Melt butter. Add flour and stir, cooking until light brown.

2. Add a spoonful of water to the sugar and stir. Add to the flour and butter pan and stir until well blended. Transfer to a serving plate and spread out. It will stiffen as it cools. Before it stiffens a lot, slice in desired size pieces.

IRON DESSERT

Ingredients:

3 eggs, 1 cup yoghurt
1 cup flour, 1/3 teaspoon salt
1 teaspoon baking powder
frying oil
walnut pieces or coconut if desired
Syrup:
3 cups sugar, 2-1/2 cups water
juice of 1/2 lemon

1. Put all ingredients into a deep bowl. Use an electric mixer and blend to a batter.

2. Pour oil in a deep pan and heat. When very hot, make the cast iron utensil(*) very hot by holding it in the hot oil. Immediately dip into the batter (keeping the top 2 mm above the batter) so that the batter clings to the bottom and most of the sides. Then plunge the iron back into the bubbling oil. Shake the iron to cause the batter to slide of into the oil. The batter will retain the pattern of the iron. When both sides are lightly browned, remove with a slotted spoon, allow to drain on oil-resistant paper and cool slightly. Dip in the warm sugar mixture and place on serving platter. Sprinkle walnuts or coconut on top if desired. This procedure is repeated until batter is finished. Each time the iron must be heated in the and the oil kept hot.

Note: *The cast iron utensil is not washed but rather is kept wrapped in clean oil paper.*

This dessert's name is taken from the fact that the batter is transferred to the oil by means of a thick cast iron utensil that has holes in it and a handle and is made in any variety of shapes (star, circle, heart, flower etc.).

FLOUR SWEETMEATS WITH GINGER

Ingredients:

4-1/2 cups flour
250 grams (1/2 lb) margarine
250 grams (1/2 lb) powdered sugar
1 tablespoon ginger
1 cup pine nuts (or walnuts or hazelnuts)

1. Brown flour in a teflon pan without oil. Remove from heat.

2. Sift flour using a wire sieve. (If a plastic one is used be sure flour is very hot when using.)

3. Add margarine all at once. Work it into the hot flour with the hands until blended.

4. Add powdered sugar and continue to work with the hands.

5. Add ginger and continue to knead dough until well blended.

6. Divide dough into two parts. Press one part into the bottom of a glass pan. Spread it evenly.

7. Spread pine nuts over it. Lay the second part of the dough on top.

8. Use a second pan the same shape to press down on the dough so that it is evenly distributed. If the second pan is lacking, press with the hands until it is smooth. Slice with a sharp knife in small rectangles and place pan in the refrigerator. When ready to serve, remove pieces one by one and stack them on a serving plate in star design. Sprinkle some nuts on top.

FLOUR SWEETMEATS WITH SYRUP

Ingredients:
1-1/2 cups flour
250 grams (1/2 lb) margarine
scant 1/3 cup pine nuts
Syrup:
2 cups sugar, 2 cups water

1. Add 2 cups sugar to 2 cups boiling water. When melted remove from heat and allow to cool until just warm.
2. Melt margarine in a pan and saute nuts until light brown. Add flour and cook over a high flame until brown. Slowly pour on the warm syrup.
3. When the syrup has evaporated remove from heat. Transfer to a serving plate with a spoon or, if allowed to cool until warm, with the hands.

Note: *This dessert is even tastier if 1cup of milk is substituted for one of the cups of water.*

NURIYE MILK DESSERT

Ingredients:
1 cup semolina
1 cup sugar
1 kilogram (2 lb) milk
50 grams (1.6 oz) cocoa
1 handful walnut pieces
1 packet (5 grams) vanilla
(1/4 teaspoon liquid)

1. Mix sugar and semolina. Add cold milk and place on the stove.
2. Stir over a high flame until it reaches pudding consistency. When about finished cooking, add vanilla, stir and remove from heat.
3. Put half the mixture in a glass pan and sprinkle half the walnuts over it. Add cocoa to remaining half. Mix and cook until it comes to a full boil twice more. Remove from heat and pour on top. Sprinkle remaining walnuts over it.
4. When cooled down enough, place in refrigerator to chill. Cut in slices and serve.

FLOUR SWEETMEATS WITH POWDERED SUGAR

Ingredients:
250 grams (1/2 lb) margarine
4 cups flour
1 box (200 grams, 6.4 oz)
powdered sugar
1 cup walnut or hazelnut pieces

1. Melt margarine, add flour and when flour begins to brown slightly add powdered sugar and walnuts or hazelnuts.
2. Cook on low flame, stirring occasionally. Place in a glass pan and spread evenly with a spoon. Slice as desired and set aside to cool.
3. When ready to serve, in order to remove the slices more easily, place another pan or plate over the top and turn upside down.

SEMOLINA SWEETMEATS WITH MILK

Ingredients:
1 cup margarine or butter
2cups semolina
3 cups sugar
2 cups milk, 2 cups water
1 handful pine nuts

1. Melt margarine. Cook nuts and semolina until light brown. Remove from heat. Add sugar and blend in well.

2. Add water and milk and return to the heat. Cook over a high flame while stirring until consistency of a stiff pudding. Remove from heat.

3. Place a clean cloth over the top of the pan and lid on top. Allow it to set awhile before serving.

Notes: *1. The cloth is used to prevent drops of water caused by the steam from getting on the food.*
2. If desired use 4 cups of water and eliminate the milk.

SEMOLINA SWEETMEAT WITH CHEESE

Ingredients:
1 cup semolina
1 cup milk, 1 cup water
1-1/2 cups sugar
100 grams (3.2 oz) butter or margarine
200 grams (6.4 oz) fresh salt-free white cheese

1. Wash and drain the cheese.

2. Cook semolina a little in melted butter.

3. Mix together in a bowl the sugar, milk and water. Add this to the pan and mix, cooking until consistency of a stiff pudding.

4. Squeeze cheese to remove any remaining water. Break into crumbs and add to pan. Stir 2-3 minutes or until cheese has melted into the mixture. Remove from heat and place in a glass pan. Bean with a spoon and smooth out flat in the pan. Draw a pattern on top as desired. May be served hot or warm.

KADAYİF DESSERT

Ingredients:
750 grams (1-1/2 lb) tel kadayif
*

250 grams (1/2 lb) margarine or
butter (or mixture of the two)
1 cup walnut pieces
Syrup:
1 kilogram (5 cups) milk
1 kilogram (2 lb) sugar

1. Place kadayif in a dish. Melt butter and pour over it and crush it.

2. Place half of it in an oven pan and the walnuts on top. Arrange remaining kadayif on top and bake until brown. Remove from oven and set aside to cool.

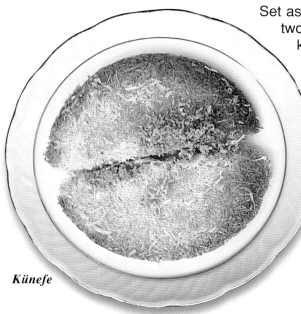

3. Heat milk, add sugar, and bring to a boil. Set aside to cool a little. Pour one or two ladles of the syrup over the kadayif that has been cooling. Ten minutes later pour on the remaining syrup and set aside to cool.

Notes: 1. * Tel kadayif is found in Turkish grocery stores, usually in 200 gram packages. It consists of very thin, wire-like dried wheat fiber formed in large flat rounds.

2. Adding the syrup in two installments prevents the kadayif from becoming too soft.

Künefe

ÇİM DESSERT

Ingredients:

750 grams (1-1/2 lb) tel kadayif *
500 grams (1 lb) cornstarch (for
rolling and handling the dough)
500 grams (1 lb) flour
1 egg, 1/3 cup milk, 1/3 cup water
250 grams (1/2 lb) margarine or oil
1 kilogram (2 lb) sugar, 4 cups water
juice of 1/2 lemon
crushed walnut pieces

1. Mix together in a deep bowl: milk, egg, water and a dash of salt. Add flour and form a soft dough. Place a damp cloth over the bowl and allow to set for 1/2 hour.

2. Place kadayif in a pan and crush it.

3. Divide the dough into egg-size pieces and on a board (using the cornstarch) roll each one into a very thin round of dough. Slice it into a half round. Sprinkle a little of the kadayif and a teaspoon of walnuts on top. Roll it up and slice in 3 cm rings. Lay the rings on their sides in a baking pan.

4. Melt butter and pour over them. Bake in oven until they sizzle.

5. Pour cooled syrup over and allow to set until the syrup has penetrated well.

6. **Syrup:** Put water to boil and add sugar, stirring until sugar is melted. Boil 10 minutes more. Just before removing from stove, add lemon juice. Set aside to cool.

HATAY CHEESE KÜNEFE

Ingredients:

750 grams (1-1/2 lb) tel kadayif *
200 grams (6.4 oz) butter
500 grams (1 lb) fresh salt-free
white cheese

Syrup:
4 cups sugar
4 cups water
juice of 1 lemon

1. Melt butter and pour over kadayif. Crush kadayif and mix in butter. Divide in two. Press half the kadayif in a greased flat pan. Crumble the cheese and spread on top. Put the remaining kadayif on top. Press down with the hands.

2. Place pan over a flame and cook while turning the pan until the bottom sizzles. Place another pan the same size over the top and turn over once. Place on stove again and turn that side around in the same way until it sizzles.

3. After both sides are browned well removed from stove and pour the cooled syrup over the top. Serve hot.

4. **Syrup:** Put water to boil and add sugar, stirring until sugar is melted. Boil 10 minutes more. Just before removing from stove, add lemon juice. Set aside to cool.

* Tel kadayif is found in Turkish grocery stores, usually in 200 gram packages. It consists of very thin, wire-like dried wheat fiber formed in large flat rounds.

KADAYIF WITH PUDDING

Ingredients:

750 grams (1-1/2 lb) tel kadayif *
250 grams (1/2 lb) margarine
Pudding:
1 liter milk, 3/4 cup flour
3 tablespoons butter
2 eggs
Syrup:
4 cups sugar, 4 cups water
half of one lemon

1. Melt margarine. Place kadayif in a pan, pour margarine over it and crush it.

2. **Pudding:** Melt 2 tablespoons butter in a pan and stir in flour. Cook until light brown. Gradually add milk, stirring constantly. Cook to a smooth pudding. Remove from heat and stir in 1 tablespoon butter. Stir occasionally until the pudding is just warm.

3. Before pudding has become warm, break 1 egg into it and mix well. Repeat with the second egg.

4. Press half of the kadayif into a baking pan and pour half of the warm pudding on top. Press remaining kadayif on top. Bake in oven until light brown.

5. Remove from oven and pour 1-2 ladles of cooled syrup on top. Ten minutes later add remaining syrup. Allow to set until syrup is absorbed. Serve warm.

6. **Syrup:** Put water to boil and add sugar, stirring until sugar is melted. Boil 10 minutes more. Just before removing from stove, add lemon juice. Set aside to cool.

FRIED VIZIER'S FINGERS (LOKMA)

Ingredients:

2 eggs
2 tablespoons yoghurt
baking powder
2 tablespoons + 2 teaspoons
margarine or butter
flour, salt, frying oil
Syrup:
2 cups sugar
2 cups water

1. Break eggs in a bowl and add yoghurt and margarine.

2. Mix baking powder with flour and add. Work it into a soft dough.

3. Divide the dough into walnut-size pieces and form into balls. Fry in hot oil.

4. Place balls in a dish and pour cooled syrup over them.

5. **Syrup:** Put water to boil and add sugar, stirring until sugar is melted. Boil 10 minutes more. Just before removing from stove, add lemon juice. Set aside to cool.

ERZURUM STUFFED KADAYIF

Ingredients:
500 grams (1 lb) kadayif *
250 grams (1/2 lb) crushed
walnuts
10 eggs
frying oil
Syrup:
3 cups sugar
3 cups water
juice of 1/2 lemon

1. **Syrup:** Put water to boil and add sugar, stirring until sugar is melted. Boil 10 minutes more. Just before removing from stove, add lemon juice. Set aside to cool.

2. Place a board or tray under the hands while working to catch crumbs. Take a little kadayif and roll in the hand. Add a spoonful of walnuts inside and roll between the hands being careful not to let walnuts drop out. Repeat until all the kadayif is rolled into pieces.

3. Beat the eggs lightly in a bowl. Moisten the pieces generously in the egg and fry in hot oil.

4. As each piece is done remove and place in syrup. When all the syrup has been absorbed, transfer to serving plate.

BAKLAVA*

Ingredients:
4 cups flour
1 egg
1/4 cup oil (if desired)
1 dash salt
1 cup walnut or hazelnut pieces
250 grams (1/2 lb) butter and oil
mixed
cornstarch as needed
Syrup:
5 cups sugar
5 cups water
juice of 1 lemon

1. Spread flour on a board. Make an opening in the middle and add 1 egg, 1/4 cup oil, a dash of salt and water. Work into a soft dough. Place a damp cloth over the dough for 15 minutes.

2. Divide into egg-size parts and using the cornstarch, roll out the pieces very thin. Layer the pieces in a large baking pan, placing some walnuts between every layer or every second or third layer.

3. Cut the dough in slices. Warm the mixture of butter and oil and pour over the baklava. Cut in diamond shapes. Bake until light brown and remove from oven.

4. **Syrup:** Put water to boil and add sugar, stirring until sugar is melted. Boil 10 minutes more. Just before removing from stove, add lemon juice. Set aside to cool.

5. If the syrup was prepared and cooled ahead of time pour it over the hot baklava. One hot and one cold helps prevent the baklava from becoming too soft.

***Note:** The Turkish type of rolling pin (oklava), which is best suited for working with baklava and similar thin pastry doughs, is much longer and thinner (about 2-3 cm in diameter) than Western types.*

TURBAN TWISTS

1. Prepare the dough and filling as for baklava, divide dough into egg-size pieces and roll out very thin on the board.

2. Layer the dough, spreading walnuts between each layer. Cut each piece in half. Using ample cornstarch, roll one part at a time completely around the rolling pin. Hold each end of the dough with the hands and push the dough toward the middle so that puckers are formed, similar to an accordion.

3. When the rolling pin is then removed, the result resembles a twisted turban. Begin laying the turbans on their puckered sides on a large round tray starting at the outer edge and adding one at a time so that they are touching. When the outer ring is complete continue with the next ring and the next and so on until the center is reached. They may also be laid out in lines until the tray is filled.

4. Just as for the previous recipe for baklava, pour the warmed butter and oil mixture over it. Bake until light brown and remove from oven. Pour cool syrup over the turbans. Allow to set until all of the syrup is absorbed.

CHEESE BAKLAVA

Ingredients:
1 package prepared dough for
baklava (phyllo)
500 grams (1 lb) fresh salt-free
white cheese
1 cup margarine and butter mixed
1/3 cup oil
Syrup:
5 cups sugar, 4 cups water
juice of 1 lemon

1. Divide phyllo leaves into 3 groups. Place the first group in layers without filling.

2. Wash cheese well. (If salty, place in water the night before in order to remove salt.) Crumble cheese and sprinkle half of it on top of the first set of layers. Place the second group of phyllo leaves in layers on top of the cheese and then sprinkle the remaining cheese on top. Then layer the third group of leaves on top (3 layers dough, 2 layers cheese). Slice in diamond or square shapes.

3. Melt margarine and butter. When hot pour over the pastry. Bake in the oven until light brown. Remove and allow it to cool slightly before pouring the warm syrup over it.

4. **Syrup:** Put water to boil and add sugar, stirring until sugar is melted. Boil 10 minutes more. Just before removing from stove, add lemon juice. Set aside to cool.

FRIED EARS IN SYRUP

Ingredients:
1 egg
as much yoghurt as egg
as much olive oil as egg
1 teaspoon baking powder,

flour
frying oil
Syrup:
2 cups sugar
3 cups water

1. Wash egg well and dry. Open the top of the egg a little and empty egg into a bowl. Fill the shell with yoghurt and add to bowl, then fill with olive oil and also add to bowl.

2. Mix baking powder and flour. Add these to the bowl. Work into a soft dough. Cover with a cloth for 5 minutes.

3. Roll out 2 mm thick on a floured board. Cut into squares. To form the "ears", pinch together 2 corners crosswise, then pinch the other 2 corners together, but back the other way. Fry the ears in hot oil.

4. **Syrup:** Put water to boil and add sugar, stirring until sugar is melted. Boil 10 minutes more. Just before removing from stove, add lemon juice. Set aside to cool. Pour over the fried ears.

LAZ BOUREK

Ingredients:

Dough:
4 cups flour
1/4 cup oil
dash of salt
milk as needed

Pudding:
1 cup flour,
1 liter milk
500 grams (1 lb) butter
3 eggs

Syrup:
4 cups sugar
4 cups water
juice of 1/2 lemon

1. **Pudding:** Melt half the butter, add flour mixing until smooth and light brown. Add milk gradually, stirring constantly until a thick pudding. Remove from heat

2. Add two more spoonfuls butter. When pudding is just warm add eggs one at a time and mix with a spoon. Allow to cool while stirring occasionally.

3. **Syrup:** Put water to boil and add sugar, stirring until sugar is melted. Boil 10 minutes more. Just before removing from stove, add lemon juice. Set aside to cool.

4. **Dough:** Put flour in a bowl. Open a hole in the middle. Add a dash of salt, oil and enough milk to work up a soft dough. Divide into parts the size of very large eggs and roll out as thin as baklava dough.

5. Cut each part into 4-finger long strips. Melt the remaining butter and butter each strip. Put about 1-1/2 tablespoons of pudding on top of one end of each strip. Fold over. Place on an oven pan so that there are no spaces between the boureks. Bake until light brown.

6. Remove from oven and using a spoon pour some of the syrup on each bourek.

REVANİ CAKE NO.1

Ingredients:
6 tablespoons yoghurt
3 cups sugar
3 cups flour
6 eggs, baking powder
Syrup:
5 cups water
4-1/2 cups sugar

1. Beat egg with sugar in a bowl. Add yoghurt.

2. Mix baking powder with flour. Add to bowl and mix well. Pour into a greased baking pan and bake in a preheated medium oven. When golden brown remove from oven. Pour cooled syrup over the cake.

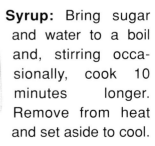

Syrup: Bring sugar and water to a boil and, stirring occasionally, cook 10 minutes longer. Remove from heat and set aside to cool.

REVANİ CAKE NO.2

Ingredients:

10 eggs

1-1/2 tablespoons semolina

3 tablespoons flour

3 tablespoons sugar

grated rind of 1 orange

Syrup:

5 cups water, 3-1/2 cups sugar

juice of 1 lemon

1. Be sure eggs are at room temperature.

2. Beat eggs in a mixer or wire whip until white.

3. Mix sugar, semolina and flour together. Add grated orange rind. Add these to the beaten eggs.

4. Mix well and pour into a deep oven pan. Bake in a preheated 150 C (300F) oven. Cake will be a dark reddish brown when done. Remove from oven and pour the cooled syrup on top.

Note: Oven temperature is very important for making this revani. If too low it will fall and if too high it will be too dark.

YOGHURT CAKE WITH SYRUP

Ingredients

3/4 cup strained yoghurt

3 eggs

1 heaping cup powdered sugar

2 tablespoons butter

1/3 teaspoon soda or baking powder

1-1/3 cups flour coconut

Syrup:

3 cups granulated sugar

3-1/2 cups water

juice of 1/2 lemon

1. Be sure all water is drained out of the yoghurt (light sour cream may be substituted), then place in a bowl and beat it with a spoon. Add eggs, melted butter and powdered sugar and mix well. Mix flour and soda or baking powder together and add to the bowl. Mix once more. Pour in a greased baking pan and place in a hot preheated oven until done.

2. **Syrup:** Mix sugar in hot water and bring to a boil. Cook 10 minutes and add juice. Remove from heat and allow to cool.

3. Pour syrup over the cake as it comes out of the oven (either the syrup or the cake should be hot if the other is cold). Allow cake to set until the syrup is absorbed. Sprinkle some coconut on top.

QUICK BREADCRUMB DESSERT

Ingredients:

3 cups dry breadcrumbs
1-1/2 cups oil
3 cups oil
1/3 cup sugar
4 eggs
250 grams (1/2 cup) raw blanched
almond pieces
1 grated orange rind
10 grams (1/3 oz) baking powder
(4 teaspoons)
Syrup:
3 cups sugar
2 cups water
juice of 1/2 lemon

1. Prepare syrup as in yoghurt cake and revani recipes. Add oil to dry breadcrumbs and mix until absorbed.

2. Mix flour, sugar, almonds, orange rind and baking powder in a bowl. Add breadcrumbs and eggs.

3. Make a dough with the hands and place in a baking pan. Bake until light brown. Remove from oven and pour cold syrup on top. Slice.

4. If desired add on top of each slice a dollop of whipped cream, or sliced fruit or berries such as banana, oranges, strawberries, cherries etc.

SHAMBABA SWEET

Ingredients:

500 grams (1 lb) semolina
1 cup yoghurt
2 cups water, 2 cups sugar
3 eggs
125 grams (1/4 lb) margarine
100 grams (3.2 oz) pistachios
1 teaspoon baking powder
Syrup:
4 cups sugar, 1-1/2 cups water

1. Mix all ingredients well and pour in a greased oven pan. Bake until browned.

2. Bring sugar and water to a boil. Pour over the cake when it comes out of the oven. (Syrup does not need to be cooled first.)

PRESSED ON THE SIEVE

Ingredients:

2 eggs
1/3 cup powdered sugar
1 cup flour
1/3 cup semolina
1/3 cup oil,
baking powder

1. Mix all ingredients together well except margarine. Melt margarine, add and mix again into a smooth dough.

2. Divide dough into small pieces. With the hands form each piece into a ball, then flatten. Press onto a sieve (kalbur) to give texture.

Note: *These may be fried in hot oil. If baked in the oven, add some walnut pieces to the dough.*

PRETTY GIRL'S LIPS

Ingredients:

1 cup oil
1 cup milk
1/3 teaspoon salt
1/3 teaspoon baking powder
flour
250 grams (1/4 lb) margarine
1 cup large walnut pieces

Syrup:
4 cups sugar
4 cups water

1. Mix together all ingredients except the margarine and, using as much flour as needed, form a soft dough.

2. Divide dough into walnut-size pieces. Roll out 10 cm diameter (3 in) wide and dust them one by one with cornstarch. Then stack them one on top of the other.

3. Roll the stack out to 1 cm thick. Using a small cutter or a glass (about 3-4 cm or 1-1/2 in wide), cut out dough rounds. Place a walnut piece on one round and another round on top. Close so that each one resembles a pair of lips. Place the lips on a baking pan.

4. Brown the margarine and spoon some onto each "lip". Place in a hot oven and bake until brown and crispy.

5. Remove from oven and allow to set a minute or two, then pour cooled syrup over them.

Syrup: Put water to boil and add sugar, stirring until sugar is melted. Boil 10 minutes more. Set aside to cool.

"DATE" DESSERT

Ingredients:

250 grams (1/2 lb) margarine
3 tablespoons olive oil
3 tablespoons yoghurt
1 egg
1 cup large walnut pieces
5 cups flour
1/3 teaspoon baking powder
dash of salt
grated rind of 1 lemon

Syrup:
3 cups sugar
3 cups water
juice of 1/2 lemon

1. Mix together in a bowl: margarine, olive oil, yoghurt, egg, salt, baking powder and lemon rind.

2. Sift flour and mix with walnuts. Add to bowl and make a dough. Divide dough into walnut-size pieces. Roll pieces into balls, then flatten. Press against a sieve to give it texture, then roll it up to resemble a (hollow) date.

3. Place them on a baking pan and bake until light brown. Remove and pour cooled syrup over it while still hot.

Syrup: Put water to boil and add sugar, stirring until sugar is melted. Boil 10 minutes more. Just before removing from stove, add lemon juice. Set aside to cool.

HAZELNUT ŞEKERPARE

Ingredients:
3 eggs
1 cup sugar
1 cup oil
1/3 teaspoon soda
3-4 drop lemon juice
1 packet baking powder
(4 teaspoons)
flour, hazelnuts

Syrup:
5 cups sugar, 6 cups water
4-5 drops lemon juice

1. Beat eggs well in a bowl. Add sugar. Continue to beat until sugar melts. Add oil and stir a little more.

2. Add lemon juice to the soda. Mix soda with the flour.

3. Add flour slowly to the egg-sugar-oil mixture and form a soft dough.

4. Divide into walnut-size pieces. Roll in the hands to form balls. Press the top of each one and place not touching on a baking pan. Place a hazelnut in the center of each one and bake in a medium oven until light brown. Remove from oven and pour cooled syrup over them.

Syrup: Put water to boil and add sugar, stirring until sugar is melted. Boil 10 minutes more. Just before removing from stove, add lemon juice. Set aside to cool.

PLAIN ŞEKERPARE

Ingredients:

1/2 cup powdered sugar
250 grams (1/2 lb) soft margarine
1 whole egg, 1 egg yolk
10 grams (1/3 oz) baking powder
(4 teaspoons)
5 grams dry vanilla (1/4 teaspoon liquid)
4 cups flour

Syrup:
4 cups sugar
4 cups water

1. Mix powdered sugar, margarine and 1 egg in a bowl. Combine baking powder and vanilla with the flour. Add to the bowl and mix well, forming a dough.

2. Divide into egg-size or walnut-size pieces and form in ovals or rounds. Place on a greased baking pan. Whip the egg yolk a little and drizzle some on each piece. Cut one or two incisions in the top of each one. Place in a hot oven.

3. When brown, remove and pour warm syrup over them.

Syrup: Put water to boil and add sugar, stirring until sugar is melted. Boil 10 minutes more. Set aside to cool.

FRIED TULUMBA

Ingredients:
2 cups flour
4 eggs
2 cups water
1-1/2 tablespoons semolina
1-1/2 tablespoons cornstarch
4 tablespoons margarine
a little salt
frying oil
Syrup:
3 cups sugar
4 cups water
juice of 1/2 lemon

1. Place water, margarine and salt in a pan and set to boil. Sift flour and mix with semolina and cornstarch. Add to pan and mix quickly with a wooden spoon to avoid sticking to the bottom. When well blended remove from heat and set aside to cool a little. While still warm mix in the eggs one at a time. Then add 1 spoonful of the syrup and mix well.

2. Using a pastry bag, either round or patterned, squeeze out the mixture and, with a knife dipped in oil, cut off in portions 3-4 cm in length.

3. Dip these pieces in warm oil and, with a slotted spoon, lift out and transfer to a pan of hot oil. While frying, stir the hot oil or shake the pan, then remove with the same spoon, drain and put directly into cold syrup. Allow to remain in syrup for 5 minutes. Transfer to serving platter.

BAKED BOHÇA WITH WALNUTS

Ingredients:
4 cups flour
4 eggs
5 tablespoons margarine or butter
100 grams (3.2 oz) walnuts
Syrup:
3 cups sugar
3-1/2 cups water
2 tablespoons lemon juice

1. Melt margarine. Sift flour into a bowl and open a hole in the center. Pour in the margarine, 1 cup water and eggs. Work into a soft dough. Set aside for 20 minutes.

2. Divide dough into 3 parts and roll out. Oil the top of each part. Stack the 3 one on top of the other. Cut into squares. Roll out each square about 1/2 cm thick, place a walnut in the middle, and form a "bag" (bohça) by pressing opposite corners together above the center. Place the bags on a baking plan.

3. Brush each one with egg. Bake in a preheated medium oven for 45 minutes. Remove and pour cold syrup over them.

Syrup: Put water to boil and add sugar, stirring until sugar is melted. Boil 10 minutes more. Just before removing from stove, add lemon juice. Set aside to cool.

SAMAKOL CAKE IN SYRUP

Ingredients:

1 kilogram milk
250 grams (1/2 lb) margarine
8 eggs
4 cups flour
Syrup:
1 kilogram (2 lb) sugar
just enough water to cover

1. Melt margarine. Add milk and stir. Place on high flame and add flour, stirring constantly and rapidly with a wooden spoon. Continue stirring until the flour no longer sticks to the spoon.

2. Remove from heat. When cooled, add eggs one at a time.

3. Thoroughly mix dough and form in desired shape. Place on a greased baking pan and bake until light brown. Remove from oven and pour cooled syrup over it. After syrup is absorbed, cake is ready to serve.

Syrup: Put water to boil and add sugar, stirring until sugar is melted. Boil 10 minutes more. Set aside to cool.

BOSNIAN DESSERT (SULPITA)

Ingredients:

6 eggs
6 tablespoons flour
1/2 liter (about 2 cups) milk
1/2 packet baking powder
(2 teaspoons)
Syrup:
3 cups sugar
3 cups water

1. Beat eggs. Add flour, baking powder and milk. Mix well and add eggs. Mix again. Grease a square glass baking dish with butter and pour in the batter. Bake in a preheated 170 (350) oven until brown.

2. Remove from oven and pour warm syrup on top.

Syrup: Put water to boil and add sugar, stirring until sugar is melted. Boil 10 minutes more. Set aside to cool.

HAZLENUT DESSERT

Ingredients:

1 tablespoon hazelnut pieces
1 egg
2 tablespoons olive oil
2 tablespoons margarine
2 tablespoons yoghurt
baking powder
flour as needed
Syrup:
3 cups sugar, 4 cups water

1. Mix all ingredients well and form into a stiff dough. Place in a greased glass baking pan and bake in the oven until lightly browned.

2. Remove from oven and pour cold syrup over it. When syrup is absorbed it is ready to serve.

BULLSEYE ROLLS

Ingredients:

2 eggs
1 teaspoon dry yeast
1 cup oil
1/2 cup milk
1/2 cup yoghurt
1 teaspoon vinegar
1 teaspoon crushed walnuts
flour as needed
Syrup:
3-1/2 cups sugar
2-1/2 cups water

1. Warm milk and add yeast. Stir. In another bowl mix egg, oil, yoghurt and vinegar. Add enough dough to form a soft dough and allow to set for 1/2 hour.

2. Divide dough into four parts. Roll out each part thin on a board. Sprinkle walnuts on top and roll up each part. Cut rolls into finger width slices. Place cut side up on an oiled baking pan and brown in the oven. Remove from oven and pour cold syrup over them. Sprinkle coconut on top.

Syrup: Bring sugar and water to a boil and, stirring occasionally, cook 10 minutes longer. Remove from heat and set aside to cool.

BOSNIAN COOKIES

Ingredients:
500 grams (1lb) margarine or part margarine,
part butter
1/3 cups sugar, 1 egg
1/3 cup strained yoghurt
1/3 teaspoon soda
flour as needed
100 grams walnut pieces

1. Melt margarine. Put in freezer. After it freezes remove and set until room temperature. Strain to remove the sediments.

2. Beat butter and sugar in a mixer until white. Add the egg and yoghurt, continuing to beat. Mix soda and flour and add, mixing until a dough is formed. Knead, adding crushed walnuts.

3. Divide dough into egg-sized pieces and form into ovals with the hands. Gently flatten each one onto the rough side of a grater to pick up the pattern. Place on a greased baking pan and place in a 150C (300F) oven until brown. Remove from oven and pour a warm syrup over them.

SIIRT İMÇERKET

Ingredients:

2 cups flour
1/3 cup water
1 walnut-size chunk margarine +
125 grams (1/2 lb) margarine
frying oil
1/3 teaspoon soda, dash of salt
1/3 cup powdered or granulated
sugar

1. Melt chunk of margarine and add 1/3 cup warm water

2. Mix flour, soda and salt. Add to margarine water and form a soft dough. Divide dough into four equal parts. Roll out each part to a thin dough. Melt 1/2 lb margarine. Spread some of it on each dough part.

3. Handle each piece of dough separately: First fold each end toward the middle. Add margarine. Then fold opposite corners inward and add margarine. Fold the short ends toward the middle and add margarine. Fold over once more. Set aside. Repeat with the other three pieces.

4. Return to the first one and roll out into a 25+ cm (10 in) square. Cut square into 4 squares. Fry squares in hot oil. Sprinkle sugar on them while hot. Repeat with the other three pieces.

Oven egg custard

MUTTON NECK DESSERT
(Award-winning recipe from Izmir)

Ingredients:

1 fresh mutton neck
750 grams (1-1/2 lb) sugar
200 grams (6.4 oz) each of dried
apricots and dried plums

1. Place neck in cold water. Change water frequently over a 24-hour period. Bring to a boil and cook until well done. Remove nerve tissue and fat. Cut remaining meat very thinly in string-like strips and place in a pot. Set to boil with sugar and 1/2 cup water.

2. Wash apricots and plums twice in hot water and add to the meat pot.

3. Boil on high flame until the fruit is soft. Transfer to a serving plate and garnish with pine nuts and cinnamon. Serve warm.

BALIKESİR HOŞMERIM DESSERT

Ingredients:

1 kilogram (2 lb) fresh saltless
white cheese
3 tablespoons flour
1 cup sugar
grated rind of 1 orange or lemon

1. Soften cheese with a fork and place in a pan. Melt while stirring over a high flame. Set aside.

2. In another pan heat the flour until light brown. Add orange or lemon rind and sugar to the flour and mix well. Return cheese pan to the stove and add flour mixture. Blend well, remove from heat and cover with lid for 10 minutes before serving.

SWEET CHEESE DESSERT

Ingredients:

1 kilogram (2 lb) fresh saltless
white cheese
3 cups sugar
2 cups water

Prepare syrup with sugar and water. Melt cheese in a pan over a high flame. Add syrup and stir until blended. Serve hot.

SWEET EGGS

Ingredients:

125 grams (1/2 lb) margarine
2 cups flour
3 eggs
1 cup grape molasses (pekmez)
(see recipe, p. 449)

Brown flour in the margarine and break eggs on top. When eggs are cooked add hot molasses. Serve hot.

Note: *A thick sugar syrup may be substituted for the molasses.*

ROSE DESSERT

Ingredients:

1 egg

1 cup oil

3-4 tablespoons yoghurt

baking powder

flour as needed

walnut halves

Syrup:

3-1/2 cups sugar

3-1/2 cups water

lemon

1. Put egg, oil and yoghurt in a large bowl and mix. Add baking powder and flour and form a soft dough. Allow to set in refrigerator for 1/2 hour.

2. Roll out dough 1/2 cm thick. Cut out circles with a 10 cm (4 in) wide cup or bowl. Cut four 1 cm incisions in each circle. Place a walnut half in the center of each circle. Draw together sides to form a rose. Place on a greased oven pan and bake until brown in a 200 (400) oven. Remove from oven and pour cold syrup over it.

Syrup: Put water to boil and add sugar, stirring until sugar is melted. Boil 10 minutes more. Just before removing from stove, add lemon juice. Set aside to cool.

OVEN EGG CUSTARD

Ingredients:

1 kilogram (liter) whole milk

1-1/2 cups sugar

5 eggs

1 packet (5 grams) dry vanilla

(1/4 teaspoon liquid)

1. Boil milk. Add sugar and stir until melted. Set aside to cool.

2. Place eggs in a deep bowl and beat with electric mixer or wire whip.

3. Add vanilla and cooled milk mixture to the eggs and mix well. Pour into an ungreased glass pan.

4. Place pan in a larger pan filled with 2 fingers of water. Place in a 170C (350F) preheated oven. Immediately turn down to 150C (300F). Bake until light brown. Remove and chill before serving.

Notes: *1. Custard may be poured into individual glass baking cups before placing in pan of water. If baked in a pan, cut portions with a spatula and transfer to individual serving dishes.*

2. This is a light dessert.

MOLASSES DESSERT

Ingredients:

1 kilogram (2 lb) flour
3 cups grape molasses (pekmez)
1-1/4 cups oil
1 cup sugar
dash of salt
1 cup walnut pieces

1. Make dough with the flour, salt, oil and warm water. Roll out 1 cm thick. Cut into 3 cm squares.

2. Allow to dry a little on the board or on a clean cloth.

3. Put to the boil: 1cup oil, 3 cups molasses, 1 cup sugar and 1 cup water. Add dough pieces to the boiling mixture. Stir with a slotted spoon and cook until the flour smell is gone.

4. Drain and place on a serving plate. Sprinkle walnuts on top.

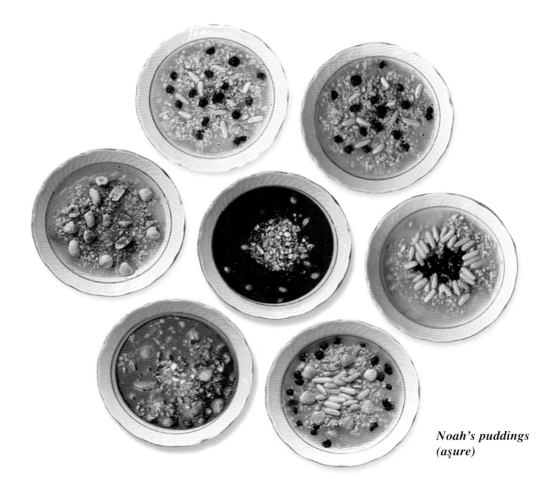

*Noah's puddings
(aşure)*

BREADS AND BOUREKS

CONTENTS

CREPES

PRACTICAL RECOMMENDATIONS

1. Flour and other ingredients mixed with it should be fresh.

2. To test the heartiness of the flour, make a small piece of dough with some flour and water. If the dough keeps splitting apart the flour is not hearty. In this situation it is helpful to add 2-3 drops of lemon juice to the dough.

3. It is important to let the dough set. It will roll more easily and be much easier to work with.

4. Preheat the oven on medium setting before baking boureks, cakes and cookies.

5. Yeast is used mainly for breads and rolls.

6. It is important to soften yeast in warm water or milk.

7. There are two ways to apply the yeast to the dough, and both ways allow the dough to set and rise:

a. Prepare dough and open a pool in the center. Place yeast in the center and warm milk or water. Add a little flour and form a sticky dough. Spread flour over the top and allow to set. After the yeast has penetrated the dough, add other ingredients and more flour until desired consistency.

b. Put the yeast in warm water or milk and allow to set for 10 minutes. Add remaining ingredients and flour and form the dough.

8. Before adding lemon juice, baking powder or soda, always mix it with the flour first, then add flour mixture.

9. For best results in making cakes and cookies, have shortening at room temperature before use (except when the recipe calls for cutting the shortening into the flour with a knife).

10. Eggs will be fluffier when beaten if they are removed from the refrigerator 1-2 hours before use.

11. After the flour has been added, other ingredients are blended in without much beating.

12. Cake batter should be the consistency of fresh, smooth yoghurt.

13. Raised doughs in recipes such as Vizier's Fingers should be the consistency of very thick yoghurt.

14. Pastry dough for noodle and bourek recipes should be stiffer than the ear lobe.

15. Dough for cookies formed with a cutter should be stiff.

16. Yeast bread doughs should be softer than the ear lobe.

17. Creamy doughs used in desserts, such as lady's navel (hanım göbeği), have to be softer than the ear lobe.

BOUREK ROLLS

Ingredients:

4 large sheets (paper-thin) phyllo dough (yufka)
1/2 cup oil
1/2 cup milk
1 egg
Filling:
3 potatoes, 1 onion
salt, black pepper

1. **Filling:** Peel and wash potatoes and onion. Cut onion in thin slices and grate potatoes. Brown them in a little oil. Stir in salt and pepper.

2. Mix milk and oil and spread out 3 phyllo sheets. Coat each one with the mixture and stack

them. Spread filling on top. Coat the 4th phyllo sheet with the mixture and place it over the filling.

3. Roll the stack tightly. Cut in finger-wide slices and place on a greased oven pan. Break the egg into the remaining milk-oil mixture and mix well. Pour over the boureks and bake until light brown.

SOUFFLE

Ingredients:
2 large sheets
phyllo dough
(yufka)
3 eggs
2 cups milk
1/3 cup oil
100 grams (3.2 oz)
white cheese or
mixture of white
and kashar

1.   Trim
phyllo leaves
into   neat
square sheets of equal size and stack. Mix other ingredients well and pour
over the leaves. Grate cheese and spread over the top.

2. Place on a greased glass oven pan and bake until light brown. Serve
hot.

SOYBEAN OIL BOUREK

Ingredients:
6 large sheets phyllo dough
1 cup soybean oil
2 cups green lentils
1 onion
2 tablespoons tomato paste
reyhan (a type of basil)
black pepper, salt, red pepper
flakes
2 tablespoons shortening

1. Wash lentils and boil in 3
cups water until soft. Add hot
water if needed to complete
cooking.

2. Slice onion thinly and saute until lightly browned. Add tomato paste and cook a little more. Add cooked lentils, then salt, basil, black pepper and red pepper. When cooked well set aside to cool.

3. Spread the sheets on a large board and spread oil all over them. Cut the sheets into 4's, then each piece into 2. Put a spoonful of filling in the wider place on each piece. Roll it cigarette style.

4. Place boureks on an oiled baking pan and bake until light brown.

PHYLLO BOUREK

Ingredients:

1 kilogram (2 lb) phyllo dough
3 eggs
2 cups milk
250 grams (1/2 lb) margarine, salt

1. Stack on a board all the dough sheets one on top of the other. Roll them together into a large roll.

2. Cut into one-finger wide slices.

3. Melt margarine and mix with milk, egg and salt. Spread this mixture over the boureks, place them on a greased oven pan and bake until done.

Note: *No filling is called for here but it may be added as desired.*

SQUASH BOUREK

Ingredients:

4 sheets phyllo dough
3 eggs
125 grams (1/2 lb) margarine
1 bottle plain soda water
Filling:
4 zucchini squash, 1 egg
1 heaping cup grated cheese
1/2 bunch parsley
1/2 bunch dill

1. Filling: Peel and grate zucchinis. Mix together well: cheese, 1 egg and minced herbs. Add to zucchini.

2. Grease an oven pan. Lay 2 phyllo sheets 1 on top of the other on the pan, pinching them at the edges to fit. Spread the filling all over the dough. Lay remaining 2 sheets over the top. Cut in slices as desired.

2. Melt margarine and add 3 eggs and soda. Beat well. Pour over the dough. Allow to set in refrigerator for one hour. Remove and bake in a hot oven.

PAN BOUREK

Ingredients:

3 sheets phyllo dough
1/3 cup oil
scant 1/3 cup water or milk
2 eggs
Filling:
a small chunk of white or kashar
cheese
1/2 bunch parsley

1. Put half the oil in a frying pan and tip to coat all surfaces well.

2. Cut off the thick outer edges of two of the dough sheets. Place one of these two sheets in the pan. Reserve the other one close by.

3. Mix remaining oil, eggs and water or milk. Grate the cheese. Spoon two tablespoons of this mixture over the dough in the pan. Place 1 uncut dough sheets lightly on top, pinching at the edges of the dough to make it. Mix together the minced parsley and cheese and spread the mixture over the dough. Place the other uncut dough sheet lightly on top.

4. Pour remaining oil and egg mixture over the top and place the remaining (cut edges) dough sheet on top. Do not add more oil. Cover pan and place over a high flame until the bottom browns slightly.

5. Use a spatula to lift and check the bottom. Serve hot.

Note: *A different filling may be used with this bourek.*

WALNUT-MEAT BOUREK

Ingredients:

2 large phyllo leaves
2 eggs
1 small onion
100 grams (3.2 oz) ground meat
1/3 cup walnuts, salt
black pepper
fine bread crumbs
1 tablespoon shortening
1 tablespoon cracked wheat
2 tablespoons water

1. Saute onion and meat in oil. Add wheat and water and cook over a low flame until water is absorbed. Add walnuts, salt and pepper.

2. Lay the sheets on top of each other and cut into 12 equal parts. Spoon filling onto each piece and roll it cigarette style.

3. Break two eggs in a bowl and beat. Dip boureks in the egg, then the bread crumbs. Place boureks on a greased oven pan (not touching).

4. Bake until light brown.

SPINACH BOUREK

Ingredients:

500 grams (1 lb) phyllo sheets
250 grams (1/2 lb) spinach (kale
or leeks may be used)
100 grams white cheese
salt, black pepper
1/3 cup oil, 1 egg yolk

1. Cut dough sheets into 4 equal parts and brush oil lightly on all of them.

2. Chop spinach finely and grate cheese. Mix together and place some on each piece of dough. Roll up cigarette style. Place on oiled pan.

3. Beat yolk with 1 teaspoon oil. Spread over boureks. Bake until golden brown.

Note: *When removing boureks from the oven a few drops of water may be sprinkled over them and then covered in order to soften them.*

PITTA

Ingredients:

2 cups milk

1/3 cup oil

1 cake yeast

salt, 1/3 cup sugar

flour as needed

topping as desired, 1 egg yolk

1. Warm milk slightly and add yeast and sugar. Allow to set awhile.

2. When yeast is raised add salt and as much flour as needed to form a dough soft as an earlobe.

3. Divide into pieces of desired size and roll out on a floured board 1 cm thick. Add toppings. Place on a greased pan. Beat egg yolk a little and spread on top. Bake until light brown.

Notes:

1. Toppings: ground meat, chopped onions, peppers, tomatoes, parsley etc. may be mixed and added along with salt and black pepper.

2. Grated cheese, parsley and black pepper can be used.

3. Cooked lentils, chopped onions, salt and black pepper can be used.

4. Just grated kashar cheese may also be a topping.

ERZURUM TATAR BOUREK

Ingredients:
1 kilogram (2 lb) flour
3-1/2 cups water, salt
1 egg
Topping:
250 grams (1/2 lb) ground meat
500 grams (1 lb) yoghurt
red pepper flakes
3-4 cloves garlic

1. Make a stiff dough with the flour, salt, egg and water and divide into 4 or 5 parts.

2. Roll out the pieces 1 cm thick. Cut in strips 2 fingers wide or as wide as desired.

3. Bring water to the boil and add salt. Add dough strips to boiling water. When they have floated to the top, allow to come to full boil once or twice more. Drain and place on a serving platter.

4. On top of the boiled boureks spread garlic yoghurt that has been prepared earlier.

5. Saute meat lightly in oil and spread over the yoghurt. Sprinkle red pepper on top and serve hot.

KADAYIF BOUREK*

Ingredients:
500 grams (1 lb) tel kadayif *
2 cups milk
3-4 eggs
1/3 cup oil
100 grams (3.2 oz) kashar cheese
100 grams sausage

1. Spread out half of the kadayif in a greased oven pan. Put thin slices of cheese and sausage on top and cover with remaining kadayif.

2. Beat together milk, egg and oil and pour over the pan. Bake in oven until light brown.

Note: *When removing from oven sprinkle a little water on top to soften it if desired.*

* Tel kadayif is found in Turkish grocery stores, usually in 200 gram packages. It consists of very thin, wire-like dried wheat fiber formed in large flat rounds.

ROLLED BOUREK (DIZMANA)

Ingredients:
2 pieces of baking dough
filling as desired

1. Press dough out flat as much as possible. Place filling in the center and roll up (not too tight).

2. Cut 2 cm wide slices and place on a greased oven pan. Bake.

BOSNIAN BOUREK

Ingredients:

1 kilogram (2 lb) flour, salt
warm water, 1/2 cup oil
1/2 cup shortening

1. Make a soft dough with the flour, salt and warm water. Place a damp cloth over the bowl and allow to set 10-15 minutes.

2. While dough is setting knead once or twice and replace the cloth over the bowl.

3. Divide dough into 30 pieces. Roll each piece out about 8 cm (3 in) in diameter.

4. Melt shortening and mix with oil. Dip each dough piece in the oil. Take two pieces and stack one on top of the other. With the fingers press the edges all around the two pieces to increase the size as much as possible.

5. Place on a board. Follow the same steps for 14 more of the pieces. Stack all of these on top of each other. Roll the stack out until it is the size of a baking pan. Use shortening to grease the pan and place the dough in it. Following the same steps for the remaining 14 pieces, place that dough on top and pinch the two layers together.

6. Pour remaining oil and shortening mixture on top. Place in a preheated 200C (400F) oven and bake until brown.

Note: After removing from oven cover with a newspaper or similar paper and a cloth over that and allow to set.

Various fillings for Bosnian bourek:

1. Mix together well: 3 eggs, 250 grams (1/2 lb) white cheese, butter (or clotted cream), and 3 tablespoons yoghurt.

2. Wash 1 kilogram (2 lb) finely chopped spinach leaves and add salt. Drain slightly. Mix with 100 grams (3.2 oz) cheese, 2 eggs and oil or butter.

3. Mix raw ground meat, chopped onion, black pepper, oil and salt.

4. Grate fresh zucchini. Rinse, add salt, drain slightly. Mix with black pepper, 2 eggs and oil.

5. Trim and wash leeks and slice very thin. Mix with 500 grams (1lb) chopped onions and a little oil. Add salt, black pepper, 2 eggs and a little butter.

YEAST BREAD

Ingredients:

1/2 liter (2 cups) milk
250 grams (1/2 lb) margarine
1 teaspoon sugar
1 yeast cake
salt
flour as needed
1 egg

1. Place yeast and sugar in 1 cup warm milk and set aside until the yeast rises.

2. Mix yeast with remaining milk, salt and melted margarine. Add enough flour to make a soft dough (soft as an earlobe). Allow dough to rise.

3. Roll up the dough and cut the thick roll into slices of desired width. Place on greased pan. Eat egg and spread on top. Sprinkle seeds on top if desired.

Note: *If desired add a filling. Serve with cheese.*

WATER BOUREK

Ingredients:

1 kilogram (2 lb) flour
8 eggs
400 grams (13 oz)
cheese or ground meat
1 bunch parsley
If meat is used:
1 onion
1 cup shortening or oil
salt, black pepper

Filling alternatives:

1. Saute chopped onion and meat in 2 tablespoons oil. Mince parsley and add. Stir in salt and black pepper.

2. Grate cheese. Add minced parsley and mix well.

Bourek:

1. Break eggs into a deep bowl. Add 1/3 cup water and a pinch of salt and beat. Add flour and knead into a stiff dough. Take 1/3 teaspoon oil in the hand and knead once more. Place a damp cloth over the bowl and allow to set for 1/2 hour.

2. Place dough on a large floured board and divide into 10 pieces. Roll all the pieces out thin (2-3 mm). Place a clean cloth over them. From time to time turn them over. When the pieces dry a little and lose their stickiness, stack them all one on top of the other.

3. Fill two large pots with cold water. Add salt to one of the pots and bring to a boil. If desired, the dough can be cut into 4's for easier han-dling. With both hands pick up one piece of the dough at a time and plunge it into the boiling water. (If done in one quick motion the dough will hold and not fall apart.) While boiling turn once with a large slotted spoon. When the dough rises to the top it is done.

4. Remove the cooked piece of dough with the aid of the slotted

spoon, let it drain a little and place in the pot of cold water. Remove with hands and drain a little. Place on a clean cloth. Repeat until all the dough has been cooked.

5. Place the first piece on a greased oven pan. Use the fingers to form some puckers in the dough so that it is not perfectly flat. Brush the dough with oil. Repeat this with each piece, making a stack. If there are more than 10 layers the filling may be added after every third or fourth layer, or just add it at the middle.

6. Bake until brown and sizzling. Allow to cool slightly, slice in squares and serve.

SAVOURY CREAM BOUREK

Ingredients:

1/2 cup milk
1 cup cream
250 grams (1/2 lb) ground meat
1 onion
2 garlic cloves
1 tablespoon oil
1 carrot
1/3 cup peas (canned or fresh)
oregano, basil
walnuts
black pepper, salt
1/3 cup dried breadcrumbs

Dough:

2 eggs (one of the yolks for the top of the bourek)
125 grams (1/4 lb) shortening
water, flour as needed

1. Parboil peas if fresh. Saute thin-sliced onion in oil. Crush garlic and add. Add ground meat and saute a little more. Cut carrot in tiny cubes. Add carrots, peas, oregano, basil salt, pepper and some of the walnuts and stir well. Add milk, cream and breadcrumbs and stir a little more. Remove from heat and set aside to cool.

2. Mix 1 egg and 1 egg white in a bowl with shortening and salt. Add flour and water to make a dough (a little stiffer than the ear lobe). Divide into 1 smaller and 1 larger part. Roll out the larger part to slightly larger dimensions than the baking pan and lay the dough in the pan. Spread filling all over it.

3. Roll out the smaller part and lay on top so it covers the filling. Cut off any dough that hangs over the edges. Roll it out and cut, using a cookie cutter. Mix together the egg yolk and 1 teaspoon oil and spread over the top of the dough. Arrange the little cut pieces on top. Bake in a medium oven until brown.

ALBANIAN BOUREK

Ingredients:

1/2 cup yoghurt
1/2 cup oil, 1 cup water
250 grams (1/2 lb) margarine
1 egg, salt
1/3 teaspoon baking powder
flour as needed
1 egg yolk
Filling: *250 grams cheese*

1. Mix together well: yoghurt, oil, water, salt and egg. Mix baking powder with flour and add. Use enough flour to form a soft dough (earlobe soft).

2. Divide dough into 20 pieces and roll out each piece to 10 cm (4 in) diameter. Brush oil on each one, making 2 stacks of 10 pieces.

3. Roll out one stack very thin. Grate the cheese and spread over the dough. Roll out second stack and lay on top. Place in a baking pan. Beat the egg yolk and spread over the top. Bake in a hot oven.

COVERED BOUREK

Ingredients:

1 kilogram (2 lb) flour
2-1/2 cups water
1 cup oil
1 egg, salt

Filling:
500 grams ground meat
2 onions, 2 tablespoons shortening
black pepper, red pepper flakes,
salt

1. Saute finely-chopped onion and ground meat in oil. Add salt, black pepper, red pepper and stir.

2. Make a stiff dough with flour, salt, egg and water. Divide into 4 parts and roll out each part to 20 cm (8 in). Oil each layer and stack them.

3. Later, again roll out each layer as wide as possible and stack. Place a clean cloth over them.

4. When the dough has raised spread the filling evenly over the dough and form an even roll and pinch the ends to close. Place on a greased oven pan. Lift one end and turn the dough inward until it is in the shape of a spiral. Bake until brown.

YEAST TWISTS (AÇMA)

Ingredients:
3 cups hot milk
1 cup oil
2 eggs
6 tablespoons sugar
1 teaspoon salt
1 yeast cake
1 kilogram (2 lb) flour
seeds

1. Separate the egg yolks. Beat whites a little and mix with milk, oil, sugar, salt, yeast and flour. Warm a steel pan, place dough inside and put lid on or put in a warm place covered with a cloth. Set aside to allow dough to rise.

2. Divide raised dough into egg-sized pieces. Cut each piece in half and form 15 cm (6 in) long pieces. Make a braid with two of the pieces and brings the ends together. Place the round rolls on a greased oven pan. Brush egg yolk on them and sprinkle seeds on top. Set to raise for 1/2 hour. Bake in a medium oven.

SESAME SEED RINGS (SİMİT)

Ingredients:
2 tablespoons yoghurt
125 grams (1/4 lb) margarine
2 tablespoons oil
1 egg yolk
2 tablespoons sesame seeds
flour, salt, soda

1. Mix salt and soda with the flour, then cut margarine into the flour. Add yoghurt, and oil. Knead to a soft dough.

2. Form dough in thick rings. Coat each one with egg yolk and sesame seeds. Bake in a medium oven.

BAKING POWDER RINGS

Ingredients:
500 grams (1 lb)
shortening
2 egg yolks
2 tablespoons sugar
3 tablespoons yoghurt
2 tablespoons vinegar
1/3 teaspoon baking
powder
flour as needed

Mix together well in a deep bowl: oil, egg yolks, sugar, yoghurt, vinegar and baking powder. Add flour and knead to a soft dough. Divide into parts as desired, roll by hand into thick cylindrical strips and join the ends to make rings. Place on a greased oven pan and bake in a hot oven.

Note: *If desired, before placing on the baking pan, dip rings in egg white and coat with sesame seeds.*

KANDIL RINGS

Ingredients:
1/3 teaspoon mahaleb powder
(mahlep)
250 grams (1/2 lb) margarine (at
room temperature)
1/2 cup yoghurt
1/3 cup oil
1 egg, salt, flour as needed
10 grams baking powder
(4 teaspoons)
1/4 cup sesame seeds

1. Separate the egg. Mix together in a deep bowl: margarine, oil, yoghurt, mahaleb and egg yolk. Mix baking powder and salt with flour and add. Mix and knead to a soft dough.

2. Divide into pieces a little larger than walnuts. Roll into thin cylindrical strips and join the ends to make rings. Dip in egg white and coat with sesame seeds. Place on a greased pan and bake in a medium oven until light brown.

LENTIL BOUREKS

Ingredients:

500 grams (1 lb) flour
300 grams (11.2 oz) lentils
250 grams (1/2 lb) margarine
1 cup oil, salt
black pepper, water

1. Wash and cook lentils until done and no water remains. Remove from heat and add salt and pepper.

2. Make a dough with flour, water and salt. Divide dough into two balls and set aside for 15 minutes.

3. Melt margarine, add oil. Allow to cool.

4. Roll out each piece of dough to 30 cm (12 in) diameter. Coat them in 3-4 tablespoons of the cooled oil mixture and stack one on top of the other. Pinch the borders all around. Slip hands under the middle of dough, lift and twirl around so that the dough spreads out as much as possible Again coat them in oil. Bring edges together from opposite sides to form a bag. Set in refrigerator for 10 minutes.

5. Place on floured board and roll out again. Cut into 15 cm (6 in) squares. Spoon lentils into the middle of each square. Join edges together to close up. Place on a greased oven pan and bake until light brown.

PASTRY SHELLS (PEKSİMET)

Ingredients:

250 grams (1/2 lb) margarine
2 eggs
1 kilogram (2 lb) flour
1 kilogram milk
1 packet dry yeast
salt

1. Melt yeast in warm milk.

2. Melt margarine. Add it to yeast and milk, along with salt and eggs. Add flour and form a dough a little stiffer than the ear lobe.

3. When mixed well, set aside to rise. The dough is ready if, when pressed with a fist, it rises up again.

4. Divide into pieces larger than a fist. Press the fist into each piece to form a pool. Press the sides higher to form a deep "pot". Place on a greased oven pan. Spread oil on them and bake until light brown.

TALAŞ BOUREK

Ingredients:

500 grams (1 lb) flour
300 grams (11.2 oz) margarine
2/3 teaspoon salt
4-5 drops lemon juice
a scant cup of water

Filling:

1 onion
500 grams (1 lb) boneless lamb cut into very thin slices
2 tablespoons shortening
1/2 bunch parsley
1/3 cup cooked peas
1 cooked carrot
salt, black pepper

1. Spread flour on the board and open a hole in the middle. Add salt, lemon juice and water and work into a dough. Cover with a damp cloth and allow to set for 20 minutes.

2. Roll out dough 2 cm thick. Place the margarine in the center of the dough. Close up like a bag from four sides. Roll out again to 4 cm thick. Place a damp cloth over it and allow to set for 20 minutes.

3. Roll out to 3 cm thickness. Divide dough in two and stack. Cover with a damp cloth and place in refrigerator for 1/2 hour.

4. Place dough again on the board and roll out stacked dough to 1 cm thickness. Cut into 10 cm (4 in) squares.

5. Spoon filling into center of each square and close up. Turn each one upside down on a greased oven pan. Coat the top of each one with egg yolk. Bake in a hot oven.

Filling: Slice onion thin and saute until light brown. Add lamb and saute a little more. When the meat juices come out add carrots, peas, salt, pepper and minced parsley. Mix well.

Notes: 1. Talaş bourek can also be made with ready phyllo dough sheets (yufka). Coat squares of the dough all over with melted shortening. Fold over to make rectangles and again coat with oil. Fold again, making squares. Cut into the middle of each of the 4 sides. Put some filling on each square. Close up like bags. Turn upside down on a greased oven pan and coat the tops with egg yolk. Bake in a hot oven.

2. Fried eggplant slices can also be used as filling.

ARM BOUREK No. 1

Ingredients:

3 prepared phyllo dough sheets (yufka)
1 cup milk
3 eggs
125 grams (1/4 lb) margarine

Filling:

150 grams (4.8 oz) white cheese or ground meat
1/2 bunch parsley

1. Beat eggs well with the milk. Melt margarine and add. Spread evenly all over the surface of each yufka. Place filling on top of each one.

2. Form them in cylindrical rolls.

Place one in the center of a greased oven pan. Join the end of the second one to the first and the third to the second and arrange as an arm in a spiral. Spread egg yolk over the bourek and bake until light brown.

Talaş Bourek

ARM BOUREK No.2

Ingredients:
flat bourek dough
oil
bourek filling

1. Divide the dough into 5 parts. Roll out to 30 cm (12 in) diameter.
2. Coat with oil. Slip hand under the middle of one dough part, lift and twirl around so that the dough spreads out as much as possible. Coat with oil and put some filling on one end. Roll up gently.
3. Place on a greased oven pan, arranging as a curved arm. Next to it place the other 4 parts all handled the same way. Bake in a hot oven.

Note: *Any of the fillings in the flat bourek recipes may be used.*

BREAD BRAID

Ingredients:
1 cup oil
250 grams (1/4 lb) margarine
1 cup yoghurt
1 egg
1/3 teaspoon mahaleb powder (mahlep)
flour as needed, salt
sesame seeds

1. Separate egg. Mix together well in a bowl: oil, margarine, yoghurt, egg white, mahaleb and salt. Add enough flour to make a soft dough. Set aside until filling is ready.
2. Prepare a filling of cheese and parsley; onion and ground meat; or onion and potatoes etc.

3. Divide dough into 2 parts. Roll out equal rectangular pieces of 1cm thickness. (The dough is oily so the shape may need to be adjusted a little by hand.)

4. Spread filling to cover the middle (1/3) of each rectangle. Cut incisions at an angle (oblique) in the edges of the dough every 2 cm around all 4 sides. Lift one end from one side and its opposite and pinch them together above the filling. Continue doing this the full length of the rectangles. Brush tops with egg yolk and sprinkle on sesame seeds on top. Place the 2 braids on a greased oven pan and bake in a medium oven until lightly browned all over.

CORN BREAD

Ingredients:

4 cups finely ground corn meal
1/3 teaspoon soda or 1/2 yeast cake
1/3 teaspoon salt
warm water

1. Sift flour. Mix all ingredients and form a dough. If yeast is used, allow to rise once. Place on a greased oven pan.

2. Bake in a preheated hot oven and bake until lightly browned.

SALTY YOGHURT CAKE

Ingredients:

3 eggs
1 cup yoghurt
1 cup oil or 250 grams (1/2 lb) margarine
3-1/2 cups flour
150 grams (4.8 oz) white cheese
fresh dill
baking powder, salt

1. Beat eggs and yoghurt. Add grated cheese, oil and minced dill. Combine flour, baking powder and salt and add to mixture. Blend well.

2. Pour in a greased pan and bake in a medium oven.

KAYSERİ FLATBREAD

Ingredients:

Enough dough for 2 breads (see yeast bread recipe)
250 grams ground meat
2 onions
1/2 bunch parsley, salt
black pepper, ground red pepper
1 tablespoon tomato paste
250 grams (about 2 cups) yoghurt
3 garlic cloves, 2 tablespoons oil

1. Roll out layers of thin dough to about a 30 cm (12 in) diameter circle and 1/2 cm thick. Heat a greased teflon pan and brown each one lightly on both sides. Lay the flat breads on a large round pan.

2. Saute ground meat and onions in oil. When almost done add salt and black pepper.

3. Spoon some of the meat mixture onto each flat bread and spread it out. Stack up all the filled flat bread layers.

4. Put garlic yoghurt on top. Fry red pepper in a little oil and drizzle over the top.

CORNMEAL SQUASH BOUREK (TİKVANİK)

Ingredients:

1-1/2 cups corn meal
3 zucchini squashes (courgettes)
1 cup milk
1/2 cup oil
100 grams (3.2 oz) white cheese
3 eggs
baking powder, a little salt
(any cream topped from the milk or the yoghurt, if available at home)

1. Mix together well: milk, oil and eggs.

2. Scrape and grate squashes and add to mixture. Add remaining ingredients and mix well. (The cream if available makes it richer.) Pour in a glass baking dish and place in a hot oven until lightly browned.

BOSNIAN LEEK BOUREK (PRAŞNAK)

Use leeks in place of squash in the preceding cornmeal squash bourek recipe. Slice leeks very thin.

BOSNIAN SPINACH BOUREK (ZELANIK)

Ingredients:

3-1/2 cups corn meal
500 grams (1 lb) spinach
1 cup milk
1/2 cup oil
100 grams (3.2 oz) white cheese
2 eggs
baking powder, a little salt
(any cream topped from the milk or the yoghurt, if available at home)
1 egg
1 tablespoon oil
1 tablespoon yoghurt

1. Mix milk, oil and 2 eggs together well. Add cream if desired. Combine cornmeal, salt and baking powder, then add to the mixture and form a dough. Divide the dough into two parts and roll out.

2. Sort spinach and wash well. Chop finely. Mix spinach and cheese together well.

3. Place one sheet of dough on a greased oven pan and spread the spinach mixture over it.

Bosnian spinach bourek

4. Place other dough on top. To arrange it more easily sprinkle a little water on the spinach. Bake in a hot oven until lightly browned. The bourek will crack in the oven. To close the cracks, mix 1 egg with 1 tablespoon each of oil and yoghurt and pour this over the bourek and continue to brown a little more. Serve hot.

Note: *Water may be substituted for the milk in this recipe.*

FORKS (ÇATAL)

Ingredients
250 grams (1/2 lb) margarine
1/4 cup oil
1/4 cup sugar
1 cup yoghurt
1/3 teaspoon salt
2 tablespoons mahaleb powder (mahlep)
10 grams baking powder (4 teaspoons)
seeds, flour as needed

1. Margarine should be at room temperature. Mix together margarine, oil, sugar, yoghurt and salt. Add mahaleb. Mix baking powder and flour together and add to mixture. Work into a soft dough.

2. Form dough into "forks" or as desired. Grease a pan with margarine and place forks on it. Sprinkle sesame or other type pastry seeds on them and bake until browned all over.

VEGETABLE STUFFED PHYLLO

Ingredients:

3 large, round phyllo pastry sheets (yufka)
200 grams (6.4 oz) fatty ground meat
1 small onion
2 medium sized carrots
1 large potato
black pepper, salt
1 tablespoon tomato paste
1/3 cup oil
1 tablespoon butter
1 cup yoghurt
2 garlic cloves

1. Mix together well: meat, coarsely chopped onions, salt, pepper and tomato paste.

2. Peel and grate potato and carrots separately.

3. Lay one phyllo dough on a board and spread 1/3 of the oil on top. Spread filling evenly over the dough. Lay one dough over the top and spread 1/3 of the oil on top. Spread grated carrot over it and place third dough on top and spread remaining oil and grated potatoes on top. Roll up tightly into a roll. Cut incisions every 2 cm the length of the roll. Place on a greased pan. Brush top with oil and bake in a medium oven.

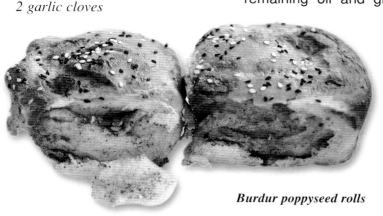

Burdur poppyseed rolls

4. When ready to serve, if desired, top with garlic yoghurt, fry some red pepper in butter and drizzle over the top.

Note: *This recipe can be made without the oil. Mix together ground meat, onion, potato and carrot. Lay half the mixture between the first and second layers of dough and the other half between the second and third layers. Form into a roll, wrap in foil and drop in a pot of boiling water for 15-20 minutes. Drain and remove from foil. Cut in 2 cm slices and serve with garlic yoghurt and fried red pepper on top.*

BURDUR POPPYSEED ROLLS

Ingredients:
1 kilogram (2 lb) flour
1 teaspoon dry yeast
1 teaspoon sugar, salt
1 heaping up poppy seeds
1 heaping up shortening

1. Place flour in a large bowl and open a hole in the middle for the yeast, sugar, salt and enough water to make a soft dough. Cover with a cloth and allow to rise.

2. When the dough has risen divide into two parts. With oil on both hands stretch each piece of dough as much as possible. Spread oil and poppyseeds all over the surface of the dough. Roll up both of them and cut in 3-4 cm long slices. Lay the pieces cut face up on a greased baking pan, spread oil on top and bake.

ERZURUM KETE

Ingredients:
1 cup oil
2 cup water
flour as needed
juice of 1/2 lemon
250 grams margarine or butter
1 egg
Filling *(if desired):*
1 tablespoon oil
2 tablespoons flour

1. Mix oil, shortening, egg, lemon juice, flour and water and form a soft dough. Allow to set at room temperature for one hour.

2. Divide dough into egg size pieces and roll them out 1/2 cm thick.

3. Melt margarine or butter and use to coat the dough pieces liberally. Fold over both ends of each piece so they meet at the middle. Roll out and repeat.

4. Now the pieces are rectangles. Cut them in squares.

5. If filling will be used, place some on each square. Join the corners of each square crosswise to form a little bag. Place them on a greased oven pan. Brush with beaten egg and bake in a hot oven until lightly browned.

Filling: *Heat oil and flour until flour is browned. Cool before using.*

KIRIKKALE TURNOVERS

Ingredients:
2 cups water
flour as needed, salt
Filling:
250 grams (1/2 lb) ground meat
500 grams (1 lb) onions
2-3 small green peppers
2 tablespoons oil
2 tomatoes or 1 tablespoon tomato paste
black pepper, salt
1 bunch parsley

1. Make a soft dough with the flour, water and salt. (Yeast may be used if desired.) Set aside until the filling has been prepared.

2. **Filling:** Saute onion and ground meat a little until light brown. Remove seeds from peppers and slice very thin. Skin the tomatoes, if used, and chop very small. Add peppers, tomatoes or tomato paste, salt and pepper to the meat and cook a little more. Add minced parsley and stir. Remove from heat and allow to cool.

3. Divide dough into egg sized pieces. Place on a floured board and roll out each piece to a 1/2 cm thick round.

4. Place a spoonful of filling on each and fold over to make a half-moon. Heat a teflon skillet and without adding oil brown each side until light brown and serve hot.

ERZURUM ROSE ROLLS

Ingredients:
1 liter milk
1 yeast cake
1 cup shortening
1 cup water
salt
1/3 cup sugar
flour as needed
1 egg

1. Mix together 1 cup warm milk, sugar and yeast. Set aside 5-10 minutes to activate yeast.

2. Separate the egg. Place flour in a bowl and open a hole in the middle. Add yeast mixture, remaining milk, egg white, water and salt. Mix well and form a soft dough. Cover with a cloth and allow to set for 1 hour.

3. Divide dough into egg size pieces. Roll out each piece very thin (2-3 mm). Melt shortening and brush all over the dough pieces. Roll each one into a long thin roll. Wind each piece around to form a rose. Place roses on a greased oven pan. Coat tops with egg yolk and bake in a hot oven until golden brown.

POTATO CRESCENTS

Ingredients:
1 cup yoghurt
1-1/2 cups mixture of margarine or
butter and olive oil
1 egg (separated)
1-1/2 teaspoons baking powder
flour as needed, salt
Filling:
4 medium size potatoes
150 grams (4.8 oz) white cheese
parsley

1. Mix together well the shortening, oil, yoghurt, baking powder and salt. Add flour and form a soft dough.

2. Divide dough into egg size pieces and roll out to 10-12 cm diameter circles.

3. Spoon some filling onto each one and fold to form crescents. Place on a greased oven pan and spread egg yolk over them.

Filling: Boil potatoes whole, cool, peel and grate. Grate cheese or mash with a fork and add. Add chopped parsley and egg white. Mix well.

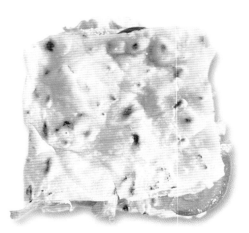

Gözleme varieties

SKILLET FLATBEAD (GÖZLEME)

Ingredients:

500 grams (1 lb) ground meat
5 onions, salt, black pepper
1 kilogram (2 lb) flour
1 teaspoon oil
2 tablespoons margarine or butter

1. Form a soft dough with flour, salt and water.

2. Divide dough into egg size parts and roll out in rounds as thin as possible.

3. Saute ground meat and chopped onions in oil. Add salt and pepper.

4. Spoon some meat filling on each dough piece and fold over. Brown on a flat skillet.

5. Melt margarine (or butter). As each one is browned remove and brush with margarine or dip a fork in melted margarine and spread over it.

MORNING CHEESE ROLLS (POĞAÇA)

Ingredients:

1-1/2 cups milk
1/3 cup oil
250 grams (1/2 lb) margarine
1 yeast cake
1/3 cup yoghurt
dash of salt, 1 teaspoon sugar
flour as needed
1 egg

Filling:

200 grams (6.4 oz) white cheese
1/2 bunch parsley
black pepper

1. Warm milk slightly and add sugar and yeast. Allow to set until yeast is activated.

2. Separate egg. Margarine should be at room temperature. Place flour in a large bowl and open a pool in the center. Add yeast mixture, margarine, oil, egg white, salt and yoghurt. Mix well and add enough flour to form a soft dough. Set aside until the dough rises.

3. Divide dough into parts about the size of two walnuts. Open each one enough to add filling and fold over to form an oval. Place on a greased oven pan and bake in a hot oven until golden brown.

Filling: Grate cheese and mix with minced parsley. Add black pepper and blend well. Or: if desired brown some ground meat and onion a little in oil and mix in the black pepper and minced parsley.

CHEESE ROLLS

Ingredients:

1 cup yoghurt
250 grams (1/2 lb) margarine
juice of 1/2 lemon
10 grams baking powder (4 tea-spoons)
1 tablespoon grated cheese
flour as needed
1 egg yolk, seeds

Filling:

100 grams (3.2 oz) white cheese
1/2 bunch parsley
ground red pepper

1. Mix oil and yoghurt well. Add salt, lemon juice and grated cheese and stir again.

2. Mix baking powder and flour together and add. Mix well and form a soft dough.

3. **Filling:** Grated white cheese and mince parsley. Mix together and add red pepper.

4. Divide dough into egg-sized pieces and round each one to a ball in the hands. Press down on the ball and place a teaspoon of filling in the center. Close up and place on a greased baking pan. Coat tops with egg yolk and seeds. Bake in a hot oven.

MEAT ROLLS

Ingredients:

1 cup yoghurt
250 grams (1/2 lb) margarine
10 grams baking powder
(4 teaspoons)
flour as needed
Filling:
1 onion
150 grams (4.8 oz) ground meat
1/2 bunch parsley, salt
black pepper, 1 tablespoon oil

1. Be sure margarine is at room temperature. Mix well with yoghurt.

2. Add baking powder and flour. Mix and add salt. Form a soft dough.

3. Saute onion and ground meat in the oil. Mince parsley and add. Add salt and pepper and mix well.

4. Divide dough into egg-sized pieces. Form them in a ball and press down. Place a teaspoon of filling in the center, close up and place on a greased oven pan. Bake in a hot oven.

PLAIN ROLLS

Ingredients:

2 prepared yeast doughs
250 grams (1/2 lb) margarine
1 egg yolk

1. Be sure margarine is at room temperature. Mix with dough and knead well.

2. If to be used right away, place in refrigerator for at least one hour. If to be used later place in the freezer and, when ready to use, remove a half hour before using and then knead a little more.

3. Divide dough into pieces, add filling as desired, close and place on a greased oven pan. Coat tops with egg yolk and bake until golden brown.

SKILLET FLATBREAD WITH GROUND MEAT

Ingredients:

1 kilogram (2 lb) phyllo dough
(yufka)
4 eggs
200 grams (6.4 oz) ground meat
2 onions
1/2 bunch parsley
salt, black pepper
2 tablespoons oil

1. Divide dough in two and trim edges to make two rectangles. Place trimmed pieces in the center.

2. Beat an egg with 3 tablespoons of water and spread over the dough.

3. Saute chopped onions a little in oil. Add ground meat. Stir and press down on meat (before juices come out). Add salt, pepper and minced parsley. Mix well and remove from heat. Spread in the center of the dough and fold each end toward the center. Fry in very little oil.

PIZZA WITH GROUND BEEF

Ingredients:
6 tablespoons yoghurt
250 grams (1/2 lb) margarine
3 eggs
baking powder, salt
flour as needed
Topping:
250 grams (1/2 lb) ground meat
2 tomatoes
2-3 small green peppers
1 onion
1 cup grated kashar cheese
Sauce:
3 tablespoons tomato paste
black pepper, oregano. Salt

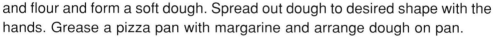

1. Melt margarine. Add yoghurt and eggs and mix well. Add baking powder, salt and flour and form a soft dough. Spread out dough to desired shape with the hands. Grease a pizza pan with margarine and arrange dough on pan.

2. Dilute tomato paste with a little water. Add salt, pepper and oregano. Mix and spread all over the dough with the hands.

3. Mix ground meat with finely chopped onion, a little salt, and pepper. Knead a little and arrange pieces of the mixture on top of the sauce. Skin and either slice thinly or cube the tomatoes. Spread these and chopped peppers on top. Bake 15-20 minutes in a hot oven.

4. Remove from oven and sprinkle grated cheese over it. Return to oven until cheese is slight-

Pizza with toppings

ly browned. Remove from oven, cut in desired size pieces and serve. (Goes well with soft drinks, yoghurt drink or tea.)

Note: *Pizza dough can also be made with simply flour, salt and yeast. If this dough is used, be sure to grease the pan liberally and to add some oil instead of water when diluting the tomato paste.*

YEAST PIZZA

Ingredients:
3 cups milk
1 egg
1 yeast cake
1-1/2 tablespoons sugar
1 cup oil
1 kilogram (2 lb) flour, salt
Topping:
1 cup grated kashar cheese
sausage and salami, one or both
2 tomatoes
2-3 small green peppers
2 tablespoons tomato paste
salt, black pepper, oregano
Sauce:
3 tablespoons tomato paste
salt, black pepper, oregano

1. Warm 1 cup of milk slightly, add sugar and yeast and allow to set for 10 minutes. Add to the bowl: oil, egg, 2 cups milk and salt and mix. Add enough dough to form a soft dough. Allow to set until it rises.

2. Grease a pizza pan liberally with margarine. Spread out the raised dough to the edges of the pan.

3. Dilute tomato paste with a little oil. Add pepper, salt and oregano. Spread mixture all over the dough.

4. Cut sausage and salami into very thin slices and arrange on top of the sauce. Skin and cube the tomatoes. Arrange tomatoes and chopped peppers on top.

5. Sprinkle with a pinch of salt and oregano and bake 15-20 minutes in a hot oven. Remove from oven and spread grated cheese on top. Return to oven until cheese melts and is slightly browned.

MUSHROOM PIZZA

Ingredients:
1 pizza dough, prepared as for
preceding yeast pizza recipe
Topping:
250 grams (1/2 lb) mushrooms
250 grams (1/2 lb) cooked
chicken meat
2 tomatoes
3 small green peppers
1 cup grated kashar cheese

1. Grease a pizza pan liberally with margarine and spread out the raised dough to edges of the pan.

2. Cut chicken into small pieces. Slice mushrooms and peppers ver thin. Skin and cube tomatoes. Mix all ingredients together and spread all over the dough. Bake in a hot oven 15-20 minutes.

3. Remove from oven and spread grated cheese on top. Return to oven until cheese melts and is slightly browned.

Note: *If desired 4-5 sliced cucumber pickles and 10 sliced green olives may be used in place of the chicken.*

SALTY COOKIES

Ingredients:

250 grams (1/2 lb) margarine
250 grams (1/2 lb) salty white cheese
1 egg
1/3 teaspoon baking soda
flour as needed

1. Separate the egg. Combine margarine and cheese and mash. Add yoghurt and egg white. Mix well and add flour and baking powder. Knead into a soft dough.

2. Divide dough into pieces as desired and arrange on a greased baking pan. Coat the tops with egg yolk and bake in a hot oven until lightly browned.

BURDUR LOKUM

Ingredients:

1 cup yoghurt
1 cup warm milk
1 egg
1 tablespoon baking powder or baking soda, salt
flour as needed
frying oil

1. Make a dough with yoghurt, warm milk, egg, salt, flour and baking powder or soda.

2. Place dough in a glass bowl, cover with a cloth and allow to set for 45 minutes.

3. Fill a deep pan with oil and heat. Dip spoon in the hot oil and use it to take walnut-sized pieces one at a time from the dough and fry in the hot oil.

Note: *If desired, use very little salt in the dough and, after the frying, place balls in a bowl of sweet syrup to make "lokma".*

PUFF BOUREK

Ingredients:

3 tablespoons yoghurt
2 eggs
10 oz baking powder (4 teaspoons)
salt, flour as needed

1. Mix all ingredients and form a dough. Knead until no longer sticky.

2. Roll dough 1/2 cm thick and use a water glass to cut out rounds. Deep fry one or two at a time in hot oil.

BOUREK FLOWERS

Ingredients:
*5 phyllo pastry dough
sheets (yufka)
100 grams (3.2 oz) white
cheese
1 egg white
frying oil*

1. Stack the dough pieces and use a water glass to cut out rounds.
2. Mix egg white with grated cheese.
3. Put a small amount of the cheese mixture between the layers of each round. Press down on each one to seal it. Heat oil in a frying pan and fry the rounds on both sides. (When they are fried the layers open slightly at the edges to resemble a flower.)

EASY BOUREK

Ingredients:
*250 grams (1/2 lb) flour
1 egg
1/2 cup water, salt*

Filling:
*250 grams (1/2 lb) ground mutton
1 onion
2 medium size tomatoes
1-1/2 tablespoons water
salt, black pepper
1 bunch minced parsley*

1. Place flour in a bowl and open a pool in the center. Add egg, water and salt and form a soft dough. Divide into egg-size parts. Place a damp cloth over them and set aside 15-20 minutes.
2. Grate onion and slice tomatoes very thin and place in a pan. Mix together with ground mutton, water, salt and half of the parsley. Saute over a medium flame. Remove from heat and mix in remaining parsley and black pepper.
3. Roll out dough 1/2 cm thick. Put filling in the middle. Fold over. Roll up any loose ends to close well.
4. Fry in hot oil. Drain and serve hot.

Puff bourek

POTATO PASTRY

Ingredients:
1 kilogram (2 lb) flour
500 grams (1 lb) potatoes
1 yeast cake, salt

1. Boil potatoes and peel. Place yeast in warm water for 10 minutes.

2. Sift the flour onto a board. Mash potatoes with a fork and add. Add yeast. Mix well and form a soft dough. Set aside to rise.

3. Divide dough into egg size pieces. Flatten each one a little with the hand. Fry in hot oil. (Good served with tea or with salad and yoghurt drink.)

SIIRT SIMEYKET PASTRY

Ingredients:
1 kilogram (2 lb) flour
500 grams (1 lb) meat preserved in brine
50 grams (1.6 oz) lamb's tail fat
2 onions
black pepper, ground red pepper
salt, 2 boiled potatoes
1 tablespoon pepper sauce

1. Grind meat and tail fat in meat grinder and combine in a bowl.

2. Slice onion very fine or grate. Add onion and all remaining ingredients. Knead well. Divide dough into pieces. Roll out 1 cm thick and fry in hot oil. (Goes well with tea or yoghurt drink).

Notes: 1. *If preserved meat is not available fresh ground meat may be used.*
2. *For a tastier dish, a few days earlier place the piece of meat in salt. When ready to use wash well. Then grind and use.*

FRIED ROLLED PASTRY (İÇİ KOF)

Ingredients:

1 cup yoghurt, 3 eggs
125 grams (1/4 lb) margarine
125 grams (1/2 lb) white cheese
flour as needed, baking powder,
salt

1. Mix together well in a deep bowl: yoghurt, eggs, margarine and cheese. Mix in a little flour, then baking powder and salt. Add enough flour to make a soft dough. Knead. Cover with a damp cloth and allow to rise (1/2 hour).

2. Roll out to a thickness of 3 mm. Cut with a knife into small pieces or cut in rounds with a water glass. Fry in hot oil and serve with tea.

Note: *If desired, eliminate salt and place fried pieces in cold syrup, then place on platter and sprinkle walnut pieces on top.*

LEEKS BOUREK (NÖBETÇİ)

Ingredients:

1 kilogram (2 lb) flour, 3 leeks
2 fresh red peppers
1 teaspoon dry yeast, salt
black pepper, frying oil
100 grams (3.2 oz) ground meat or
cheese

1. Melt yeast in warm water. In a deep bowl, make a dough with flour, yeast and warm water. Knead and cover with a damp cloth until it rises.

2. Slice leeks and red peppers very thin. Mix together well with ground meat or cheese.

3. Divide dough into walnut-sized pieces. Roll out pieces and place a teaspoon of the filling in the center of each one and seal. Fry in hot oil and remove to drain on paper towels. Serve after cooling slightly.

CREPES

OVEN MUSHROOM CREPES

Ingredients:

2 eggs
2 cups milk
1/3 cup oil
1 cup flour, salt
Filling:
1/4 lb mushrooms, 1 onion
2 small green peppers, 1 tomato
2 tablespoons oil, salt, black
pepper

1. Mix together well eggs, milk and oil. Add flour and salt and blend into a batter.

2. Heat a teflon (crepe) pan (without oil) and pour one ladle full of batter so that it just covers the bottom of the pan. Brown on both sides and remove. Repeat until all batter is used.

3. Chop mushrooms and peppers very small. Skin tomato and chop the same size. Slice onion thin and saute a little in oil. Add remaining vegetables and mushrooms and continue cooking. Add salt.

4. Place a tablespoon of the filling on each crepe and close. Place on a greased oven pan. On top of each one place a thin slice of kashar cheese and, if desired, a thin slice of tomato. Bake until cheese has melted.

Note: *If desired, omit cheese and tomato and, instead of putting the crepes in the oven, simply put the filling on the crepes, fold over and serve.*

CREPES SÜZETTE

Ingredients:

4 eggs
2 cups milk
1-1/2 cups flour
4 tablespoons melted margarine
(1 for the batter and the rest to grease the pan)
grated lemon rind
dash of salt
1/3 cup marmalade

1. Mix together well eggs, flour, salt and grated lemon rind. Add 1 spoonful of the margarine. Mix well. Pour milk on top and blend until no lumps remain.

2. Heat the greased crepe pan. Pour 1 ladle (or 1/2 if desired) into the hot pan. Tip the pan to cover the bottom, as the batter bubbles, flip the crepe over, cook a little more and transfer to serving platter. Repeat until all batter is used. Place a teaspoon of marmalade (or pudding) in the center, fold over or roll up, and serve.

MOLASSES CREPES

Ingredients:

4 cups flour
dash of salt, water or milk
1 cup walnut pieces
100 grams (3.2 oz) butter
2 cups grape molasses (pekmez)

1. Make a thin batter with the flour, salt, and water or milk. Pour 1 ladle into a hot teflon pan (oil a little if desired). Tip the pan to cover the bottom. As the batter bubbles burst, flip the crepe over. When done place on a glass platter.

2. Sprinkle some walnuts on top. Continue making layers with each crepe and walnuts. On top do not put the walnuts. Melt the butter and mix with molasses. Pour this over the top of the stack of crepes. When the molasses is absorbed the dish is ready to slice and serve.

GREEN ONION CREPES

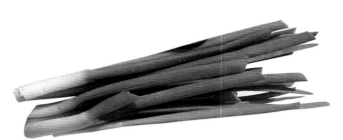

Ingredients:
5 eggs
1-1/2 tablespoons flour
3-4 green onions
1/2 bunch parsley, salt
oil

1. Mix eggs and flour and beat well. Chop onions finely and mince parsley. Mix onions and parsley together with salt. Add to egg mixture and mix well.

2. Pour a ladle into a greased teflon pan and fry briefly. Continue until all the batter is used. Serve hot.

CHEESE CREPES (AKITMA)

Ingredients:
2 eggs
2 cups milk
1/3 cup oil
1 cup flour, salt

1. Mix together well the eggs, milk and oil. Add flour and salt. Blend to a thin smooth batter.

2. Heat a teflon skillet (no oil) and pour in 1 ladle. Tip pan to cover the bottom. When bubbles burst, flip the crepe with the pan or using a spatula. When the other side is cooked remove from the pan and continue until all batter is used.

3. A variety of possible fillings include mashed potatoes, grated cheese, ground meat with onion saute, etc. Add filling, roll up each crepe and place on serving plate.

Note: *If a teflon pan is not available, a stainless steel pan may be used with a little hot oil.*

COOKIES
AND TARTS

352

COOKIES AND TARTS

SUGAR COOKIES

Ingredients:

2 cups sugar
1 cup yoghurt
1 cup maragarine
3 eggs, baking powder
flour as needed
egg white and sugar

1. Combine in a bowl 3 eggs and 2 cups sugar. Mix slightly. Melt margarine and add. Mix in yoghurt. Mix together baking powder with flour and add to the bowl. For a soft dough.

2. Divide into pieces about the size of 2 walnuts. Form into balls in the hands. Gently flatten them. Dip each one in egg white, then sugar. Place (not touching) on a greased cookie sheet. Bake in a pre-heated medium oven until light brown.

Note: *If the dough sticks to the fingers use a little oil on the hand. Egg yolk instead of egg white and sugar may be used to coat the cookies before baking.*

CRESCENT COOKIES

Ingredients:

1 cup eggs (3)
1 cup sugar
1 cup oil or shortening
1/2 teaspoon baking soda
flour as needed
powdered sugar

1. Mix together well all ingredients to form a soft dough.
2. Divide dough into parts and shape into crescents. Bake in a medium oven until white. Remove from oven and sprinkle powdered sugar on them while still hot.

BERSEN COOKIES

Ingredients:

250 grams (1/2 lb) margarine
1 cup oil, 1 cup sugar
2 egg yolks, 1 egg white
3 tablespoons milk
10 grams baking powder (4 teaspoons)
5 grams dry vanilla (1/4 teaspoon liquid)
walnut pieces
flour as needed

1. Mix oil and margarine until soft. Beat until it whitens. Add sugar and beat. Separate eggs. Add egg yolks and beat in. When well blended add milk and stir a little more.
2. Add baking powder and vanilla to flour and add to above mixture. Knead into a stiff dough. Divide into small pieces and make balls with the hands. Dip in egg white and roll in crushed walnuts. Arrange on a greased cookie sheet. Place in a preheated medium oven. Turn down oven to low and bake until light brown.

CORNSTARCH COOKIES

Ingredients:

500 grams (1 lb) cornstarch
1 cup powdered sugar
2 eggs
250 grams (1/2 lb) margarine
10 grams baking powder (4 teaspoons)

1. Have all ingredients ready in advance. Soften margarine and add remaining ingredients and form a dough. If dough seems a little too soft, up to 1/4 cup flour may be added.
2. Form pieces of desired shape, such as round or in rolls. Arrange on a greased cookie sheet and bake in a preheated medium oven until done. Cookies will remain white.

FLOUR COOKIES

Ingredients:

1 tablespoon yoghurt
250 grams (1/2 lb) margarine
1 cup powdered sugar
1 egg white
10 grams baking powder
(4 teaspoons)
5 grams dry vanilla (1/4 teaspoon
liquid), flour as need to make stiff
dough

1. Margarine should be at room temperature. Combine baking powder and vanilla with flour. Add margarine and mix well. Add remaining ingredients and form a stiff dough.

2. Form pieces in rolls and press down on top a little. Cut slashes on the tops about 3-4 cm apart. Mark the tops with a fork. Bake in a preheated medium oven. The cookies will remain white. Remove from oven and coat with powdered sugar.

HAZELNUT BALLS

Ingredients:

5 tablespoons powdered sugar
250 grams (1/2 lb) shortening
3-1/2 cups flour
10 grams baking powder
(4 teaspoons)
1/3 cup hazelnut pieces
1/3 cup powdered sugar
1/3 teaspoon cinnamon

1. Remove shortening from refrigerator an hour ahead of time. Mix well with 5 tablespoons powdered sugar. Add baking powder and flour and mix well. Add chopped hazelnuts, stir again.

2. Divide into pieces of desired size. Form balls with the hands. Dust a cookie pan with flour. Bake in a low oven. These cookies will remain white. When ready to serve sprinkle over them a mixture of cinnamon and powdered sugar.

EGG WHITE COOKIES

Ingredients:
3 egg whites
1 cup sugar
1/2 packet dry vanilla
(1/8 teaspoon liquid)

1. Mix egg white and sugar with an electric mixer until sugar is melted. Add vanilla. Whip until stiff.

2. Spread aluminum foil on a cookie sheet and drop spoonfuls of the mixture onto the foil so they are not touching. Bake in a very low temperature oven for 20-25 minutes.

Notes: 1. *Be sure no egg yolk is mixed with the whites when separating the eggs. Before starting be sure the bowl and beaters have no water on them.*
2. *A pastry bag can be used to squeeze out the mixture onto the pan.*
3. *Check oven temperature carefully to be sure the cookies do not burn.*

WALNUT COOKIES

Ingredients:
250 grams (1/2 lb) margarine
(at room temperature)
1 cup powdered sugar
3 eggs (1 separated)
10 grams baking powder
(4 teaspoons)
5 grams dry vanilla
(1/4 teaspoon liquid)
1 cup walnut pieces
flour as needed

1. Mix margarine and powdered sugar with the hands until creamy. Add 2 eggs and 1 egg yolk and mix well.

2. Add vanilla and baking powder to flour. Add to the mixture and form a soft dough. Divide into pieces the size of 2 walnuts. Form in balls in the hands. Dip in egg white, then roll in crushed walnuts. Arrange on a greased cookie sheet and bake in a preheated medium oven until light brown.

PUDDING COOKIES

Ingredients:
250 grams (1/ 2 lb) margarine (at room temperature)
3-1/2 to 4 cups flour
3 tablespoons yoghurt
10 grams baking powder (4 teaspoons)
5 tablespoons powdered sugar
Pudding:
2 cups milk
3 tablespoons flour
5 tablespoons sugar
vanilla
grated lemon rind

1. Mix margarine, sugar and yoghurt together well. Add baking powder to flour and add this to wet mixture. Form a soft dough.

2. **Pudding:** Mix sugar and flour in a pan. Add milk and place over a high flame. Stir well so there are no lumps. Add vanilla and lemon peel. When pudding consistency remove from heat and set aside to cool.

3. Divide cookie dough into egg-sized pieces. Form balls with the hands. Open the center of each and insert some of the pudding. Close up the seam well. Place seam side down on a greased cookie sheet and bake in a medium oven.

Note: *A fruit pudding or chocolate pudding may be substituted for the filling.*

PISTACHIO COOKIES

Ingredients:
6 cups flour
2/3 cup powdered sugar
375 grams (3/4 lb) margarine
1 cup pistachios (hazelnuts may be substituted)
1/3 teaspoon baking soda
3-4 drops lemon, cinnamon

1. Mix 6 tablespoons of the powdered sugar with the flour. Melt soda in the lemon drops and add. Melt margarine and add to flour. Knead into a somewhat stiff dough. Add chopped nuts and knead until stiff.

2. Knead until the dough can be held and squeezed in the hand without sticking. Form into balls and flatten a little. Arrange on a cookie sheet dusted with flour and bake 40-45 minutes in a medium oven. Removing from the oven, coat the hot cookies with a mixture of the remaining powdered sugar and cinnamon, and set on a serving platter to cool.

MALATYA COOKIES

Ingredients:

3 cups pastry flour
1 cup coarse flour
2 cups powdered sugar
500 grams (1 lb) unsalted butter
1 cup olive oil
dash of salt
walnuts, hazelnuts or almonds

1. Melt butter the night before and place in refrigerator.

2. Place butter in a large mixing bowl and whip until white. Add olive oil and mix a little. Add sugar and eat until dissolved. Add flour and salt and mix. Knead into a soft dough.

3. Divide dough into egg-sized parts and arrange on a cookie sheet. Place a nut on top of each and bake in a medium oven until light brown.

TAHIN COOKIES

Ingredients:

4 cups flour
1 cup sugar
1 cup tahin
200 grams (6.4 oz) margarine
1/3 cup crushed walnuts
10 grams baking powder
(4 teaspoons)
1 egg
5 grams dry vanilla (1/4 teaspoon liquid)

1. Be sure margarine is at room temperature. Separate the egg. Mix together well the sugar and tahin. Add margarine, vanilla and egg yolk. Mix well. Add baking powder and flour and knead to a thick dough.

2. Divide into walnut-sized pieces and form into balls in the hands. Coat with egg white and roll in the walnuts. Arrange on a greased cookie sheet and bake in a medium oven for 15-20 minutes.

RAISIN COOKIES

Ingredients:

250 grams (1/2 lb) margarine
1 cup powdered sugar
10 grams baking powder (4 tea-
spoons)
5 grams vanilla
(1/4 teaspoon liquid)
1 egg
flour as needed
1/3 cup seedless raisins

1. Mix margarine and powdered sugar by hand. Add egg and raisins and mix. Mix baking powder and vanilla with the flour and add to the wet mixture. Blend well but not beating the dough too much.

2. Divide into pieces and roll in the hands, forming in desired shape. Bake in a light oven until light brown.

"MUSHROOM" COOKIES

Ingredients:

250 grams (1/2 lb) margarine at
room temperature
1 cup flour
1-1/2 cups powdered sugar
2 eggs
1-1/2 cups cornstarch
10 grams baking powder (4 tea-
spoons)
5 grams dry vanilla (1/4 teaspoon
liquid)
1/4 cup cocoa

1. Mix margarine, eggs and powdered sugar. Add cornstarch, flour, baking powdered and vanilla and make a smooth dough. Form into balls and place on a greased cookie sheet.

2. Take a narrow glass (no more than 4 cm or 1-1/2 inch across) and dip the lip in cocoa. Press this into the top of each ball so that a dark ring is formed. Bake in a medium oven. When done it will resemble a mushroom.

COCONUT COOKIES

Ingredients:
2/3 cup powdered sugar
2/3 cup coconut
250 grams (1/2 lb) margarine
flour as needed
1/3 teaspoon baking soda
5 grams dry vanilla (1/4 teaspoon liquid)
3 eggs
some coconut for the top

1. Separate 1 of the eggs and reserve 1 egg white. Mix together well: sugar, eggs, coconut, margarine, flour, baking soda and vanilla. Form a soft dough.

2. Divide into pieces the size of 2 walnuts. Form in balls. Flatten slightly. Dip in egg white and roll in coconut. Arrange on a greased cookie sheet and bake in a medium oven. Do not brown.

PHYLLO TAHIN COOKIES

Ingredients:

3 phyllo dough sheets (yufka)
1 cup + 2 tablespoons tahin
5-6 tablespoons oil
(only as needed)
1 heaping cup sugar
1 heaping cup finely chopped
walnuts
1/4 cup sesame seeds
1 egg yolk

1. If the tahin is very thick, mix in just enough oil to thin out.

2. Spread out the yufka. Coat all of them all over with tahin. Sprinkle 1/3 of the sugar on top, then 1/3 of the walnuts. Fold over one edge 2cm wide, then continue by making a roll of the whole piece. Repeat with other two sheets.

3. Cut the rolls crosswise in desired length and shape (such as diamond shape) and place pieces on a greased cookie sheet. Coat with egg yolk and sprinkle sesame seeds on top. Bake in a low oven until light brown.

4. When removed from the oven if the cookies appear too dry, sprinkle them with a few drops of water and place a clean cloth over them for 10-15 minutes and then serve.

APPLE TART

Ingredients:

2 cups flour
1-1/2 cups rice starch
250 grams (1/2 lb) margarine
3 tablespoons sugar
1 egg
1/3 teaspoon baking powder
grated lemon rind
Filling:
3 apples
1/3 cup sugar
cinnamon

1. Be sure margarine is at room temperature. Mix flour and rice starch. Open a pool in the middle and add margarine, egg, sugar, baking powder and grated lemon rind. Mix and knead.

2. Divide dough into 3 parts. Roll out 2 parts to form a 25-30 cm (10-12 in) long piece to fit the baking pan. Arrange on the (greased) baking pan. Slice apples thinly and arrange on the dough. Spread 1/3 cup sugar and cinnamon over the apples. Roll out the remaining dough to fit on top and pierce dough in a few places to allow for steam (or cut dough in strips and arrange as cross-strips on top). Bake in a medium oven until light brown.

ORANGE TART

Ingredients:

3 tablespoons yoghurt
1 egg
250 grams (1/2 lb) margarine
10 grams baking powder (4 tea-spoons)
3 tablespoons powdered sugar
3 cups flour
1 cup rice flour
Filling:
peels of 4 oranges
2 cups sugar

1. Mix flour and rice starch. Melt margarine. Add to flour along with egg, yoghurt baking powder and powdered sugar. Form a soft dough.

2. Candied orange peels: Peel oranges and place peels in a pan. Cover with water and bring to a boil once or twice. Drain. Again place in water and bring to a boil once or twice. Repeat once or twice more. This both softens the peels and gets ride of the bitterness.

3. Drain and add sugar. Mix well and work the sugar in. Set aside.

4. Divide dough into 3 parts. Roll out 2 parts 1/2 cm thick, forming a long piece to fit the baking pan. Arrange on the (greased) baking pan. Arrange candied orange peels on top. Roll out remaining dough and fit over the top. Bake until brown. Turn upside down onto a serving platter. Sprinkle powdered sugar over it.

APPLE PIE

Ingredients:

3 cups flour
250 grams (1/2 lb) margarine
1/4 cup yoghurt or milk
10 grams baking powder (4 tea-spoons)
1 grated lemon rind
Filling:
4-5 apples
1/3 cup sugar
2-3 tablespoons cinnamon

1. Peel and grate apples. Mix one of the grated apples in a pan with the sugar and cook a little. Remove from heat and addd remaining grated apple. Add cinnamon. Mix and set aside to cool.

2. Be sure margarine is very soft. Put flour on a board and open a pool in the center. Add margarine, yoghurt or milk, grated lemon rind and baking powder. Form a dough and set aside for 5-10 minutes.

3. Divide dough into two parts. Roll out to thickness of 3-4 cm. Arrange one dough in the baking pan and arrange the apple over it. Lay the remaining piece of dough over and seal the edges. Pour some water on top and bake in a medium oven until golden brown.

Apple tart

PROFITEROLES

Ingredients
250 grams (1/2 lb) margarine
1 cup flour, 4 eggs
pinch of salt, 1 cup water
Cream filling:
1 egg, 1 cup sugar, 5 tablespoons
flour, 1/2 liter milk
1 grated lemon rind
100 grams (3.2 oz) margarine
5 grams dry vanilla (1/4 teaspoon
liquid)
Chocolate sauce:
1/2 cup granulated sugar
1/2 cup cocoa, 2 eggs
100 grams (3.2 oz) margarine

1. Bring to a boil water, margarine and dash of salt. Sift flour and dump all at once into the boiling water. Cool while stirring for 10 minutes. Remove from heat. When cooled break eggs one at a time into the mixture. Knead into a soft dough.

2. Fill a pastry bag with the dough. squeeze out small portions (smaller than a walnut) onto a greased cookie sheet. Place them touching. Bake in a medium oven 30-35 minutes. As they bake the centers will become empty. Remove from oven and allow to cool a little. Pump the cream into each one. Pour the chocolate

sauce on top.
To prepare the filling:
1. Place egg, sugar, flour and lemon rind in a pan. Mix. Slowly add milk, stirring constantly. Place on the stove and cook until pudding consistency.
2. When cooled add margarine and vanilla. To prevent lumping, stir from time to time.
To prepare the sauce:
Beat egg with a mixer. Add sugar and beat a little more. Add cocoa and margarine (melted but not hot) and beat until creamy.

TEA COOKIES

Ingredients:

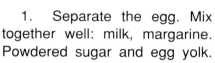

3 tablespoons powdered sugar
250 grams (1/2 lb) margarine
1 egg
3 tablespoons milk
10 grams baking powder
(4 teaspoons)
flour as needed
1/3 cup crushed hazelnuts

1.   Separate the egg. Mix together well: milk, margarine. Powdered sugar and egg yolk. Mix baking powder and flour and add. Form a dough slightly stiffer than the ear lobe. (so it can be rolled out easily). Allow to set for 15 minutes.

2. Roll out dough. Use cutters or the rim of a small glass to cut into shapes. Dip in egg white and roll in crushed nuts. Place on a greased cookie sheet and bake in a medium oven until golden brown.

SABLE COOKIES

Ingredients:
3 eggs
1-1/2 cups powdered sugar
250 grams (1/2 lb) margarine
10 grams baking powder
(4 teaspoons)
5 grams dry vanilla (1/4 teaspoon liquid)
flour as needed
1/3 cup mixture of sesame seeds and crushed hazelnuts

1. Have margarine and eggs at room temperature. Separate 1egg and set aside the white. Mix margarine and powdered sugar well.

2. Mix baking powder and vanilla with flour. Add to margarine-sugar mixture. Form a dough slightly stiffer than the ear lobe (so it can be rolled out easily).

3. Roll out dough to 1 finger thickness. . Use cutters or the rim of a small glass to cut into shapes. Dip in egg white and roll in crushed nuts and seeds. Place on a greased cookie sheet and bake in a medium oven until golden brown.

TWO-COLOR COOKIES

Ingredients:
300 grams (9.6 oz) flour
1-1/2 cups powdered sugar
3 egg yolks
50 grams (1.6 oz) cocoa
1 grated lemon rind
5 grams vanilla (1/4 teaspoon liquid)
1/3 teaspoon baking soda

1. Put flour on a board and margarine on top. Cut margarine into the flour with a knife. Add powdered sugar, egg yolks, lemon rind, vanilla and soda. Form a dough slightly stiffer than the ear lobe.

2. Divide dough into 2 parts and set aside for 15 minutes.

3. Add the cocoa to one part of the dough and knead. Roll out the other dough to 1 cm thickness. Roll out the chocolate dough the same and place on top of the other dough. Make a roll of the two together. Cut roll crosswise in 2 cm wide slices. Arrange on a greased cookie sheet and bake in a medium oven until lightly browned.

4. Another way is to make slices of each type of dough separately, half of one type being cut into rounds that are twice as wide as half of the other. Place the smaller rounds in the center of the larger ones. Then do the opposite with remaining halves of the 2 doughs. Bake until lightly browned.

CAT'S TONGUE COOKIES

Ingredients:
125 grams (1/4 lb) margarine
1/2 cup powdered sugar
8 tablespoons flour
2 egg yolks
1 grated lemon peel
1/2 teaspoon dry vanilla (few drops liquid vanilla)

1. Place baking paper in a baking pan, oil it and dust with flour. If the paper is not available be sure to grease pan very well and dust with flour. Preheat oven at medium temperature.

2. Cream softened margarine and powdered sugar in a porcelain or glass bowl. Add egg yolks one at a time and mix well. Mix vanilla and lemon peel with flour. Then add and mix well.

3. Fill a pastry bag and squeeze flat pieces onto the baking pan (like a cat's tongue).Bake in oven 10-15 minutes or until lightly browned.

APPLE COOKIES

Ingredients:
3 cups flour
250 grams (1/2 lb) margarine
4-1/2 tablespoons yoghurt
1/4 cup powdered sugar
juice of 1/2 lemon
10 grams baking powder (4 tea-spoons)
5 grams dry vanilla (1/4 teaspoon liquid)
Filling:
3 apples
1/3 cup sugar
1 handful walnuts or hazelnuts
cinnamon

1. Peel and grate apples. Place in a pan with sugar, nuts and cinnamon. Cook until apples are soft. Remove from heat and set aside to cool.

2. Put flour on a board. Add margarine, yoghurt, lemon juice, baking powder and vanilla. Make a dough and allow to set 10-15 minutes.

3. Divide dough into walnut-sized pieces. Roll in the hands and press down a little with the thumb. Place some of the apple mixture in the center of each and close up. Arrange on a cookie sheet and bake in a medium oven until done.

4. Roll each coookie in powdered sugar and place on a serving platter.

"For the hungry a bitter onion is like baklava." old saying
"A full stomach feels like the whole world is full."
"The hungry one thinks there is no bread in the world." - Sabayi

CAKES AND TORTES

CONTENTS

TIPS FOR SUCCESSFUL BAKING *

1. For best results use only fresh, high-quality flour.

2. Measurements are particularly important to observe in cake preparation.

3. Sifting the flour once or twice before use prevents lumping and helps the batter rise better.

4. Adding lemon juice before adding the flour helps the batter to rise and enhances the aroma.

5. Ingredients, particularly the eggs, should be at room temperature before using.

6. Beat eggs in a glass, stainless steel or copper bowl. Aluminium can alter the color of the eggs.

7. When using a mixer it is not necessary to separate the eggs. If using a fork to beat the eggs:

   a. Separate the eggs first.

   b. Beat the yolks with sugar until sugar is melted.

   c. Beat whites in a separate bowl until white and at desired stiffness.

   d. Add beaten yolks to beaten whites. Then add lemon juice and other ingredients. The flour, mixed with baking powder and dry vanilla*, is added last.

8. Once the flour is added, stop beating and continue mixing with a spoon.

9. Grease the bottom and sides of the cake pans. To prevent the cake from sticking to the pan after baking, dust the bottom with flour and the sides with sugar.

10. Always preheat the oven.

11. To test the doneness of the cake insert a sharp knife near the center. If batter sticks to the knife it is not done. The knife should come out clean.

12. Decorate the cake only after it has cooled.

_____

(*) 1 packet dry vanilla contains about 4 teaspoons, of which about 10% is vanillin. In these recipes it equals about 1/4 teaspoon pure liquid vanilla. If liquid is used, add toward the end of the mixing, not with the flour.

TOPPINGS AND FILLINGS

CHOCOLATE CREAM

Ingredients:

4 cups milk
3 tablespoons flour
3 eggs
50 grams cocoa
1 cup sugar
1 cup hazelnuts or walnuts
5 grams dry vanilla (1/4 teaspoon liquid)

1. Bring milk to a boil and set aside to cool. Separate eggs. Mix together well: egg yolks, sugar, cocoa and flour. Add cooled milk slowly, mixing constantly. Place on stove and cook until thick and smooth.

2. Beat eggs whites with mixer until white. Add 2-3 tablespoons cream and mix well. Add remaining cream and bring to a boil once or twice. When almost done add vanilla. Use with a cake or torte recipe or pour into individual bowls and garnish with nuts.

STRAWBERRY CUSTARD

Ingredients:

4 tablespoons cornstarch

3 tablespoons strawberry cream (see recipe in this chapter)

1 cup sugar

4 cups water

1. Mix cornstarch, strawberry cream and sugar in a pan. Slowly add water while stirring. Place on stove cook until thickened.

2. If desired, whip in mixer until creamy.

Note: If available, 3 tablespoons of the product "Oralet" may be used in place of strawberry cream.

VANILLA CUSTARD

Ingredients:

1 liter milk

2 scant cups sugar

2 tablespoons potato starch

1-1/2 tablespoons cornstarch

3 egg yolks

5 grams dry vanilla (1/4 teaspoon liquid)

1/3 teaspoon salt

1. Mix together well in a pan: potato starch, cornstarch, sugar, salt and egg yolks.

2. Boil milk and chill. Add milk very slowly while stirring. Be sure all lumps are out and put on a high flame, cooking until thickened. When almost done add vanilla. Remove from stove and set aside to cool. From time to time stir.

3. Add to a cake or torte, either with a spoon or in a pastry bag, or fill individual serving cups and garnish with crushed hazelnuts, pistachios, walnuts, coconut and/or grated chocolate as desired.

HAZELNUT SAUCE

Ingredients:
3 eggs
1 cup sugar
1/3 cup hazelnuts or walnuts
2 cups milk
1/3 cup cornstarch
5 grams dry vanilla (1/4 teaspoon liquid)

1. Mix together well in a pan: eggs, sugar and cornstarch. Boil milk and chill. Add milk very slowly while stirring. Place on stove and cook until thickened.

2. Remove from stove and add nuts and vanilla. Allow to cool, stirring from time to time. Use to garnish cakes and puddings.

CHESTNUT PUREE

Ingredients
500 grams (1 lb) chestnuts
1 cup sugar
1-1/2 cups milk or water
5 grams dry vanilla (1/4 teaspoon liquid)

1. Remove outer shells of chestnuts and place in a pan. Cover with water and bring to a boil. When the inner skins start to come off remove from stove. Allow to cool a little and put in food processor to make a puree.

2. Meanwhile mix milk or water with sugar and bring to a boil once. Slowly add to puree, stirring constantly. Add vanilla. Continue stirring while bringing to a boil once more. Remove from heat and cool.

3. Use as is to decorate cakes. Or, mix in a little fruit jam and fill individual serving cups. Add a spoonful of whipped cream or vanilla custard (see recipe above) on top.

BUTTER FROSTING

Ingredients:
125 grams (1/4 lb) margarine
1 handful powdered sugar

1. Place softened margarine (or butter) in a porcelain or glass bowl, add sugar and use an electric mixer or wooden spoon to beat until creamy.

3. Put in a pastry bag and decorate the top of a cake as desired.

WHIPPED CREAM

Ingredients:

1 cup fresh whole cream
1-1/2 tablespoons powdered sugar
vanilla

1. Beat ingredients with an electric mixer to desired thickness.

2. Do not to beat too long or it will turn to butter.

MOCK WHIPPED CREAM

Ingredients:

4 egg whites
1 cup sugar
dash of salt

1. Place sugar in a pan and add just enough water to cover. Boil until blended.

2. Separate eggs, being sure there is no yolk in the white.

3. Add a dash of salt to the whites and whip until white.

4. Add sugar to whites and quickly stir once or twice (If stirred too much white will become watery.)

5. Allow egg whites to cool. Put in a pastry bag and decorate cake as desired.

Notes: 1. *This fatless topping is low calorie.*

2. *If 125 grams (1/ 4 lb) margarine is added and beaten until frothy it becomes like whipped cream.*

CHOCOLATE ICING

Ingredients:

200 grams (6.4 oz) chocolate
100 grams (3.2 oz) margarine

1. Put ingredients in a pan and set in a larger pan of boiling water. Allow them to melt and stir well.

2. When cooled spread on cake. Other garnitures such as whipped cream can be added on top.

CANDIED ORANGE RINDS

Ingredients:

3-4 orange rinds
1 cup sugar

1. Remove white pith from inside the orange rinds. Cut into half-matchstick size.

2. Place in a pan and add just enough water to cover. Bring to a boil for 5 minutes. Drain. Repeat 4-5 times in order to remove bitterness. Then add sugar. Add 1 tablespoon more of water and return to stove. Cook until water has evaporated but the orange has not become dried. Use with cakes and tarts.

CAKES AND TORTES

SPONGE CAKE (PANDİSPANYA)

Ingredients:

6 eggs
1-1/2 cups powdered sugar
1-1/2 cups flour
5 grams dry vanilla (1/4 teaspoon liquid)
10 grams baking powder (4 teaspoons)
dash of salt
grated lemon rind

1. Break eggs into a glass, porcelain or copper bowl. Add sugar and beat with a mixer until foamy.

3. Sift flour 2-3 times. Add baking

powder, salt and vanilla. Add to egg mixture and mix well with a wooden spoon. Mix in grated lemon rind.

3. Grease a baking pan and dust with flour. Pour batter in pan and bake in a preheated medium oven for 20-25 minutes.

PARFAIT

Ingredients:

3 eggs
1/4 cup sugar
75 grams (2.4 oz) dry whipping cream
1 cup cold milk
200 grams petit beurres (butter cookies)
dash of salt
1/3 cup coarsely chopped walnuts

1. Separate eggs.
2. Blend egg yolks and sugar.
3. Put egg whites in a bowl, add dash of salt and beat until foamy.
4. In another bowl mix cream and milk until foamy.
5. Put all 3 mixes together in a large glass or porcelain bowl and beat with a wooden spoon.

6. Divide mixture into three parts. Finely crush the cookies and add to 1 part. Mix and transfer to a glass pan. Put remaining 2 parts on top. Sprinkle walnuts on top. Allow to set in refrigerator for 2-3 hours or overnight.

Note: *If desired, add walnuts before putting to remaining mixture on top. Then pour some chocolate sauce over it.*

ICE CREAM COOKIE TORTE

Ingredients:

200 grams (6.4 oz) petit beurres (butter cookies)
150 grams (4.8 oz) dry whipping cream
2 cups milk
4 eggs
3 tablespoons cocoa
4 tablespoons powdered sugar

1. Combine cream and milk and whip.
2. Separate whites and yolks into two bowls and beat each separately with mixer.
3. Fold beaten whites into the yolks. Add cocoa and sugar. Beat with mixer.
4. Pour half of this mixture into a pan. Dip cookies in milk and arrange on top. Add remaining mixture. Place in freezer. When frozen spread whipped cream on top and return to freezer until frozen.

PRINCESS DESSERT

Ingredients:
1 liter milk
1/2 cup flour
1/ 2 cup sugar
200 grams (6.4 oz) margarine
5 grams dry vanilla (1/4 teaspoon liquid)
coconut
Topping:
1/2 cup sugar
1/2 cup cocoa
2 eggs
100 grams (3.2 oz) margarine

1. Melt 200 grams margarine in a pan and remove from stove. Add sugar, flour and milk. Mix well, removing all lumps. Return to stove and cook until thick and smooth. When almost done add vanilla. Beat the hot mixture with a mixer for 10-15 minutes until thick. Transfer to a glass pan and set aside to cool.

2. Meanwhile, melt 100 grams margarine and allow to cool. Break eggs into a deep bowl. Beat a little with the mixer. Add sugar and beat a little more. Add margarine and cocoa. Beat until creamy. Spread over first layer in glass pan. Sprinkle coconut on top and allow to set in refrigerator for 2 hours or over night.

Note: If desired, first put some plain vanilla or chocolate cookies in the glass pan. Put half the pudding on top, then as second layer of cookies and the rest of the pudding. Chill in refrigerator.

EASY TORTE

Ingredients:
150 grams (4.8 oz) dry whipping cream
1-1/2 cups milk
1 200-gram (6.4 oz) package plain chocolate cookies
1 200-gram package vanilla cookies
1 tablespoon powdered sugar
1 cup hazelnuts

1. Beat whipping cream and milk in a deep bowl to soft peak stage. Add powdered sugar, nuts and crushed cookies. Mix well.

2. Use a glass pan, cake pan or a deep bowl. Stretch plastic or aluminum wrap across the insides and extending well over the edges. Place the mixture inside the container. Fold the ends of the wrapper to cover. Seal and press down a little. Set in refrigerator 3-4 hours or over night. Remove 5 minutes before serving. Open covering and turn upside down onto a serving platter and remove covering. Slice and serve.

BIRTHDAY CAKE

Ingredients:
4 eggs
1 cup powdered sugar
1 cup flour
10 grams baking
powder (4 teaspoons)
5 grams dry vanilla
(1/4 teaspoon liquid)
Filling:
250 grams (1/2 lb)
margarine
3/4 cup flour
3/4 cup granulated
sugar
1 liter milk
Topping:
125 grams (1/4 lb)
margarine
3 tablespoons
granulated sugar
3 tablespoons cocoa
1 egg

1. Break eggs (room temperature) into a glass, porcelain or copper bowl. Add powdered sugar. Whip with an electric mixer until frothy.

2. Sift flour 2-3 times. Add baking powder and vanilla. Add flour mixture to egg mixture and blend well with a wooden spoon.

3. Grease and flour a large round cake pan and transfer batter to pan. Bake in a preheated medium oven 20-25 minutes.

4. After the cake has cooled remove from pan and split into two layers. Spread half the fillling over the top of one layer, place second layer on top and spread remaining filling on top. Set aside to cool. Meanwhile prepare the topping.

Filling:

1. Combine (melted but not hot) margarine and flour. Mix lightly. Mix sugar and milk and slowly pour into flour mixture, stirring constantly. Place over a high flame, stirring until thickened.

2. While still hot, beat 15 minutes with electric mixer.

Topping:

1. Combine sugar and cocoa. Add egg and stir a little more. (Food processor or electric mixer is recommended.)

2. Melt margarine but do not heat. Add margarine and beat until creamy.

3. When the cake has cooled spread on top and set in refrigerator for at least 2 hours.

CAT'S TONGUE COOKIE TORTE

Ingredients:

500 grams (1 lb) cat's tongue cookies (see recipe in "Cookies and Tarts" chapter)
1 liter milk
125 grams (1/4 lb) margarine
3/4 cup flour, 3/4 cup sugar

Filling:

200 grams (6.4 oz) margarine
3 eggs, coconut
3 tablespoons sugar
3 tablespoons cocoa

1. Combine margarine and flour. Mix lightly. Mix sugar and milk and add. Beat well with the mixer. Place over a high flame, stirring until thickened. Remove from heat and beat 15-20 minutes with mixer.

2. Completely cover bottom of a baking pan with cookies. Spread half the filling on top, and make another layer each of cookies and filling. Set aside to cool.

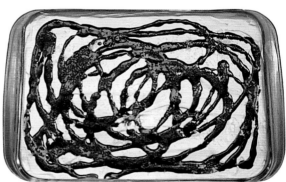

Petit beurres with chocolate cream

Topping:

1. Mix sugar, eggs and cocoa together. Beat well while adding melted margarine (should not be hot). Beat in food processor or mixer until creamy.

2. Spread on top of dessert, sprinkle coconut over it and place in refrigerator. Best if allowed to set over night.

CUPCAKES WITH CHOCOLATE CREAM

Ingredients:

1 package paper cupcake holders
2 eggs
125 grams (1/4 lb) margarine
5 grams baking powder (2 teaspoons)
1 cup granulated sugar
1/2 cup milk
2-1/2 cups flour
Topping:
1/2 liter milk
2 tablespoons cornstarch
2 tablespoons cocoa
1 cup granulated sugar
50 grams (1.6 oz) margarine
1 egg

1. Do not preheat oven. Beat 2 eggs and 1 cup sugar. Melt margarine and add. Add milk. Combine baking powder with flour and add to mixture. Mix well.

2. Spoon 1 tablespoon of cake batter into each cup. Put in unheated oven. Set oven on a medium temperature and bake.

3. Mix cornstarch, cocoa and sugar together. Add milk and place on stove. Stirring constantly cook until consistency of pudding. Remove from heat and add margarine and egg. Beat with mixer. Spoon onto cupcakes when they come out of the oven. Allow to cool.

CUPCAKES WITH SYRUP

Ingredients:

1 package paper cupcake holders
4 eggs
1/2 cup milk
1/ 4 cup oil
10 grams baking powder (4 teaspoons)
5 grams dry vanilla (1/4 teaspoon liquid), 1-1/2 cups flour
1 cup sugar
chocolate pudding (homemade or store bought)
Syrup:
3 cups sugar, 2-1/2 cups water

1. Do not preheat oven. Beat eggs and sugar. Add oil and milk. Combine baking powder and vanilla with flour and add. Mix well. Beat with a wooden spoon.

2. Spoon 1 tablespoon of cake batter into each cup. Put in unheated oven. Set at medium temperature and bake. Remove from oven and pour 1 tablespoon syrup over each cake.

3. Make a packaged chocolate pudding. Spoon some hot pudding on top of each cake. Allow to cool and place in refrigerator.

APPLE CAKE

Ingredients:

1 cup sugar
1 cup yoghurt
1 cup oil
2 eggs
10 grams baking powder
(4 teaspoons)
flour as needed

Filling:
4 medium sized apples
4 tablespoons sugar
1 teaspoon cinnamon
1/ 4 cup powdered sugar

1. Peel and grate apples. Combine with 4 tablespoons sugar and cinnamon and cook until soft.

2. Combine: eggs, sugar, yoghurt and oil. Combine baking powder with flour and add. Makle a soft dough and knead.

3. Set aside one handful of the dough. Arrange remaining dough in a greased pan and spread apple mixture over it. Mix handful of dough with flour until it is stiff enough to grate. Grate over the apples. Bake in a medium oven until lightly browned. After it has cooled sprinkle powdered sugar on top and serve.

PETIT BEURRES WITH CHOCOLATE CREAM

Ingredients:

2 packages (400 grams, 12.8 oz)
plain chocolate cookies
100 grams (3.2 oz) margarine
1/3 cup sugar
1/3 cup cocoa
2 eggs
2 cups milk
1 package (150 grams, 4.8 oz) dry
whipping cream

1. Arrange a layer of cookies to cover a square glass baking dish. Moisten by spooning cold milk on them.

2. Mix sugar, cocoa and egg in the food processor or mixer. Add melted (but not hot) margarine, beating until creamy. Pour a layer of this sauce over cookies in the baking dish.

3. Add another layer of cookies and moisten with milk. Pour another layer of sauce. Layer remaining cookies on top and more sauce. Save 1 tablespoon of sauce.

4. Combine 1 cup milk with whipping cream and beat to soft peaks with a mixer. Spread cream on top.

5. Drizzle 1 tablespoon of sauce on top. Use a fork to make designs on the top, creating a swirls effect with some of the white cream and chocolate sauce. Chill in refrigerator.

MELBA TOAST CREAM TORTE

Ingredients:

250 grams (1/2 lb) rush bread (melba toast or Turkish "Etimek")
2 cups sugar
1 cup water, 1 liter milk
250 grams (1/2 lb) margarine
3/4 cup flour, 3/4 cup sugar

Topping:

1 package (150 grams, 4.8 oz) dry whipping cream
1 cup water or milk

1. Cover the bottom of a rectangular glass pan with the melba toasts.

2. Make a syrup combining 1 cup sugar and 1 cup water and bring to boil twice. Spoon all of the syrup onto the toasts. Set aside to let syrup be absorbed.

3. Combine flour and margarine and mix lightly. Add remaining sugar and the milk. Use mixer to blend. Cook on a high flame and bring to a pudding consistency, stirring constantly. Remove from heat and beat 15-20 minutes with the mixer until very thick.

4. Spread pudding over melba toasts in the pan. Set aside to cool.

5. Meanwhile, combine whipping cream and milk or water and beat to soft peak stage. Spread on top of the pudding in the pan. Allow to set in refrigerator.

__Note:__ If desired carmelize the syrup by first heating sugar in a pan and then adding the water and bring to a boil. Boil 1-2 minutes, then pour over toasts.

GERMAN CAKE

Ingredients:
2 eggs
1/3 cup yoghurt
2/3 cup granulated sugar
1 cup flour
10 grams baking powder
(4 teaspoons)
powdered sugar
Filling:
1/2 liter milk
1 egg
5 tablespoons flour
1/3 cup sugar
60 grams (2 oz)
margarine
1 or 2 bananas

1. Beat granulated sugar and eggs a little. Mix in the yoghurt. Combine flour and baking powder and add. Mix a little and pour in a greased round cake pan. Bake in a hot oven.

2. Filling: Combine in a pan all ingredients except margarine. Cook until thickened. Remove from heat and add melted margarine. Beat with electric mixer.

3. After cake has cooled split into 2 layers. Spread pudding on one layer and put other layer on top. Cover cake with remaining pudding. Arrange banana slices on top and dust liberally with powdered sugar. Chill in refrigerator.

Fruit garnish with kiwi

BANANA CAKE ROLL

Ingredients:

4 eggs
1 cup sugar
1 cup flour
1/3 teaspoon baking soda
3 bananas
Cream topping:
2 cups milk
1 cup sugar
3 tablespoons flour
1-1/2 tablespoons cornstarch
5 grams dry vanilla (1/4 teaspoon liquid)
125 grams (1/4 lb) margarine
coconut

1. Beat until blended: eggs, sugar and flour. Add soda and mix. Pour in a greased baking pan. Bake 10 minutes in a preheated medium oven. Set aside to cool.

2. **Cream:** Combine milk, sugar, flour, cornstarch and vanilla in a pan and cook until creamy and thick. Remove from heat and add melted margarine. Set aside to cool, stirring from time to time to prevent separation.

3. Spread cooled cream over the cake and arrange sliced bananas on top. Make a roll and sprinkle coconut on top. Allow to set in refrigerator for at least 1-2 hours.

ITALIAN TORTE

Ingredients:

2 prepared cake layers (or see recipe in this chapter for Sponge Cake)
2 cups milk
200 grams (6.4 oz) soft cream cheese
2 tablespoons flour
2 bananas
1 egg
1/3 cup sugar
1/3 cup black coffee
baking chocolate

1. Prepare coffee. Place one cake layer in a pan and moisten with half of the coffee.

2. Combine milk, flour, sugar and egg. Place over a flame and cook until it thickens. Add cheese and stir until cheese melts. Remove from heat.

3. Spread half of the filling all over the layer in the pan. Moisten second cake layer with coffee and place on top. Arrange sliced bananas over it and spread remaining filling over the bananas. Sprinkle with grated chocolate and allow to set in refrigerator for 2-3 hours.

APPLE PUDDING DESSERT

Ingredients:

3 apples
3 tablespoons sugar
1 teaspoon cinnamon
Pudding:
1/2 liter milk
125 grams (1/4 lb) margarine
5 tablespoons sugar
3 tablespoons flour
5 grams dry vanilla (1/4 teaspoon liquid)
2-3 bananas
1 cup walnut pieces

1. Peel and grate apples. Combine with 3 tablespoons sugar and cinnamon and place over a high flame, cooking until apples are soft. Pour into a flat glass dish and set aside to cool.

2. **Pudding:** Heat milk in a pan on the stove and add margarine. Combine sugar, flour and vanilla and add to milk, stirring constantly. Bring to pudding consistency. Remove from heat and beat 10 minutes with a mixer. Pour pudding over apples, arrange walnut pieces and banana slices on top, and chill.

STRAWBERRY CREAM TORTE

Ingredients:

150 grams (4.8 oz) dry whipping cream mix
1 cup milk
1 cup strawberry flavored or plain milk
1 cup sugar
2 egg whites
500 grams (1 lb) strawberries
10 grams vanilla (1/2 teaspoon liquid)
15-20 cat's tongue cookies (see recipe in "Cookies and Tarts" chapter)

1. Separate egg whites carefully so that no yolk remains. Beat whites and sugar until foamy.

2. Wash strawberries and (setting aside some for the top) make a puree in the food processor.

3. Add to puree: 1 cup milk, vanilla and dry whipping cream. Beat with a mixer. When it thickens fold in the beaten egg whites mixture and beat a little more.

4. Cover the bottom of a glass pan with cookies and moisten them with the strawberry or plain milk (if desired, do this in individual serving bowls). Add some strawberry slices, a layer of cream and more strawberry slices as desired. Allow to set in refrigerator 1-2 hours or overnight.

ORANGE PUDDING TORTE

Ingredients:
3 oranges
1/2 liter milk
1 egg
1-1/2 tablespoons cornstarch
6 tablespoons flour
1 cup sugar
1 cup water
200 grams (6.4 oz) plain
chocolate cookies
75 grams (2.4 oz)
margarine
coconut, cinnamon

1. Mix together well in a pan: flour, cornstarch, egg and water. Squeeze juice out of oranges and add. Add milk and oil and, stirring constantly, cook until consistency of a pudding.

2. Pour half the pudding into a glass pan. Arrange cookies on top. Add remaining pudding and arrange another layer of cookies. Sprinkle coconut and cinnamon on top and chill.

Note: *Sponge cake (recipe in this chapter) may be used in place of cookies.*

TEA CAKE

Ingredients:

3 eggs
1,5 cups sugar
250 grams (1/2 lb) margarine or
1 cup oil
4 cups flour
1 cup cold tea
1 tablespoon cocoa or instant
coffee powder
1 teaspoon baking soda, vanilla
1 teaspoon cinnamon
1/3 cup walnut pieces

1. Beat well with a mixer the eggs and sugar. Add margarine or oil, tea, cinnamon, cocoa or coffee, and walnuts. Sift flour and combine with vanilla and soda. Add to wet mixture and mix a little with a wooden spoon.

2. Pour batter into a greased baking pan dusted with flour. Bake in a hot oven.

YOGHURT CAKE

Ingredients:

3 eggs
1-1/2 cups sugar
1 cup yoghurt
1 cup oil
2-1/2 cups flour
10 grams baking
powder (4 teaspoons)
dash of salt

1. Separate eggs into 2 bowls. Beat egg yolks. Add yoghurt and oil and beat a little more.

2. Put dash of salt in egg whites and beat until foamy. Gradually fold into egg yolk mixture.

3. Sift flour and combine with baking powder. Gradually add to egg mixture. Mix well.

4. Grease baking pan. Coat bottom with flour and sides with granulated sugar (to prevent cake from sticking when being removed from pan). Pour batter into pan and bake in a medium preheated oven.

EASY CAKE

Ingredients:
250 grams (1/2 lb) margarine
4 eggs
1-1/2 cups sugar
1 cup milk
juice of 1/2 lemon
500 grams (1 lb) flour
5 grams vanilla (1/4 teaspoon liquid)
10 grams baking powder (4 teaspoons)

1. Beat eggs with sugar. Melt margarine and combine with milk. Add to eggs and beat a little more.

2. Sift flour and combine with baking powder and vanilla. Gradually add to egg mixture.

3. Grease baking pan. Coat bottom with flour and sides with granulated sugar. (This prevents cake from sticking when being removed from pan.) Bake in a medium preheated oven.

CREAM CAKE

Ingredients:
3 eggs
1 scant (7/8) cup sugar
1 cup flour
5 grams dry vanilla (1/4 teaspoon liquid)
2 tablespoons shortening
cream (one of two varieties)
1st cream:
1 tablespoon cornstarch
1 egg yolk
2 cups milk
5-6 tablespoons sugar

200 grams (6.4 oz) shortening, more or less
2nd cream:
5-6 tablespoons sugar
2 cups milk
5 tablespoons flour
4-5 tablespoons (or to taste) cocoa or strawberry mix
2 egg yolks
1 whole egg
1/2 teaspoon dry vanilla (a few drops)
50 grams (1.6 oz) butter

Cake: Set mixing bowl into a container of boiling water. Put sugar and eggs in mixing bowl and beat a full 10 minutes. Set bowl aside. Add vanilla and gradually add flour while mixing. Add melted shortening. Stir once. Pour in a greased pan and bake in a hot oven.

1st cream:

Combine all ingredients except the shortening and cook until pudding consistency. Remove from flame and set aside. When room temperature add melted shortening and mix. Chill, stirring from time to time to avoid separation. Spread on top of the cake and chill in refrigerator a few hours.

2nd cream:

Combine in a pan: 2 egg yolks and whole egg, sugar, vanilla and cocoa or strawsberry mix, and mix well. Warm the milk in a pan. In another bowl blend a half ladle of milk with the flour. Pour remaining warm milk in the bowl and mix well. Add this mixture to the egg mixture and cook until pudding consistency. Stir in butter, continuing to stir. Stir 3-4 more times to prevent lumping. When ready spread on top of cake. Chill in refrigerator a few hours.

PLAIN CAKE

Ingredients:

1 scant (7/8) cup oil
3 eggs
1 cup milk
1 cup sugar
500 grams (1 lb) flour
10 grams baking powder (4 teaspoons)
5 grams dry vanilla (1/4 teaspoon liquid)
3 tablespoons raisins, if desired

1. Beat eggs and sugar. Add milk and oil and beat a little more.

2. Sift flour and combine with baking powder. Add to egg mixture and mix well. Stir in raisins.

3. Grease baking pan. Coat bottom with flour and sides with granulated sugar. (This prevents cake from sticking when being removed from pan.) Bake in a medium preheated oven.

BURSA OVMA CAKE

Ingredients:

250 grams (1/2 lb, about 1 cup) yoghurt
3 eggs
125 grams (1/4 lb) margarine
500 grams (1 lb) granulated sugar
1 packet dry yeast
1 teaspoon rezene (a type of basil)
1 teaspoon mahaleb powder (mahlep)
1 treaspoon tumeric

1. Mix yeast in 1/2 cup water with 1/3 teaspoon sugar. Allow yeast to activate.

2. Combine yoghurt with sugar. Break eggs into mixture and beat. Melt margarine. Add margarine and yeast. Add rezene, mahaleb and tumeric to flour. Add flour mixture to batter and knead to a stiff dough resembling bread dough.

3. Place in a greased pan and spread out by hand. Bake in a medium oven until lightly browned. Remove, allow to cool and serve.

Note: *This traditional cake of the Bursa district is served on holy days.*

EASY SWIRL CAKE

Ingredients:
3 eggs
2 cups sugar
1 cup milk
1/ 2 cup oil
1/ 2 cup margarine
3-1/2 cups flour
2 tablespoons cocoa
juice of 1 lemon
10 grams baking powder
(4 teaspoons)
5 grams vanilla
(1/4 teaspoon liquid)
1/3 cup raisins or
walnuts, as desired

1. Beat eggs and sugar well. Add lemon juice, oil, melted margarine and melt and mix well. Sift flour twice and mix with baking powder and vanilla. Add flour to egg mixture and mix well.

2. Thoroughly grease cake pan, dust bottom with flour and sugar on the sides.

3. Pour half the batter into the pan. Add cocoa to the remaining half and mix well. Pour at random into the pan. Hold the pan with both hands and tip slightly from side to side to distribute the cocoa mixture and create swirls. Bake in a medium oven.

Note: *If nuts or raisins are to be used. Mix them with the flour before adding.*

FRUIT JUICE CAKE

Ingredients:
4 eggs
3 cups flour
2 cups sugar
1 cup orange juice or other juice
10 grams baking powder (4 teaspoons)
5 grams vanilla (1/4 teaspoon liquid)
Custard:
1/2 liter milk
1 tablespoon flour
1-1/2 tablespoons cornstarch
1/2 cup + 2 tablespoons sugar
1 egg yolk
1/2 tablespoon butter or margarine if desired
cocoa, if desired

1. Beat eggs and sugar. Add fruit juice. Sift flour and mix with baking powder and vanilla. Add to egg mixture. Grease baking pan with butter or margarine. Pour batter in pan and bake in a medium oven.

2. **Custard:** Mix together well all ingredients and cook until thickened. Add butter, if desired, and blend in, add cocoa, if desired, and beat until smooth and creamy.

3. Split cake into 2 layers. Cover 1 layer with custard , place remaining layer on top and remaining custard on top. If desired, arrange fruit slices on top. Allow to set in refrigerator for a few hours before serving.

COLA CAKE

Ingredients:
1 cup cola
1 cup olive oil
1 cup sugar
4 eggs
2-1/2 cups flour
10 grams (4 teaspoons) baking powder
1 packet dry vanilla (1/4 teaspoon liquid)

1. Beat eggs with sugar. Add oil and cola and mix well. Mix flour and baking powder together and add to liquid mixture. Add vanilla.

2. Pour batter in a greased, loured baking pan and bake in a preheated hot oven.

CARROT CAKE

Ingredients:
4 eggs
2 cups sugar
2 cups flour
1 cup walnut pieces
1 cup grated carrot
10 grams (4 teaspoons) baking powder
1 teaspoon cinnamon
1/3 cup oil
Frosting:
2 cups milk
3 tablespoons cornstarch
1cup sugar
60 grams (2 oz) margarine
1 packet dry vanilla (1/4 teaspoon liquid)

1. Beat eggs and sugar well. Mix in walnuts, cinnamon and carrots. Sift four twice and mix with baking powder. Combine with mixture and stir just enough to blend. Do not beat.

2. Pour batter into a greased, floured baking pan and place in a hot preheated oven.

Frosting:

1. Mix cornstarch in 1/3 cup milk. Add remaining milk and sugar and cook, stirring constantly until thickened. Remove from heat and set aside to cool.

2. When cooled, add vanilla and margarine (not melted) and beat 10-15 minutes.

3. Split cake into 2 layers. Spread half of the frosting on 1 layer, place 2nd layer on top and cover top and sides with remaining frosting.

Note: *If desired, whipped cream may be added to the top of the cake.*

WET CAKE

Ingredients:
3 eggs
2 cups sugar
1 cup milk
250 grams (1/2 lb) margarine
3 cups flour
2/3 teaspoon baking powder
1 packet dry vanilla (1/4 teaspoon liquid)
50 grams (1.6 oz) cocoa
coconut

1. Beat eggs and sugar with hand or electric mixer. Melt margarine. Add milk, margarine and vanilla. Mix well.

2. Remove 1 cup of the batter from the bowl. Sift flour twice and mix with baking powder. Add flour to bowl and stir just enough to mix. Pour batter in a greased pan and bake in a hot oven.

3. When the cake is removed from the oven spread the reserved cup of batter over the top. Sprinkle coconut on top and allow to cool before serving.

PLAIN CUPCAKES

Ingredients:

2 eggs
1 cup sugar
1/3 cup yoghurt
1/3 cup oil
2 cups flour
1 packet dry vanilla (1/4 teaspoon liquid)
10 oz (4 teaspoons) baking powder

1. Beat sugar and eggs together. Add yoghurt and oil and mix a little. Add flour, baking powder and vanilla and continue to mix.

2. Fill cupcake holders half way with the batter and arrange on an oven pan. Bake in a hot oven.

ORANGE MOSAIC

Ingredients:

2 oranges
400 grams (12.8 oz) petit beurres (butter cookies)
1/2 cup flour
1/2 liter milk
1 cup sugar
125 grams (1/4 lb) margarine
1 egg
1 packet dry vanilla (1/4 teaspoon liquid)

1. Squeeze oranges. Crush cookies in a bowl and pour juice over them. Stir them a little.

2. Mix egg, sugar, flour and milk and cook until mixture thickens. Remove from heat to cool. When lukewarm, stir in margarine.

3. Pour mixture over cookies in bowl. Stir and transfer to oiled paper. Roll up or fold over in 3's. Allow to set in refrigerator for 1 day. When ready to serve, cut in slices.

RAISIN CAKE

Ingredients:

4 eggs
2 cups sugar
3 cups flour
1 cup cornstarch
1 cup milk
1/2 cup oil
10 grams (4 teaspoons) baking powder
1 grated lemon rind
1 teaspoon lemon juice
1 handful seedless raisins
2 teaspoons cocoa

1. Beat eggs and sugar. Add milk and oil. Sift flour twice and combine with cornstarch and baking powder. Stir flour into liquid mixture.

2. Add grated lemon rind and lemon juice. Mix a little flour with the raisins and add. Mix the batter well. Set aside 3 tablespoons. Pour remaining into a greased, floured baking pan. (If possible, also coat sides of pan with sugar.)

3. Mix 3 tablespoons batter with the cocoa. Spread mixture on top of batter. Bake 45 minutes.

Note: *Adding the lemon juice gives the cake a golden color.*

COLD DRINKS

CONTENTS

LEMON SODA

Ingredients:
1 bottle soda
juice of 1 lemon
1-1/2 tablespoons
sugar
2-3 ice cubes

Mix all ingredients well and pour over ice.

CHERRY SODA

Ingredients:
1 bottle soda
1/2 cup sour cherry syrup (home made or prepared)
2-3 ice cubes

ORANGE SODA

Ingredients:
1 bottle soda
1/2 cup orange syrup (home made or prepared)
2-3 ice cubes

LEMONADE

Ingredients:
5-6 lemons
10 cups water
1-1/2 cups sugar

Wash lemons and put in food processor. Add sugar, mix well and add water. Strain with a fine sieve. Pour over ice cubes and serve immediately or allow to set in refrigerator a short time.

GRAPEFRUIT DRINK

Ingredients:
3-4 grapefruits
2 cups sugar
10 cups water

Remove grapefruit rinds and seeds. Put grapefruits in food processor. Add sugar and continue mixing well. Add water, mix and serve cold.

ORANGE DRINK

Ingredients:
3-4 oranges
1-1/2 cups sugar
10 cups water

Remove orange rinds and seeds. Put oranges in food processor. Add sugar and continue mixing well. Add water, mix and serve cold.

Note: *An easier and healthier way is simply to squeeze the juice from the oranges and serve.*

Orange juice

Grapefruit juice

COLD DRINKS WITH MILK

PEACH MILK

Ingredients:
2 cups milk
3 peaches
4-1/2 tablespoons sugar
2-3 ice cubes

Peel peaches and remove pits. Blend with milk, sugar and ice in food processor.

STRAWBERRY MILK

Ingredients:
2 cups milk
8-10 strawberries
3 tablespoons sugar
4-5 ice cubes

Remove strawberry stems and wash. Blend together with milk, sugar and ice in food processor.

BANANA MILK

Ingredients:

2 cups milk
2 bananas
3 tablespoons sugar
2-3 ice cubes

Boil milk and chill. Blend together with bananas, sugar and ice in food processor.

APRICOT MILK

Ingredients:

2 cups milk
5-6 fresh apricots
6 tablespoons sugar
juice of 1/2 lemon
5-6 ice cubes

Peel apricots and remove pits. Blend together with milk, sugar, lemon juice and ice in food processor.

CHOCOLATE MILK

Ingredients:

2 cups milk
1/4 cup cocoa
1/2 cup sugar
1 egg
5-6 ice cubes

Blend all ingredients together in a food processor.

CHERRY JAM MILK

Ingredients:

2 cups milk
1-1/2 tablespoons sour-cherry jam
4-5 ice cubes

Blend all ingredients together in a food processor.

COMPOTES

SOUR CHERRY COMPOTE

Ingredients:
500 grams (1lb) sour cherries
1-1/2 cups sugar
3 cups water

1. Wash cherries and remove stems. Boil together with sugar and water.

2. When soft, remove from heat, cover with lid and set aside to cool.

STRAWBERRY COMPOTE

Ingredients:
500 grams strawberies
1 cup sugar
3 cups water

1. Put strawberries in water 3-4 times. Each time remove them gently from the water with the hands. Remove stems and wash once more.

2. Boil water and sugar in a pan for 5 minutes. Add strawsberries and bring to a boil again. Remove from heat, cover with lid and set aside to cool.

PEACH COMPOTE

Ingredients:
500 grams firm peaches
1 cup sugar
4 cups water

1. Wash peaches by rolling them in the hands under water. Cut in two and remove stones. Cut into pieces of desired size.

2. Place in pan with sugar and water and cook until done but not mushy. Remove from heat, cover with lid and set aside to cool.

APPLE COMPOTE

Ingredients:
1 kilogram (2 lb) apples
1-1/2 cup sugar
5 cups water

Peel apples and remove seeds and stems. Cut into pieces of desired size. Place in pan and cover with water. When almost done add sugar. return to boil and simmer until done. Cover with lid and set aside to cool.

QUINCE COMPOTE

Ingredients:
1 kilogram (2 lb) quinces
2 cups sugar
4-5 cups water

1. Peel quinces and remove seeds and stems. Cut into pieces of desired size. Place pieces into cold water as they are cut to prevent them from turning brown. If a dark reddish color is desired, boil seeds and stems in 4-5 cups water 5-10 minutes.

2. Drain quince pieces, place in a pan. Drain seeds and stems and add the water (not the seeds and stems) to the quince pan. Add sugar and bring to the boil. Simmer until done but not mushy. Cover with lid and set aside to cool.

APRICOT COMPOTE

Ingredients:
500 grams (1 lb) fresh apricots
1 cup sugar
3 cups water

1. Wash apricots and remove puts.

2. Boil water and sugar for 5 minutes. Add apricots and simmer until soft. Cover with lid and set aside to cool.

SHERBETS

DRIED APRICOT SHERBET

Ingredients:
500 grams dried apricots
1 cup sugar
4 cups water
juice of 1/2 lemon

Soak apricots in some water for 1/2 hour. Strain and wash. Place in a pan with water, sugar and lemon and cook until soft.

Note: *Apricots and raisins cooked together are also delicious. Raisins take longer to cook so start to cook them first, then add apricots.*

RAISIN SHERBET

Ingredients:
1 cup raisins (seedless is best)
1 cups sugar
4-5 cups water
juice of 1/2 lemon or 2 teaspoons citric acid

Wash raisins a few times, each time allowing to soak in water 1-2 minutes. Drain. Place in pan and coverf with water. Bring to a boil and simmer. When done add sugar and lemon and bring to a high boil 1-2 times more. Remove from heat and set aside to cool.

SOUR CHERRY SHERBET

Ingredients:
1 heaping cup sour cherries
2 cups sugar
6 cups water
juice of 1/2 lemon

Soak cherries in water 1-2 hours. Wash twice, drain. Bring to a boil with only the water and simmer until soft. Add sugar and lemon and boil 5 more minutes. Remove from heat.

Note: *Lemon juice may be omitted.*

PRUNE SHERBET

Ingredients:
·1 heaping cup prunes
2 cups sugar
6 cups water
juice of 1/2 lemon

Soak dry prunes in water 1-2 hours. Bring to a boil with only the water and simmer until soft. Add sugar and lemon juice and boil 5 more minutes. Remove from heat.

OTHER DRINK VARIETIES

LOHUSA SHERBET

Ingredients:
500 grams lohusa sugar *
6 cups sugar
5-10 whole cloves
1-2 cinnamon sticks
1 cup finely chopped walnuts
4-5 liters water

1. Combine in a big pot, water, sugar, lohusa sugar and bring to the boil. Tie cloves and cinnamon in a bag and add to pot. Bring to a boil once or twice. Serve cold or hot.

2. After filling the drinking glasses sprinkle a little walnuts on top.

* Lohusa sugar is a red-colored rock sugar traditionally intended for making sherbet for women who are pregnant or have female problems.

BOZA (FERMENTED WHEAT DRINK)

Ingredients:
500 grams cracked wheat
1/3 cups rice
2 cups sugar
5 grams dry vanilla (1/4 teaspoon liquid)
2 yeast cakes or 1/3 cup old boza

1. Rinse wheat and boil until very soft. Add more hot water as necessary.
2. In a separate pan, boil rice until very soft. (Rice is used to make the boza white.)
3. Put wheat and rice through the food processor or press through a sieve.
4. Add sugar and bringto a boil once or twice until a thick soup. Remove from heat and set aside until lukewarm. Stir from time to time. Add yeast or old boza and set aside to rise for 2-3 days. Stir frequently. When boza appears to be ready add vanilla and, if needed, a little more sugar. Mix and store in refrigerator. When ready to serve, pour in cup and sprinkle cinnamon on top. Traditionally boza is serve with roasted chickpeas.

Note: *Boza should be made in a porcelain, glass or enamel container.*

MELON MILK

Ingredients:
1 ripe melon
4 cups milk
1/3 cup sugar
juice of 1/2 lemon

Remove rind and seeds, wash and slice. Place slices in a pan and cook to a puree consistency while stirring. Add sugar and milk, mix well and add lemon. Allow to cool and chill in refrigerator.

Vanilla ice cream

Chocolate ice cream

ICE CREAMS
AND ICES

CONTENTS

ABOUT MAKING ICE CREAMS AND ICES

1. The quality of the container used is very important. Use of a bad quality or a aluminum container causes the milk to darken when boiled.

2. When pouring the cooked mixture into serving bowls do not fill all the way to the top.

3. After the mixture has cooled sufficiently, place in the freezer compartment or deep freeze.

4. During the freezing process, stir the mixture frequently to prevent ice crystals from forming on the surface or the bottom and to give the frozen mixture a slightly chewy consistency.

5. Fruit ices in particular need to be stirred often while freezing because they freeze more quickly than creams.

6. If the amount of sugar is reduced by much, the mixture will form ice crystals or even turn to ice. Therefore it is necessary to use the amount of sugar that is specified.

Sayings about hunger

"A hungry person never looks at the cook's faults."

"If the load on the camel is dinner, it looks like very little to a hungry person."

" Hunger can hook even the smartest fish."

"If they think their deaths are near the healthy will eat sweetmeats every day."

PISTACHIO ICE CREAM

Ingredients:
1 liter milk
1 cup sugar
1-1/2 teaspoons sahlep (orchid root powder)
2-3 pieces mastic
100 grams (3.2 oz) shelled pistachios

1. Beat the mastic to a powder. Combine and mix well in a good quality pan: sugar, sahlep, mastic. Slowly add milk, stirring. Place over a flame and continue to stir until the mixture thickens. Remove from heat.

2. Crush the shelled pistachios and add to mixture as soon as it is removed from the stove. Allow to cool, mixing frequently. Fill individual cups and freeze.

3. From time to time stir the edges and bottom to prevent ice crystals and to give the frozen mixture a creamy, slightly chewy consistency. Freeze as long as desired and serve.

VANILLA ICE CREAM

Ingredients:
1 liter milk
1 cups sugar
5 egg yolks
1-1/2 tablespoons flour
10 grams dry vanilla (1/4 teaspoon liquid)

1. Boil the milk. Mix together in a bowl: egg yolks, flour and sugar. Slowly add hot milk and stir until well mixed. Place over a flame and bring just to the boiling point. Remove from flame immediately. Add vanilla. Allow to cool, mixing frequently.

2. Fill individual dishes and place in deep freeze. Stir frequently to prevent ice crystals from forming.

Note: *The flavor of the vanilla ice cream may be enhanced by adding roasted, crushed hazelnuts to the mixture after it is removed from the flame.*

PLAIN ICE CREAM

Ingredients:
1 liter milk
1 cup sugar
1-1/2 teaspoons sahlep (orchid root powder)
2-3 pieces mastic

1. Beat the mastic to a powder. Combine and mix well in a good quality pan: sugar, sahlep, mastic. Slowly add milk, stirring. Place over a flame and continue to stir until the mixture thickens. Remove from heat

2. Remove from heat. Allow to cool, stirring frequently. Pour into individual dishes and place in deep freeze. Stir frequently to prevent ice crystals on the sides and bottom. If this is done often the ice cream will be creamy and gummy. Freeze as much as desired and serve.

CHOCOLATE ICE CREAM

Ingredients:
1 liter milk
1 cups sugar
5 egg yolks
1-1/2 tablespoons flour or
3 tablespoons cornstarch
100 grams (3.2 oz) baking
chocolate or 6 tablespoons cocoa

1. Boil the milk. Mix together well the egg yolks, flour and sugar. Slowly add hot milk while stirring.
Place on stove and bring just to the boiling point. Immediately remove from heat. If chocolate is used, grate it and add to the cooling cream. Stir once or twice, just enough to make the cream chocolate colored. If cocoa is used, add when the cream comes to a boil and stir.

2. Fill serving dishes and place in the deep freeze. Stir mixture from time to time to prevent sides and bottom from forming ice crystals. Return to freezer. If this procedure is done frequently the ice cream will be smooth and creamy. Freeze as long as desired and serve.

FRUIT ICES

CHERRY ICE

Ingredients:
500 grams (1 lb) sour cherries
2 cups sugar
2 cups water

1. Place sugar and water in a pan and boil 5-10 minutes. Remove from heat and allow to cool.

2. Remove cherry stems and wash 3 times. Add cherries to cooling syrup and mix well. Pour through a wire strainer and then pour cherry liquid into individual serving dishes. Place in freezer. To prevent ice crystals from forming, stir frequently (Because fruit ices freeze so quickly, stir more often than the ice creams). Return to freezer until ready to serve.

ROKOKO

1. Line a bowl with plastic wrap. Be sure there is plenty of wrap hanging over the edges. Spread chopped nuts in the bottom.

2. In another bowl, add 1 box of the whipping cream to half of the fruit-flavored milk and beat with electric mixer until thick and creamy. Pour this mixture evenly on top of nuts and place in freezer immediately

Ingredients:
450 grams (14.5 oz) dry whipping cream (3 boxes)
500 grams (1 lb) fruit-flavored milk (2 boxes)
250 grams chocolate milk (1 box)
1 cup walnut or hazelnut pieces
200 grams (6.4 oz) petit beurres (butter cookies)

(in order to spread the other cream mixture on top later).

3. Beat together well in a bowl one box of whipping cream with the chocolate milk. Remove the slightly hardened cream from freezer and spread the chocolate cream on top. Return to freezer.

4. Combine the remaining box of whipping cream and other half of the fruit-flavored milk and beat together well until thick and creamy. Again remove bowl from freezer and add this layer on top. Arrange the cookies to cover the top and fold the plastic wrap over the cookies. If there is not enough to cover, place another plastic sheet across the top of the bowl. Allow to remain in freezer 4-5 hours or over night before serving.

STRAWBERRY ICE

Ingredients:

500 grams (1 lb) strawberries

2 cups sugar

2 cups water

juice of 1 lemon

1. Sort straweberries, remove leaves and wash 3 times. Squeeze lemon juice on berries to prevent darkening. Combine sugar and water in a pan and boil 5-10 mnutes. Remove from heat and allow to cool.

2. Add strawberries to cooling syrup and mix well. Pour through a wire strainer and pour liquid into individual serving dishes. Place in freezer. To prevent ice crystals from forming, stir frequently (Because fruit ices freeze so quickly, stir more often than the ice creams). Return to freezer until ready to serve.

PEACH ICE

Ingredients:

500 grams (1 lb) peaches

1-1/2 cups sugar

1-1/2 cups water

juice of 1 lemon

1. Combine sugar and water in a pan and boil 5-10 minutes. Remove from heat and allow to cool. Wash peaches 3 times and cut in pieces. Squeeze lemon juice on them to prevent darkening.

2. Add peaches to cooling syrup and mix well. Pour through a wire strainer and pour liquid into individual serving dishes. Place in freezer. To prevent ice crystals from forming, stir frequently (Because fruit ices freeze so quickly, stir more often than the ice creams). Return to freezer until ready to serve.

APRICOT ICE

Ingredients:

500 grams (1 lb) apricots
1-1/2 cups sugar
1-1/2 cups water
juice of 1 lemon

1. 1. Combine sugar and water in a pan and boil 5-10 minutes. Remove from heat and allow to cool. Wash apricots 3 times and cut in pieces. Squeeze lemon juice on them to prevent darkening.

2. Add apricots to cooling syrup and mix well. Pour through a wire strainer and pour liquid into individual serving dishes. Place in freezer. To prevent ice crystals from forming, stir frequently. (Because fruit ices freeze so quickly, stir more often than the ice creams). Return to freezer until ready to serve.

ORANGE ICE

Ingredients:

5 juice oranges
1-1/2 cups sugar
3 cups water
1 lemon

1. Combine sugar and water in a pan and boil 5-10 minutes. Remove from heat and allow to cool

2. Squeeze oranges and lemon and mix the juices together. Pour through a wire strainer and pour liquid into individual serving dishes. Place in freezer. To prevent ice crystals from forming, stir frequently. (Because fruit ices freeze so quickly, stir more often than the ice creams). Return to freezer until ready to serve.

LEMON ICE

Ingredients:

3 lemons
1-1/2 cups sugar
2 cups water
1 grated lemon rind

1. Combine sugar and water in a pan and boil 5-10 minutes. Remove from heat and allow to cool.

2. Grate one of the lemon rinds. Squeeze the lemons and mix with grated rind. Pour through a wire strainer and pour liquid into individual serving dishes. Place in freezer. To prevent ice crystals from forming, stir frequently. (Because fruit ices freeze so quickly, stir more often than the ice creams). Return to freezer until ready to serve.

SYRUPS, MARMALADES, PRESERVES

CONTENTS

Syrups

Marmalades

Preserves

Fruit gelatins

Fruit juice puddings (pelte)

PRACTICAL INFORMATION

1. Jars and bottles must be perfectly clean. It is recommended to boil the containers and keep in the boiled water until just before filling.

2. Too much stirring when hot can cause the syrup to become sugary.

3. Immediately after filling containers allow them to cool down in a cool place away from sunlight.

4. Do not reduce the amount of sugar specified in the recipe.

5. It is necessary to stir the marmelade after sugar is added to prevent sticking to the pan.

6. To capture the full flavor and aroma do not over-boil.

7. To assure preserves will keep a long time without molding, the measurement of sugar should be 1-1/2 to 2 times the measurement of fruit.

8. Lemon is added to the preserves just at the point the pan is ready to come off the stove. If added while cooking, lemon can change the color of the preserves.

9. Remove the foam from the top of the preserves after the pan comes off the stove.

10. Do not cap the lids tightly on the preserve jars until completely cooled.

11. The preserves are done when:

a. A spoon is dipped into the pan and the preserves slide off the spoon in long threads.

b. A spoonful is placed on a plate, the preserves are spread out with a finger and the preserves merge again very slowly. If they merge quickly, they need to boil a little longer.

c. The end of a spoon is dipped in the preserves and when dripped into water the preserves form little balls or droplets. If instead the preserves spread out in the water, they need to boil a little longer.

SYRUPS

ORANGE SYRUP

Ingredients:

15 oranges

10 cups sugar

5 cups water

5 grated orange rinds

citric acid

Grate 5 of the orange rinds and set aside the rind. Squeeze all 15 oranges. Combine sugar and water and bring to a boil. When the sugar has melted add orange juice, grated rind and some citric acid. Bring to a boil once or twice. When cooled, strain into jars or bottles.

CORNELIAN CHERRY SYRUP

Ingredients:
1 kilogram (2 lb) ripe cornelian cherries
2 kilograms (4 lb) sugar
juice of 1 lemon or 1-1/2 table-spoons citric acid

1. Sort and remove stems from cherries. Wash a few times in plenty of water. Cover with water in a pan and bring to a boil. When it comes to a boil strain cherries. Save juice. Do this two more times: cover, bring to a boil, strain and save juice (or repeat until the color is all gone from the cherries).
2. Add sugar and lemon juice or citric acid to the hot juice and boil until mixture thickens. Remove from heat and spoon off the foam. Cover pot with lid and set aside to cool. When cooled, fill bottles.

BLACK MULBERRY SYRUP

Ingredients:
1 kilogram (2 lb) black mulberries
2 kilograms sugar
juice of 1/2 lemon

1. At least 1 night before cooking: sort berries carefully, wash gently, place in a cooking pot and cover with sugar.
2. Place over a low flame and cook in its own juice, stirring ocasionally. Spoon off foam. Add lemon juice and bring to a boil. Remove from heat and cover. When cooled, strain and fill bottles.

SOUR CHERRY SYRUP

Ingredients:
1 kilogram (2 lb) sour cherries
2 kilograms (4 lb) sugar
1/3 cup citric acid or juice of
1 lemon

Wash cherries, cover with water and bring to a boil. Immediately strain them and reserve juice. Again cover cherries in water and strain. Combine 2 hot juices and add sugar and lemon or citric acid. Boil until thickened. Remove foam from syrup and cover. Allow to cool. When cooled, fill bottles.

LEMON SYRUP

Ingredients:
10-15 lemons
15 cups sugar
3 cups water
4 grated lemon rinds

1. Boil sugar in water. When sugar is completely melted remove from heat.
2. Grate 4 lemon rinds very finely. Squeeze the lemons. Add juice and rinds to pan and stir well. Do not boil. Allow to cool and fill bottles. (When ready to use syrup, thin if necessary with a little water.)

PLUM SYRUP

Ingredients:
1 kilogram (2 lb) plums
2 kilograms (4 lb) sugar
1/3 cup citric acid or juice of 1 lemon

Cover plums with water and bring to a boil. Immediately strain. Reserve juice. Repeat this process and mix the two juices. Add sugar and lemon or citric acid to hot juice. Boil until thickened. Remove from flame and spoon off foam. Cover and allow to cool. When cooled fill bottles.

ROSE SYRUP

Ingredients:
2 kilograms (4 lb) preserves-type roses
100 grams (3.2 oz) sugar
1/3 cup citric acid or juice of 1 lemon

1. Prepare roses the same as for rose preserves (see recipe this chapter).
2. A few leaves and poppies (with the black part removed) may be added to the roses. The syrup should be thinner than the preserves.

MARMALADES

QUINCE MARMALADE

Ingredients:
1 kilogram (2 lb) quinces
5 cups sugar
juice of 1 lemon or 1/3 cup citric acid
3 cups water

1. Peel quinces, remove centers and seeds and grate. Bring to a boil in 3 cups water. When soft add sugar and lemon juice or citric acid.
2. Cook until thick, remove from stove and cover. When cooled fill jars. Store in a cool place away from sunlight.

Note: *If reddish colored preserves are desired, put quince seeds in a small cheesecloth bag, tie tightly and boil with the fruit. Remove after cooking.*

ORANGE MARMALADE

Ingredients:

1 kilogram (2 lb) thin-skinned juice oranges
1-1/2 kilograms (3 lb) sugar
juice of 1 lemon or 1/3 cup citric acid

1. Remove outer (orange) peels from oranges and bring to a boil once or twice to eliminate bitterness. Strain peels and set aside to cool. Discard the bitter water.

2. Remove white pith and seeds from oranges. Put in food processor along with boiled and cooled outer peels. Place mixture in a pot and cook until thick. Cover and allow to cool. When cooled, fill jars and close very tightly. Store in a cool place away from sunlight.

PEACH MARMALADE

Ingredients:

1 kilogram (2 lb) ripe peaches
1 kilogram sugar
juice of 1 lemon or 1/3 cup citric acid

1. Wash peaches and remove stones. Put in food processor. Place in pan, put sugar on top and allow to set 1 hour.

2. Cook until thickened. When about to remove from flame add lemon juice or citric acid. Cover and allow to cool, then fill jars and close very tightly. Store in a cool place away from sunlight.

PLUM MARMALADE

Ingredients:

1 kilogram (2 lb) plums
2 kilograms (4 lb) sugar
juice of 1 lemon or 1/3 cup citric acid

1. Remove stems from plums and wash. Boil in a little water until skins burst. Allow to cool. Strain and pass plums through a sieve back into the juice.

2. Add sugar and cook until thickened. When about to remove from flame add lemon juice or citric acid. Cover and allow to cool. Store in a cool place away from sunlight.

CORNELIAN CHERRY MARMALADE

Ingredients:
1 kilogram (2 lb) cornelian cherries
2 kilograms (4 lb) sugar
juice of 1/2 lemon

Bring cherries to boil in very little water. When soft, pass cherries through a perforated skimmer. Add sugar and cook until thickened. When about to remove from flame add lemon juice. Remove from heat and cover. When cooled, fill jars.

Note: *Unlike sour cherries, the stones of cornelian cherries cannot be removed before cooking. If you have the time and patience try to remove them one by one after cooking.*

PRESERVES

QUINCE PRESERVES

Ingredients:
1 kilogram (2 lb) quinces
6 cups sugar
3 cups water
1/3 teaspoon citric acid or juice of 1 lemon

1. Wash, slice and peel quinces. Boil cores and seeds in 3 cups water (to help thicken and give color). Strain and reserve juice.
2. Cut fruit in hazelnut size cubes or as desired. Boil in juice until soft.

3. When soft add sugar and lemon juice and simmer 5-10 minutes longer. Remove from stove, cover and allow to cool. When cool fill jars. Store in a cool place away from sunlight.

SOUR CHERRY PRESERVES

Ingredients:

1 kilogram (2 lb) sour cherries
2 kilograms (4 lb) sugar
juice of 1/2 1emon or 1/6 teaspoon
citric acid

1. Sort cherries and wash 2-3 times. Place in pan and cover cherries with all the sugar. Allow to set at least 12 hours.

2. Cook in its own juice over a low flame until thickened. A few times during the cooking spoon off the foam from the top. Just before removing from the stove add lemon juice or citric acid.

3. When cooled fill jars and cap them tightly. Store in a cool place away from sunlight.

SWEET CHERRY PRESERVES

Ingredients:

1 kilogram (2 lb) sweet cheeries
1-1/2 kilograms (3 lb) sugar
juice of 1 lemon or 1/3 teaspoon
citric acid

1. Sort cherries and wash 2-3 times or more. Remove seeds. Place in pan and cover cherries with all the sugar. Allow to set overnight, at least 10-12 hours.

2. Bring just to boiling point, then allow it to simmer in its own juice over

a low f lame about 5-10 minutes. Set aside for 10 minutes. Return to stove and simmer a little more. Repeat this process again. Each time spoon off the foam. When about to remove from stove the third time, add lemon juice or citric acid.

3. When cooled, fill jars and cap tightly. Store in a cool place away from sunlight.

AMBER PRESERVES

Ingredients:
1 apple
1 orange
1 lemon
1 grapefruit
2 tangerines
1-1/2 heaping cups sugar for each heaping cup of fruit

1. Wash all the fruit well and remove peels. Rinse again and drain off water. Cut fruits to desired size pieces. Mix all pieces together and measure in heaping cupfuls. Place all fruit in a pot and cover with measured sugar (1-1/2:1). Allow to set over night.

2. Place pot over a medium flame and cook in its own juices until thickened.

ORANGE PRESERVES

Ingredients:
1 kilogram (2 lb) thick-skinned juice oranges
1-1/2 kilograms (3 lb) sugar
juice of 1 lemon or 1/3 teaspoon citric acid

1. Wash oranges well and grate rinds off 2 oranges.

2. Boil oranges in plenty of water. Strain and discard water. Peel oranges and remove the white pith. Slice oranges and remove any seeds. Place oranges in large pan (or 2 pans) and add grated rinds and sugar. Simmer over a low flame until thickened. When about to remove from stove add lemon juice or citric acid. When cooled fill jars.

APRICOT PRESERVES

Ingredients:
1 kilogram (2 lb) apricots (or peaches)
1 kilogram (2 lb) sugar
1/3 teaspoon citric acid

1. Wash apricots and remove stones without cutting the fruit in two. Cover with sugar and a little water and boil until the fruit has a rich, dark color. Remove from heat and allow to set overnight.

2. Bring just to boiling point, then allow it to simmer in its own juice over a low f lame about 5-10 minutes. Set aside for 10 minutes. Return to stove

and simmer a little more. Each time spoon off the foam. When about to remove from stove the second time, add citric acid. When cooled, fill jars and cap tightly. Store in a cool place away from sunlight.

Notes: 1. *Apricots may be prepared like other fruits that are simply covered uncooked with sugar and set over night. However, doing this the apricots turn out quite mushy.*
   2. *Peaches may be cut to desired size pieces and prepared in the same way as the apricot preserves recipe.*

STRAWBERRY PRESERVES

Ingredients:

1 kilogram (2 lb) strawberries
1-1/2 kilograms (3 lb) sugar
juice of 1 lemon or 1/6 teaspoon
citric acid

1. Soak strawberries in plenty of water for 1-2 minutes. Remove with the hands and repeat once or twice – or as often as is necessary to be sure all the sand is off the berries.

2. Remove stems and wash once more. Strain and place in a pan. Cover with the sugar and allow to set at least one night.

3. Without adding water simmer on low flame until thickened. When about to remove from the stove add lemon juice or citric acid. Cover and allow to cool. Fill jars. Store in a cool place away from sunlight.

ROSE PRESERVES

Ingredients:

2 kilograms (4 lb) roses
for preserves
100 grams citric acid
1 cup sugar
5-6 red roses

1. Put roses in water and strain. Remove stems along with the white part on the underneath layer of the roses. Add pounded citric acid and sugar and mix well with the hands. Continue to rub and press with the hands until the juices come out.

3. Fill jars with this mixture and cap very tightly. Store in a cool place away from sunlight. This is the basic mixture for making preserves whenever needed, as follows: Place 500 grams (1 lb) sugar in a pot and enough water to cover. Bring to a boil. When it thickens add 1 tablespoon of the roses and boil for 5 minutes (if boiled longer the color will be lost). Cover and allow to cool. Fill jars and store in a cool place away from sunlight.

BLACK MULLBERRY PRESERVES

Ingredients:
1 kilogram (2 lb) black mulberries
1-1/2 kilograms (3 lb) sugar
juice of 1/2 lemon or 1/6 tea-
spoon citric acid

1. Mulberries crush very easily so sort berries carefully and wash gently. Put in a cooking pot one at a time

2. Add a little water and lay sugar on top. Allow to set at least 12 hours. Place on stove and simmer slowly on a low flame, stirring only once. When almost ready to remove from stove, add lemon or citric acid and cook 2 minutes longer. Cover and allow to cool. Fill jars and store in a cool place away from sunlight.

Notes: 1. *While the mullberries are cooking the seeds come to the top. If desired, these can be removed with a slotted spoon.*

2. *Black mulberry syrup and preserves are a good choice if one has a stomach ache or sores in the mouth.*

3. *Raspberries may be prepared according to this recipe.*

FRUIT GELATINS

Gelatins are made by boiling fruit juice with sugar.

PRACTICAL TIPS

1. Not every fruit makes a good gelatin. The best choices are tart varieties of apples, pears, plums, quinces, grapes and sour grapes.

2. The stronger the aroma of the fruit, the better the flavor and color of the gelatin.

3. Boil the fruit only briefly.

4. While cooking, the juice is stirred to aereate it.

5. The faster the mixture is cooked the faster it jells.

6. After the sugar is added the foam that rises to the surface is removed.

7. To test for doneness, a few drops of the gelatin are placed on a cold plate. If the drops do not spread out, it is done and should be removed from the stove. Or, the same applies: Squeeze the drops between the fingers. If the fingers separate easily it needs more cooking but if the drops stick to the fingers, it is done.

8. Fill serving cups when the gelatin is hot. (Cups should be sterilized.)

9. When the cups of gelatin are cold remove carefully, cut if desired and add coconut or granulated sugar on top if desired.

10. A good quality gelatin is transparent and shiny.

APPLE GELATIN

Ingredients:
1 kilogram (2 lb) tart, juicy apples
3 cups sugar

1. Wash and trim apples. Cut into small pieces. Put an equal amount of apples and water in a pan and boil until soft. Process in a

juicer and pour juice in a pan. Set aside for awhile. Add sugar and boil over a high flame, stirring constantly and whipping up the mixture frequently to aereate it. Cook as quickly as possible.

2. Keep spooning off the foam. When it thickens, transfer a few drops onto a plate. If the drops do not spread out or if they stick to the fingers when squeezed between two fingers, the gelatin is done.

3. Remove from heat and immediately pour into cups (with lids but do not cover yet). When cooled, cover each cup with a piece of parchment dipped in alcohol, then cover tightly with the lid. If candied gelatin is desired instead, fill icecube trays with the hot liquid and chill. When ready to serve spoon gelatin cubes into a dish of coconut or granulated sugar. Squeeze the drops between the fingers. If the fingers separate easily it needs more cooking but if the drops stick to the fingers, it is done.

QUINCE GELATIN

Ingredients:

1 kilogram (2 lb) quinces
3 cups sugar

1. Wash and trim quinces. Cut into small pieces. Put an equal amount of apples and water in a pan and boil until soft. Process in a juicer and pour juice in a pan. Set aside for awhile. Add sugar and boil over a high flame, stirring constantly and whipping up the mixture frequently to aereate it. Cook as quickly as possible.

2. Keep spooning off the foam. When it thickens, drop a few drops onto a plate. If the drops do not spread out or if they stick to the fingers when squeezed between two fingers, the gelatin is done.

3. Remove from heat and immediately pour into jars that have lids but do not cover yet. When cooled, cover each jar with a piece of parchment dipped in alcohol, then cover tightly with the lid. If candied gelatin is desired instead, fill ice-cube trays with the hot liquid and chill. When ready to serve spoon gelatin cubes into a dish of coconut or granulated sugar.

PLUM GELATIN

Ingredients:

1 kilogram (2 lb) plums

3 cups sugar

1. Sort and wash the plums. Cut and remove stones. Place in a pot with just enough water to cover. When soft remove from stove. Process in a juicer and pour juice in a pan. Set aside for awhile. Add sugar and boil over a high flame, stirring constantly and whipping up the mixture frequently to aereate it. Cook as quickly as possible.

2. Keep spooning off the foam. When it thickens, transfer a few drops to a cold plate. If the drops do not spread out or if they stick to the fingers when squeezed between two fingers, the gelatin is done.

3. Remove from heat and immediately pour into cups (with lids but do not cover yet). When cooled, cover each cup with a piece of parchment dipped in alcohol, then cover tightly with the lid. If candied gelatin is desired instead, fill icecube trays with the hot liquid and chill. When ready to serve spoon gelatin cubes into a dish of coconut or granulated sugar.

SOUR GRAPE GELATIN

Ingredients:

4 cups sour grapes

4 cups sugar

1. Sort and wash grapes and remove stems. Process in a press or juicer and place in a pan.

2. Add sugar and boil on a high flame, stirring constantly and whipping up the mixture frequently to aereate it. Spoon off the foam. When it thickens, transfer a few drops to a cold plate If the drops do not spread out or if they stick to the fingers when squeezed between two fingers, the gelatin is done.

3. Remove from heat and pour into cups while still hot.

Notes: 1. When the grapes are very small they don't give juice. They are best when brownish spots have formed on them.

2. An alternative method is to boil the grapes in very little water and drain instead of using a press or juicer.

FRUIT JUICE PUDDINGS (PELTE)

ORANGE PUDDING

Ingredients:

4 sour oranges

6 tablespoons cornstarch

1-1/2 cups sugar

2 cups water

(1 cup to mix with cornstarch)

    1. Squeeze juice from oranges and mix juice with 1 cup water and sugar in a pan. Set to boil. Mix 1 cups water with cornstarch. Drizzle slowly into boiling juice while stirring constantly to avoid sticking or lumps.

    2. When thickened remove from heat and pour into bowls.

RİZE GRAPE PUDDING (PEPEÇURA)

Ingredients:
1 liter (Concord type purple)
grape juice
2 cups granulated sugar
1 cup corn flour
1 cup walnuts
1 cup hazelnuts and/or pistachios

1. Wash and drain grapes in a colander. Crush out the juice.

2. Bring grape juice to a boil. When it comes to aboil add sugar. Mix corn flour with a little water and stir to a smooth liquid paste. Add very slowly to the boiling grape juice, stirring constantly. Continue cooking to thick pudding consistency.

3. Pour the pudding into individual serving dishes and sprinkle crushed nuts on top.

LEMON PUDDING

Prepare as for orange pudding in this chapter. In place of orange juice use the juice of two lemons.

Fig pudding
(paluze)

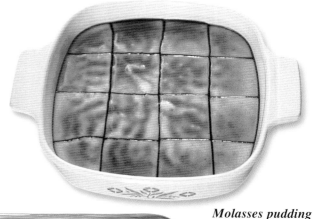

Molasses pudding
(asita)

Molasses
pudding
(gebole)

FIG PUDDING (PALUZE)

Ingredients:

100 grams (3.2 oz) dried figs
1/3 cup grapes
2 medium sized apples
2 tablespoons cornstarch
1 scant (7/8) cup sugar or molasses
1 handful each walnuts and hazelnuts
1/3 teaspoon grated orange rind

1. Sort and wash grapes. Wash figs and cut into small pieces. Bring about 2 liters water to a boil.

2. Add grated or finely chopped orange rind, grapes and figs. Bring to a boil once or twice again. Mix cornstarch in a little cold water and very slowly stir into the boiling juice. Continue stirring until it returns to a boil.

3. Add sugar or molasses and the coarsely chopped nuts. Bring to a boil once or twice again. Remove from heat and chill before serving.

MOLASSES PUDDING (GEBOLE)

Ingredients:

3 tablespoons flour
2 tablespoons butter, olive oil,
OR 1/3 cup walnuts
5 cups water
1 cup molasses

1. Mix flour with 1 cup of water until smooth and put in a pan. Add 4 cups of water and butter or olive oil. (If oil-free dessert is desired, add the walnuts.)

2. Stir while cooking to a pudding consistency. Then add molasses and bring to a boil twice. Pour into a glass dish. Allow to cool slightly. Serve warm.

Note: *If desired, prepare a sugar syrup and add in place of molasses. Or, honey may be used.*

MOLASSES PUDDING (ASITA)

Ingredients:

3-4 tablespoons wheat starch
4 cups water or milk
1/3 cup molasses

1. Mix starch with 1 cup water until smooth.

2. Put 4 cups water or milk in a pan and mix in the starch.

3. Cook until pudding consistency and pour in a glass dish. Allow to cool until warm. Pour molasses over it, cut slices and transfer to individual serving plates. Or, pour hot pudding into individual bowls and allow to set until warm, spoon molasses on top, and serve warm or cold.

TANGERINE PUDDING

Ingredients:

8 tangerines
6 tablespoons cornstarch
2 cups water (1 cup to mix with starch)
1 cup sugar

1. Squeeze juice from tangerines and mix in a pan with 1 cup water and sugar. Set on stove to boil. Mix starch with 1 cup water until creamy. Drizzle very slowly into the boiling juice while stirring constantly.

2. Be careful to avoid sticking on the bottom or lumping. When thickened, remove from heat and pour into individual serving bowls.

Eating and Drinking Customs in Turkish Culture

1. To wash the hands and clean the teeth both before and after the meal.

2. To begin with grace and to give thanks at the end. To meditate during the meal about food, food consumption and nourishment … to offer compliments and thanks to the host and the chef. Not to sit down at the table with a frown and a long face. Not to refer to sickness, death and upsetting topics during the meal.

3. Not to sit down at the table without an appetite and not to overeat. To wait until all family members have come to the table before beginning the meal, if at all possible.

4. To use the right hand to bring food to the mouth (except when holding a knife, the left hand holds the fork). It is seen as useful to use the left hand for holding the bread.

5. Not to speak with food in the mouth. Not to stuff the mouth too full with food. To eat slowly.

6. Not to smack the lips or slurp the soup. If hot, not to blow on the food. Not to chew with the mouth open. Not to cough, sneeze or laugh loudly with food in the mouth.

7. To take on the plate only as much food as can be consumed and finish what is on the plate.

Pickled red peppers

Gherkin pickles

Tomato pickles

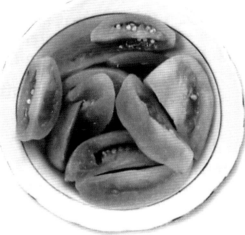

Mixed pickles

PICKLES

CONTENTS

PICKLING TIPS

1. Reasons for formation of mold, slime or white spots on pickles:
   a. not enough salt and vinegar used,
   b. stored in a hot place,
   c. water used was not pure,
   d. air allowed to seep inside jar,
   e. vegetables used were not fresh or healthy.

2. Although the amount of salt used may change according to taste. Do not use less than 3 tablespoons per liter of water. More may be used. In addition pickling salt, not refined salt should be used.

3. Water pickles in which no vinegar is used are more susceptible to molding. Therefore it is useful to first boil and chill the water before using.

4. To prevent molding it is suggested to add potassium sorbate (calcium sorbate), which is harmless and organic and available from druggists.

5. Before use in making pickles it is very important for the flavor of the pickles to rid the jars of any food flavors lingering from prior use.

VINEGARS

DENIZLI WINE VINEGAR

Fill a very large glass container with grapes that have been sorted one by one and the stems removed. Add just enough water to cover. To start the fermentation, add 1 cup of vinegar. (Use 1/3 cup for every 5 to 6 kilograms, or 10-12 lb, of grapes.) If allowed to set in a hot sunny spot it will become vinegar in 40 days. If set in a cool or sunless place it may take longer.

BURDUR ROSEHIPS VINEGAR

Wash the amount of rosehips to be used and place in a large container. Add just enough hot water to cover. Allow to cool and strain. Discard rosehips and fill a large jar with the juice. It will be vinegar in a few months.

BURDUR APPLE OR PEAR VINEGAR

As the apples or pears are consumed, collect the peels in jars and add enough water to cover. Close jars very tightly and allow to set in a cold place. When the color turns yellow the vinegar is ready to use.

PICKLES

PICKLE GARNISH

Ingredients:

1 cup salt	1 handful chickpeas
1/4 teaspoon citric acid	leaves from 1 bunch parsley
1/3 cup vinegar	leaves from 1 bunch celery
2 grated tomatoes	1 head garlic, crushed
1 handful seedless grapes	

Combine these ingredients and mix well. Combine in any type of pickles.

TRAKYA PICKLED RED PEPPERS

Ingredients:

2 kilograms (4 lb) red
pimento peppers
3 garlic cloves
1 bunch parsley
1 cup vinegar
1/3 cup lemon juice
1/3 cup oil
pickling salt as needed

1. Broil peppers in the oven or over an open flame until they blister. When cooled remove outer skins. Split down the middle and remove stems and seeds.

2. Mix together thinly slices garlic and parsley and add to peppers. Mix well and fill a large jar.

3. Meanwhile, combine vinegar, lemon juice, salt and oil and mix until salt is dissolved. Pour over peppers. Cover tightly and store in a cold place.

PICKLED PIMENTOS

Ingredients:

5 kilograms (10 lb) pimento peppers

salt, vinegar and olive oil

2 heads garlic

1. Broil peppers over an open flame (or on a grill or in oven broiler) until they blister. Instead, peppers may be boiled 1-2 minutes in a little water. When

slightly cooled, remove outer skins and set aside to cool.

2. Put peppers in a large jar. Peel garlic, separate the cloves and wash. Add garlic to the jar and fill to the top with a mixture of one-half vinegar and one-half olive oil. Close lid tightly and store in a cool place.

HOT ALBANIAN PEPPER PICKLES

Ingredients:
2 kilograms Albanian peppers
1/4 cup vinegar
1/3 cup olive oil
2 large tomatoes
1 head garlic
1 tablespoon sugar

1. Wash peppers and fill a jar with them. Grate tomatoes. Peel garlic and slice thin. Mix tomatoes with oil, vinegar, sugar and garlic. Mix into a sauce and pour on top of the jar of peppers.

2. Mix water and salt until salt is dissolved (3-4 tablespoons salt to 1 liter water). Pour over the peppers and cap very tightly. Store in a cold place. When the green peppers in the jar turn yellowish, pickling is finished.

PICKLED GREEN CHILES

Ingredients:
4-5 kilograms (8-10 lb) green chile peppers
3-4 heads garlic
2-3 lemons
2 tablespoons granulated sugar
1 slice bread
1 handful chickpeas
1 tablespoon cardamon seed
1 cup vinegar
water and salt as needed (3-4 tablespoons salt to 1 liter water)

1. Cut off tips of pepper stems, as desired. Wash thoroughly.

2. Wash chickpeas. Peel and wash garlic. Place slice of bread and chick-

peas in the bottom of a large container to be used for the pickles. Place peppers and garlic cloves in alternating layers in the jar.

3. Wrap cardamon seed in a clean cloth or bag and tie tightly. Add among peppers in the jar.

4. Dissolve 2/3 teaspoon sugar in water. Add vinegar. Sqeeze lemons and add lemon juice (or add sliced lemons). Pour this mixture into the jar so it is filled.

5. Cap tightly and store in a cool place.

6. When the peppers turn a yellow color in the jar the pickling is finished.

PICKLED BELL PEPPERS

Ingredients:

1-1/2 kilograms (3 lb) bell peppers

1 small head cabbage

4-5 red chili peppers

1 bunch parsley

leaves of 10-12 celery stalks or

celery roots

2 cups vinegar

salt and water (1-1/2 tablespoons

salt to 4-5 cups water)

1. Wash peppers and remove stems and seeds. Fill a large container.

2. Chop finely: cabbage, red peppers, garlic and parsley and celery leaves. Mix together and stuff into container.

3. Mix salt in the water until dissolved. Add vinegar and mix well. Pour over peppers. Place a weight firmly on top of the peppers in the jar so that all the liquid comes to the top. Cap tightly and store in a cool place.

ULUBORLU EGGPLANT AND BEAN PICKLES

Ingredients:

3 kilograms (6 lb) eggplants
(aubergine)
2 kilograms (4 lb) green beans
500 grams (1 lb) cabbage
500 grams (1 lb) red chili peppers
2 heads garlic
1 cup vinegar, salt, water
1 tablespoon sugar
1 bunch fresh mint

1. Wash eggplants and place in a pan. Add water to cover and boil 1-2 minutes. Discard water and allow to cool.

2. Wash cabbage and peppers. Remove stems and seeds from peppers. Chop finely the cabbage and peppers. Mix together well. Split eggplants lengthwise and spoon out some of the insides. Fill with the cabbage and pepper mixture. Close up each eggplant again and use a clean string to tie them back togetgher. Place them in a large container.

3. Trim ends off beans, wash well and place in a pan. Add water to cover and boil 1-2 minutes. Discard water and allow to cool. Put on top of the eggplants in the jar. Peel garlic and wash. Trim and wash mint. Add garlic and mint on top of the beans. Mix vinegar and sugar together and add. Dissolve salt in water (3 tablespoons to 1 liter water) and fill container to the top. Cap tightly and store in a cool place.

MIXED PICKLES NO 1

Ingredients:

1 large cabbage
2 kilograms (4 lb) pickling cucumbers
2 kilograms green tomatoes
2 bunches celery leaves
2 bunches parsley
2 kilograms red chili peppers
1 kilogram carrots
1 kilograms small green peppers
3 kilograms eggplants
250 grams (1/2 lb) garlic
hot peppers as desired
1-1/4 liters vinegar
salt

Wash all vegetables and chop the size of walnuts (carrots a little smaller). Mix all except eggplants together in a very large bowl. Bring water to boil in a pan and add chopped eggplant. Boil 1-2 minutes and discard water. Allow to cool and add to container. Add salt to 1/2 liter vinegar and pour over vegetables. Mix well. Fill one or more large jars with the vegetables and any juices in the container. Pour remaining 3/4 liter vinegar over the vegetables and vaccum seal the jar(s). Store in a cool place.

MIXED PICKLES NO 2

Ingredients:

green peppers
pickling cucumbers
apples, pears, quinces, grapes, carrots, okra, celery root leaves, bay leaves
1-2 lemons, vinegar, garlic chickpeas, bread, a little granulated sugar
Water and salt (1 liter to 5 tablespoons)

1. Exact measurements of the ingredients are not needed for this recipe. Whatever is available at home can be added as desired from the list above.

2. Be sure the grapes are firm and fresh. Wash one by one and add. Scrap carrots and slice in large pieces or add whole. Remove stems and seeds from pears. Peel apples and remove seeds.

Wash okra and add without cutting off stems.

3. As with other pickles place one or two slices of bread and a handful of chickpeas in the bottom of the pickling jar(s). Garlic is peeled and washed and placed among other vegetables. Wash celery root leaves and bay leaves and place on top of the other vegetables. Slice lemons and add. Dissolve salt in water, add sugar and mix well (1 liter water: 5 tablespoons salt: 1 teaspoon sugar). Cap very tightly and store in a cold place.

PICKLED BEETS

Ingredients:
1 kilogram (2 lb) red beets
1 cup vinegar
1 cup water
1 head garlic
2 teaspoons salt

1. Wash beets and place in a pan of water. Cook beets but not too soft. When cooled slightly, peel and slice in rounds. Place in a jar.

2. Crush garlic with the salt. Add vinegar and water and mix. Pour over the beets. Shake the jar a little so the liquid spreads well. Cap the jar and allow to set for a day before serving.

PICKLED CABBAGE

Ingredients:

1 medium sized cabbage
1 head garlic
2-3 hot peppers
1 teaspoon sugar
1 handful chickpeas
teaspoon dry yeast
water, salt (5 cups water:
1-1/2 tablespoons salt)

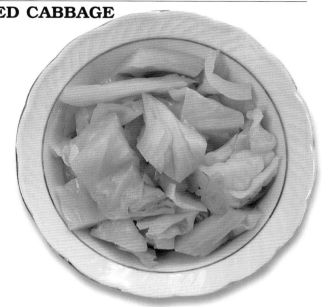

1. Remove outer leaves of cabbage and wash well. Chop in large pieces and place in a glass jar. Crush garlic

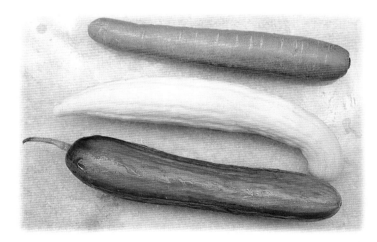

with the salt. Add garlic, red peppers and chickpeas.

2. Mix together salt, sugar and dry yeast. Add to water. Fill jar to top.

3. Stir once or twice daily. Store in a cool place. Pickling is completed in 15-20 days.

CUCUMBER PICKLES

Ingredients:

5 kilograms (10 lb) pickling
cucumbers
1 cup vinegar
1 cup oil
1 head garlic

1. Put cucumbers to soak for a little while and wash one by one, scrubbing if necessary, until clear of all traces of dirt.

2. Place in a pot with enough water to cover and parboil. When color turns a little remove from heat and set aside to cool. Do not discard water. When cooled fill one or more large jars with cucumbers. Peel and slice garlic and add. When cooking water has cooled, measure it. Add 4 tablespoons salt for every liter of water. Mix vinegar and oil with water and pour over cucumbers. Close tightly and store in a cold place.

QUICK PICKLED PEPPERS

Ingredients:

500 grams (1 lb) peppers
2 cups sumach juice or juice of
2-3 lemons
3-4 garlic cloves
dry mint

1. Cut peppers into 2 or 3 pieces and boil. Strain and allow to cool.

2. Crush garlic in a deep bowl and stir in sumach or lemon juice. Add peppers and stir again. Allow to set 2-3 hours before serving.

PICKLED PEPPERS IN TOMATO SAUCE

Ingredients:

5 kilograms (10 lb) Italian
tomatoes
500 grams (1 lb) tiny hot peppers
2-3 bunches each parsley and dill
500 grams (1 lb) garlic
250 grams (1/4 liter) vinegar
1 cup olive oil
1 cup sugar
1/2 cup salt

1. Grate tomatoes and Chop parsley, dill and garlic. Do not cut peppers. Combine all vegetables in a bowl.

2. Mix together olive oil., sugar, salt and vinegar and pour over vegetables. Mix well and fill bottles. Cap bottles very tightly and store in a cool place. The pickles will be ready in 15 days.

Note: *When the bottle is opened the first time, some of the contents may burst out. Therefore it is advisable to open very slowly or open it over a bowl.*

BURDUR MIXED PICKLES

Ingredients:

Carrots, cabbage, green tomatoes, red peppers, green peppers, red tomatoes, garlic, parsley, dill, cucumbers (different types) 1 cup sugar, 1/2 cup salt, 250 grams vinegar, with these proportions repeated as necessary depending on volume of vegetables

1. Wash all vegetables. The amount of each is not important. Chop all vegetables and fill containers.

2. Mix sugar, salt and vinegar and pour over vegetables. Mix more in same proportions, as needed to fill containers.

CUCUMBER PICKLES

Ingredients:

5 kilograms gherkin (very small) cucumbers
1 cup vinegar or more as desired
2 tablespoons sugar
1 or 2 slices bread
1 cup chickpeas
2 tablespoons cardamon seed, if desired
3-4 heads garlic
water and pickling salt as needed (1 liter water:3 tablespoons salt)

1. Wash cucumbers one by one with the hands under running water. Use a fork or knife to cut 1 or 2 incisions in each one.

2. Place bread slices in the bottom of a big jar. Wash chickpeas and put on top of bread.

3. If used, wrap cardamon seed in cheesecloth, tie tightly to prevent leaking and add.

4. Separate, peel and wash garlic and place some cloves in the bottom of the jar and mix the rest with cucumbers.

5. Fill jar with cucumbers.

6. Mix salt in water until it dissolves. Add sugar and vinegar and stir again. Pour over cucumbers (or add vinegar separately at the end).

7. Cap jar tightly and store in a cool place.

Note: *Vinegar may be omitted. In this case, boil the water first and allow to cool before proceeding, and add lemon slices and a few grated tomatoes to the cucumbers.*

A FEW WINTER PREPARATIONS

CONTENTS

WINTER PHYLLO DOUGH (YUFKA)

Ingredients:
3 kilograms (6 lb) flour
10 eggs
2 kilograms (2 liters) milk,
a little salt

1. Mix milk and eggs together. Add salt. Add flour very slowly while mixing and knead to a soft dough.

2. Roll out dough and form thin rounds. Place one by one on a hot saç (or similar round flat pan) and brown slightly on both sides (no oil is used). Set to dry in an airy place. Layer all of them in a stack for later use as needed in making pan boureks.

ULUBORLU DRY GRAPE LEAVES IN SALT

Ingredients:
fresh grape leaves
salt

1. Wash each leaf and sprinkle both sides all over with a thin layer lof salt. Make stacks of 10-15 leaves. Place stacks next to each other in a wide container.

2. Set aside for 2-3 days. Wash off excess salt and roll up each leaf.

3. Store in a large jar and store in a cool place. (No water is used in this method.)

4. When ready to use the leaves in a recipe, wash leaves in warm water 3-4 times, drain and allow to set in warm water 1-2 hours. When using these leaves for stuffed grape leaves, omit the salt in the filling.

BOTTLED GRAPE LEAVES

1. Select very thin, fresh grape leaves. Stack 2-3 leaves together and roll up tightly. Fill a plastic water bottle with these rolls.

2. If the bottle is capped very tightly, the leaves will keep a long time. When ready to use, cut open the bottle with a knife. Put a little salt in a pot of boiling water, turn down to simmer, add the leaves and simmer briefly. Remove from water and rinse leaves in fresh water. Proceed with stuffed grape leaves recipe.

Note: Using this method, salted water can also be added to the bottle if desired, as is done with the recipe (this chapter) for seedless grape leaves. This can improve the flavor. Before using the leaves simply wash them in warm water and proceed.

GRAPE MOLASSES

1. Squeeze juice from grapes. This can be done in the food processor if desired. If a very large amount of grapes are to be used, place them in a large burlap bag and crush them, squeezing out the juice.

2. For 20 kilograms grape juice, add 2 kilograms of topsoil.

3. Allow juice to set in soil for 1 hour to ferment. Put fermented juice through a filter to remove all soil. Bring juice to a boil in a large pot. Strain again into another pot and allow to cool. When cooled, strain once again to remove all residues. Pour into a shallow pan and put to the boil again. When it acquires a molasses consistency remove from stove.

Note: 10 kilograms of grapes make approximately 1 kilogram of molasses.

DENİZLİ SOUP MIX (TARHANA)

Ingredients:
1 kilogram (2 lb) red peppers (hot or sweet)
2 kilograms (4 lb) tomatoes
500 grams (2 lb) black-eyed peas or white beans
1 kilogram (2 lb) onions
2 kilograms (4 lb) strained yoghurt
flour as needed, salt

1. Boil peas or beans until soft. Place tomatoes, peppers and peas or beans in the food processor. Add to this mixture salt, yoghurt and as much flour as needed to make a dough (a little stiffer than the ear lobe).

2. Put dough in a clean pastry bag and tie tightly. Place in a cool place and allow to set for one week. Every day knead the dough inside the bag. After a week remove and place on a board covered with a clean pastry cloth. Divide dough into walnut-sized pieces. Allow to dry for 1 day. When dried crush into a coarse flour consistency. Spread out on yet another clean cloth and allow to dry completely.

Note: *When the dough is in the bag, as well as when it is laid out to dry, it should be in a shady place, not in direct sunlight.*

PEPPER SAUCE (ÇEMEN)

Ingredients:

1 kilogram (2 lb) garlic
250 grams (1/2 lb) ground red sweet pepper
250 grams ground red pepper
2 tablespoons cumin
1 tablespoon black pepper
3-4 whole cloves
1 teaspooon salt
1/3 teaspoon ginger

Peel and separate garlic and crush. Mix with peppers. Crush cloves and add. Mix remaining ingredients together and add. Add as much warm water as needed to make a thick sauce. Fill jars, cover tightly and store in a cool place.

SEEDLESS GRAPE LEAVES IN SALT WATER

Ingredients:

5 kilograms (10 lb) fresh leaves of seedless green grapes
5 liters water
1 kilogram (2 lb) salt

1. Wash leaves, drain and place in a large bowl.

2. Boil water and add salt.

3. If the leaves are hard, pour boiling water on top. If very fresh, allow water to cool down a little first. Allow to set 1-2 days until leaves turn yellowish.

4. Place leaves in a very large jar. Pour remaining water from bowl into jar. Store in a cool place. Check frequently during 10-15 days. As water level goes down, mix more salt water in the same proportions, boil and add. The leaves should be kept in water until they are used.

TURKISH CANDY (LOKUM)

Ingredients:

4 cups water
1 kilogram (2 lb) sugar
1/2 cup cornstarch
1 cup roasted hazelnuts
1 cup coconut

1. Mix sugar and water and bring to a boil. While boiling, spoon off foam. Mix cornstarch in a little cold water. Very slowly add to the syrup while stirring constantly, and continue until thickened. To test for doneness dip a cold spoon in the bubbling mixture and set aside to cool. If the candy flows very slowly on the spoon like gum, it is done.

2. Spread coconut all over a platter. Transfer candy to platter and spread evenly over coconut. Spread cornstarch all over the candy. Allow to set one day. After one day brush off the cornstarch. Sprinkle a little water on the candy. Spread hazelnuts on one end. Make a roll with the candy and seal. (The water helps the roll to stick together.) Cut slices crosswise of desired thickness. Roll pieces in coconut.

Note: *Omit nuts, if plain lokum is desired, or substitute walnuts or pistachios for hazelnuts.*

AFYON TOMATO SAUCE

Ingredients:

5 kilograms (10 lb) tomatoes
1 cup vinegar
1cup olive oil
2 teaspoons salt
1-1/2 heads garlic
250 grams (1/2 lb) hot peppers
(miniature decorative type)

1. Wash, peel and grate tomatoes. Cook in a large pot for one hour.

2. Add vinegar, olive oil, salt and crushed garlic.

3. Trim stems and wash peppers. Add to bubbling tomato mixture and cook 15 minutes more.

4. Fill jars and cap very tightly. Store in a cool place. Or, fill freezer bags, seal tightly and store in deep freeze. Remove from freezer one hour before use.

What dishes should or should not be combined in one meal?

• Vegetables stuffed with meat and rice are not served with pilaf, macaroni, bourek and similar foods.

• A heavy dessert is not served after a meal containing pilaf, macaroni, bourek and similar foods.

• More than one dish containing the same type of ingredients, such as yoghurt ravioli (mantı), ayran, yoghurt soup and milk pudding, which all contain dairy, are not included in the same meal.

• More than one juicy dish, dry dish, bread dish, or vegetable dish are not served in the same meal.

• Both a soup and a juicy meat dish are not served together.

• Soups are best served in the evening and dried legume dishes at noon.

• Two cold olive oil dishes are not served together.

• A green leafy salad goes well with fried or grilled fish. A cold bean salad goes well with Albanian liver.

• Breakfast selections from the milk, meat, oil or butter, and sweet categories are best varied from day to day. According to season, various fruits and vegetables are also served, such as oranges, apples, grapes, green peppers and tomatoes. Milk, tarhana soup or fruit juices may be substituted for tea.

"The worst meal is a wedding banquet to which only the well-fed are invited and the hungry are left out." Prophet Mohammed

"Food allowed to sit too long will take revenge and cause illness."
                                                                    Cenap Şahabettin

"I can do without food you offer me in a humiliating manner." Sheik Sadi

"A bear will eat the meat only after it goes rotten." Seyrani

"The one who is ignorant of how the meat tastes falls in love with the liver." Old saying

"Spoiled meat is an inviting feast for the flies." Old saying

"A wealthy Muslim should spend less for pleasure and more according to need." Old saying

FOOD SHOPPING

SPECIAL POINTS REGARDING SHOPPING

1. Quality is the first step before taste and economy in selection of goods.

2. When shopping it is important to consider all aspects of the variety of products, each of which has its own special shape, appearance, taste and aroma.

3. Fruits and vegetables are best purchased in season. Out-of-season greenhouse raised foods are under-ripened and are expensive – as well as lower in food value.

4. Stay away from produce containing hormones. Odd or over-sized shapes are good indications of these.

5. Think about what is needed before going shopping and make a list in order to avoid buying unnecessary products.

6. Buy fruits and vegetables only in volumes necessary and be sure they are very fresh. Do not let the seller include any spoiled ones.

7. It is best to carry foods home in paper or plastic bags to keep germs away. However, one can feel more confident about the quality of what is purchased if it is carefully examined first rather than bought pre-packaged.

8. As soon as possible after shopping, place the fresh foods in the appropriate compartments of the refrigerator in order to prevent the flavors from mixing.

9. To get rid of or avoid an accumulation of unwanted odors in the refrigerator, place half a cup of milk uncovered in the refrigerator.

10. Some hard sausages will mold if stored in the refrigerator.

11. It is not necessary to store cookies, crackers, honey or preserves in the refrigerator.

12. If cooked food is to be stored, place in refrigerator only after it is cooled. Wrap all cooked foods in plastic or aluminum foil or cover tightly before storing in the refrigerator.

13. Food should be cooked fresh daily. When this is not possible, do not store it in the refrigerator for more than 2-3 days and only reheat the portion to be eaten at a particular meal.

14. Frozen meat is best removed from the freezer and placed in the refrigerator compartment one day before use. Meat that has been thawed should not be re-frozen.

15. Frozen meat thaws more quickly when rinsed with vinegar water.

MEAT:

Be particularly careful to buy only meat that bears the stamp of approval of health authorities. The meat of unhealthy animals is harmful and should never be used.

MILK:

Milk varies according to the breed of cow it comes from and the season. Fresh milk of the best quality is slightly yellowish, has a slightly sweet taste, is fatty and without odor and does not separate when boiled.

If water has been added to milk it has a bluish appearance and does not coat the sides of its container.

Skim milk has no cream.

The practice of adding soda to milk to prevent it from going sour is just a trick to fool the consumer.

After raw milk has come to the boiling point it should be boiled at least 10-15 minutes. In less time than this all germs are not destroyed.

CHEESE:

Bad cheese is apparent by its unpleasant taste and smell. It is hard and slimy and may appear pale, dull and chalky. Sharper cheeses are very compact and mild cheeses are flaky and loose. If the cheese has big holes or is spongy it is gassy.

Definitely do not buy fresh cheese that is badly shaped, spotted or dirty.

Good quality white cheese is the color of fresh cream. If, when sliced in half there is a hole in the middle, the hole was formed by unwanted microbes.

Tulum cheese (a soft type of cheese made in a goatskin) that is bitter or too salty should be avoided.

Do not buy kashar cheese that looks dull in color, has colored spots, is dirty or swollen, or especially if it has red mold on it.

The best place to store cheese in the refrigerator is in the vegetable compartment. Remove from refrigerator 1/2 hour before use.

If the cheese is too hard, place in a glass jar and cover with pure olive oil to soften. If desired, add bay leaves, oregano, dill and/or black pepper.

Cheese   *Yoghurt*

BUTTER:

Fresh butter has the aroma of fresh hazelnuts. It should not have a layer of moisture on it.

FRUITS AND VEGETABLES:

Green beans should be crisp and green

Cauliflower should be well-formed, ivory white and firm to the touch.

Potatoes that are green or sprouted are harmful to eat. If potatoes stored at home start to become green or sprouted, those parts should be trimmed completely off before cooking.

Dry (winter) potatoes are best for cooked foods and salads. New potatoes are excellent for frying.

Onions should have round, shiny skins and be hard and firm.

Uncooked garlic and onions eaten together cause fermentation in the intestines and stomach ache.

Eggplants (aubergine) should have long, green and lively leaves, be a black or dark purple color, and soft to the touch but not spongy inside.

How to choose for different recipes:

a. For split eggplants with ground meat (karnıyarık) or eggplant in olive oil (imam bayıldı), they should be straight and thin.

b. For stuffed eggplant they should be straight and a little fat.

c. For eggplant puree they should be big and fat.

d. For stews and other mixtures they should be straight and medium sized.

e. For kebabs any type is fine.

Squashes (zucchini): should be fresh, green, lively and not too big. Very large ones too often are soft inside and the seeds too big.

Tangerines should have thin rinds.

Watermelons should be eaten ripe. 95% of the nutritive value is in the rind.

Sometimes the rinds are useful for making drinks and preserves. The white part is a useful source of vitamins and minerals.

Melons are a source of very high food value that can alone provide sufficient nutrition. The juice can be drunk. Peel off only a thin layer of the outer rind.

PRACTICAL TIPS

Walnuts: The nut meat should be plentiful and white. Store in a cloth bag to preserve freshness.

Hard walnuts: Soak 1 day in salt water for easier cracking.

Honey: If it becomes sugary or cloudy, set the jar in a pan of hot water for awhile and it will become clear again.

Squeezing lemons: Wash and soak 2 minutes in hot water first to make all the juice flow out better when squeezed.

If only half a lemon is used, to prevent molding of the unused half, put a little vinegar on a small saucer and place the cut side of the lemon down on it.

Leftover orange and lemon peels:

If there is a heating stove in the home, put 1 or 2 rinds on the stove to replace unpleasant odors with a pleasant one.

One peel placed in the corner of the kitchen sends away ants or other unwanted crawlers.

The dried peels can add a pleasant aroma to some sauces, desserts and cookies.

Eggs and eggshells:

Put boiled eggs immediately into cold water to stop the cooking and make them easier to peel.

To use up egg whites left over from recipes calling for yolks only, beat with sugar (1 egg white to a scant teaspoon of sugar) until it forms soft peaks and use as a garnish on desserts.

Using the cooled water from boiled eggs to water the plants gives minerals to the soil.

Mix the shells with used coffee grinds and tea leaves and use as fertilizer.

Dry beans, chickpeas and lentils: To protect from insects during storage, sprinkle some salt on top and stir from time to time.

Do not store in a damp place.

Ground coffee: If it becomes stale, re-roast it by spreading it out in an open pan over a very low flame.

Olive oil: To remove bitterness (for a 5-liter container of olive oil): Mix 1/3 cup sugar and 1/4 cup old oil together. Heat until sugar melts. Pour mixture into the 5-liter container and stir.

Salt: Prevent dampness in the shaker by first placing a few grains of rice in the bottom before filling.

Bread: To prevent mold from forming in the bread container, set one or two sugar cubes inside the container along with the bread.

Peeling onions: To avoid tears, put each onion as it is peeled into a bowl of water.

Red (ground) pepper: Add when the food is almost cooked. If added at the beginning, the flavor will be bitter.

Hot green peppers: Remove stems and seeds and chop thin before adding to the cooking.

Carrots, radishes, turnips etc.: The vitamin-rich greens of these vegetables are valuable additions to soups and salads.

CLEANING THE REFRIGERATOR

1. When the refrigerator is empty or appears almost empty is the ideal time for cleaning. In this way food is not left sitting out to spoil during the cleaning and defrosting period.

2. Pull the plug or turn the temperature button to "off."

3. The best way to get rid of the ice in the freezer is to wait for it to melt.

4. Soap and detergent should not be used inside the refrigerator. Add pure soda to water and wipe all surfaces, then repeat with plain water.

5. After all surfaces are dry allow refrigerator to air out for 15 minutes before starting up.

REFRIGERATION PERIODS FOR VARIOUS FOODS (0-4C – 32-40F)

Ground meat and meatballs: 1 day
Fresh milk: 2 days
Preserved milk: 4 months
Meat, chicken and sausages: 3 days
Vacuum packed sausages, dried meats: 3 months
Butter: 1 months

Vacuum packed white cheese: 6-12 months
Yoghurt: 10 days
Canned fish: 1 year
Fresh, cleaned fish: 1 day
Fruits and vegetables: 3-4 days

ABOUT OVENS

The evenness of the oven and accuracy of temperature are as important as the cooking method and the ingredients of the dish. Some doughs will not rise if the oven too cool, and will rise but remain raw in the middle if the oven is too hot.

Gas and electric ovens function quite differently. Ovens that have no accurate temperature control make it particularly difficult to prepare baked goods. The gas oven is ideal.

In order to get good results one needs to acquire a good working knowledge of the particularities of the oven to be used.

Meat dishes call for a very hot oven to sear the meat at the beginning. The temperature is then reduced for the remainder of the cooking. Pan drippings prevent the meat from becoming dry. As soon as the juices become to come out, reduce the temperature and allow the meat to cook slowly, in this way remaining moist and retaining its flavor.

Cookies and crackers are baked in a medium oven. Cakes are baked in a slightly hotter oven.

When baking a cake with an old-fashioned oven in which the temperature cannot be regulated accurately, first preheat the oven, top and bottom, then put the cake in the oven and turn off the top part. When the bottom half of the cake has risen turn off the bottom part of the oven and re-light the top part. Bake until the cake fragrance comes out. Prick the center of the cake with a knife. If it comes out clean the cake is done.

When putting a meat dish in the oven place a small pan of water next to it to prevent the food from drying out too much.

INDEX